# Reality TV

# TV Genres

*Series Editors*
Deborah Jermyn, Roehampton University
Su Holmes, University of East Anglia

Titles in the series include:
*The Quiz Show*
by Su Holmes
978 0 7486 2752 3 (hardback)
978 0 7486 2753 0 (paperback)

*The Sitcom*
by Brett Mills
978 0 7486 3751 5 (hardback)
978 0 7486 3752 2 (paperback)

*Reality TV*
by Misha Kavka
978 0 7486 3722 5 (hardback)
978 0 7486 3723 2 (paperback)

Forthcoming titles include:

*Crime Drama* .
by Sue Turnbull

*Animation*
by Nichola Dobson and Paul Ward

Visit the TV Genres website at www.euppublishing.com/series/edtv

# Reality TV

Misha Kavka

EDINBURGH
University Press

Edinburgh University Press Ltd
22 George Square, Edinburgh

www.euppublishing.com

Typeset in 10/12 Janson Text
by Servis Filmsetting Ltd, Stockport, Cheshire, and
printed and bound in Great Britain by
CPI Group (UK) Ltd, Croydon, CR0 4YY

A CIP record for this book is available from the British Library

ISBN 978 0 7486 3722 5 (hardback)
ISBN 978 0 7486 3723 2 (paperback)
ISBN 978 0 7486 3724 9 (webready PDF)
ISBN 978 0 7486 5435 2 (epub)
ISBN 978 0 7486 5434 5 (Amazon ebook)

# Contents

# Acknowledgements

I am indebted most of all to the series editors, Deborah Jermyn and Su Holmes, for their tireless and stimulating engagement with this project. Deborah and Su inspired me to write the book and kept me at it with invaluable feedback at every stage of the process. I am also grateful to the University of Auckland and the Department of Film, Television and Media Studies for financial assistance with research trips and research support. Thanks goes, moreover, to the colleagues and students who have broadened my reality TV horizons as well as my personal archives, particularly Scott Wilson, Pip Howells, and the enthusiastic students in my 'Reality TV' class. I am also indebted to my summer scholar Tessa Clews for her astute comments on the manuscript. Finally, I am extremely grateful to my family, who created the time and space for this book to happen: they have encouraged my obsessions, made me cups of tea and, most importantly, watched television with me. No one can go it alone, certainly not when it comes to reality TV.

# Introduction: What is Reality TV?

When I began studying reality television, many years ago now, I
found myself collecting episodes of *Cops* (1989–), footage from Court
TV (launched 1991), pratfalls from *America's Funniest Home Videos*
(1989–99, 2001–) and seemingly endless hours of highway pursuits
filmed from helicopters and police cruisers. I was drawn to these programmes by the appeal of the raw footage, which looked so different
from the slick sitcoms, dramas and even newscasts on other channels. I
was drawn, too, by the counter-intuitive appeal of slow-paced, trivial,
repetitive events screened on television, where every minute is worth a
small fortune and 'dead time' is anathema. When, I asked myself, had
tedium on the small screen become compulsive viewing? In 2000, I
joined the ranks of viewers the world over who were glued nightly to
the first season of *Big Brother* (1999–). Despite the different premise
and viewing experience of *Big Brother*, this show struck me as a con-
tinuation of the techniques from *Cops* and *America's Funniest Home
Videos*. The camerawork and the unrehearsed performances of people
engaging with the trivia of everyday life made the link seem obvious.
Reality TV innovations since then – and there have been too many to
count – have similarly been absorbed into the programming slipstream
they have helped to create, even though now there is probably not a
single feature that is shared by all of the programmes which fall under
the rubric of 'reality TV'.

As I write, the TV discussion sites and review pages are abuzz
with debates about *Jersey Shore* (2009–) on MTV and *My Big Fat
Gypsy Wedding* (2010–) on Channel 4 in Britain. As hyperbolic representations of social and personal identity, these two very different
programmes probably have something in common, but it is far less
clear how they link back to the mundanity of a show like *Cops*. Even
in the current environment of 2011/12, it is difficult to articulate the
connections among programmes like *Jersey Shore*, which is a *Real
World* (1992–) offshoot for Italian American youths; *My Big Fat Gypsy*

*Wedding*, which is a sociological series about marriage rituals amongst Britain's traveller communities; *Who Do You Think You Are?* (2004–), which is a genealogy series that traces the family tree of celebrities; *Tabatha's Salon Takeover* (2008–), which is a makeover series helmed by an Australian hairstyling diva; and the popular *American Idol* (2002–)/*MasterChef* (1990–2001; 2005–)/*Project Runway* (2004–) talent quests. There also seems little to connect the humdrum aesthetic of a programme like *16 and Pregnant* (2009–), an MTV observational series about pregnant teens, with the VH1 celebrity mini-industry that began with *The Surreal Life* (2003–6) and led to the rapper/rocker dating shows *Flavor of Love* (2006–8) and *Rock of Love* (2007–9), the spin-off etiquette programme *Charm School* (2007–9) and the catch-all hybrid *I Love Money* (2008–10), which collects together D-list denizens of the previous programmes to squabble in a shared house while competing for cash. All of these programmes are regularly referred to by viewers, commentators and industry professionals as 'reality TV', yet the framework that allows them to be grouped together is less than obvious.

Despite its generic haziness, one cannot overestimate the impact of reality TV. In just two decades, it has transformed programming schedules, branded satellite and digital channels, created a celebrity industry in its own right and turned viewers into savvy readers of – not to mention potential participants in – the mechanics of television production. Some critics have gone so far as to declare that reality TV has 'remade' television culture (Murray and Ouellette 2004). Yet, despite the wide circulation of the term 'reality TV' and its comparatively short tenure on our screens, its genre status, cultural significance and even history are all heavily contested. On the one hand, programmers, viewers and commentators use the term in full confidence that they will be understood, whether it is meant as an industry pitch, a statement of viewing preference, a marketing tool or the topic of a university course. On the other hand, there is confusion about what constitutes and delimits 'reality television' as a grouping or genre, in part because of its format hybridity and in part as a result of the sheer volume and changing nature of the programmes themselves. As a populist form, moreover, reality TV sits at the intersection of numerous extra-televisual discourses, from trade magazines, viewing guides and official websites, to the tabloid press, unofficial webpages and television discussion forums. Reality TV thus does not just consist of programme texts but also of the entire discursive field that surrounds them.

This discursive field now includes a considerable amount of

academic scholarship. Key areas of study to date have focused on reality television's associations with documentary, its hybridisation of fictional and factual programme styles, its intersection with everyday life and ordinary people, its representation of social identities (such as gender, sexuality, class, ethnicity and race), and its participation in the production of makeover culture as well as media celebrity. Of these areas, the study of reality television's relation to documentary film and realism was the earliest and most influential academic approach, especially in the British television context (Biressi and Nunn 2005: 1). From the mid-1990s to the early 2000s, as the phrases 'reality TV' and 'docudrama' began to enter the academic lexicon, scholars defined reality TV as a televisual form that blurs traditional distinctions between information and entertainment, documentary and drama, public and private discourses (Kilborn 1994; Nichols 1994; Bondebjerg 1996). Focusing on the crime/emergency programmes and docusoaps of the 1990s, these studies framed their investigation of reality TV through concepts like realism, hyperreality and/or its claims to the 'real' (Friedman 2002; Cummings 2002). This often meant, however, that reality TV was positioned as documentary 'lite' and associated with the decline of public service television; it was considered to be either a cheap form of 'trash TV' aimed at entertaining the masses or a postmodern 'nightmare' that took hybridisation and surveillance technology too far (Dovey 2000: 83). While John Corner has consistently argued that the legacy of documentary is still at work in reality TV, albeit in revised form (2000, 2002), this legacy has also meant that reality TV continues to be judged as either 'dumbed-down' television or 'lowest-common denominator' programming which presents nothing of social value.

    With the appearance of the highly popular *Big Brother* in 1999/2000 and the introduction of fabricated competitive environments to reality TV, other scholarly approaches and methods began to be applicable. Reality TV became an important site of discussion for scholars of surveillance culture (Andrejevic 2004) as well as those interested in the relation between television and everyday life (Bonner 2003), and public and private spheres (van Zoonen 2004). *Big Brother* further led to the first sustained audience and fan studies of reality TV (Hill 2002, 2005; Jones 2003) as well as industry analyses (Ritchie 2000) and studies of the intersection between television and new media (Jones 2004). Since *Big Brother* the rise of competition programmes as well as shows that promise self-improvement for ordinary people has meant a growing critical interest in the interventionist role of reality TV, from DIY programmes to the parenting and lifestyle shows

that appear to teach audiences how to better manage themselves
(Ouellette and Hay 2008). Although reality television's many detractors remain, within academic scholarship as well as among public
commentators, the tendency in recent years has been to study reality
TV from the perspective of its continuing popularity rather than
condemning its populism: critics now ask which forms of reality TV
appeal to viewers in which contexts, how reality TV intersects with a
multitude of social discourses, and what role particular programmes
play in helping viewers to negotiate the social, political and technological forces that shape their lives. In keeping with this attitude, this
book will not seek to assess the value of reality TV in comparison
with other genres or media forms. Rather, I wish to investigate reality
TV on its own terms, as a form whose stubborn ability to renew and
extend itself indicates just how well integrated it has become into
contemporary social structures.

This book does not attempt to subscribe to any one method or
perspective for studying reality TV but rather to include the range of
critical approaches as part of its broader discursive context. I aim to
navigate a path through this rich territory by tracing reality TV as a
textual, social and cultural formation with an entangled programming
and critical history. If, as Jason Mittel has argued, '[g]enres operate
in an ongoing historical process of category formation' (2004: xiv),
then the book offers a textured account of the rise and development
of reality television in a way that ties genre to history and emphasises
its cultural, industrial and conceptual contexts. To achieve this, I have
chosen a methodology which I call genealogical, in recognition of
Foucault's understanding of genealogy as a way of 'doing' history that
does not involve finding singular stories with a beginning, a middle
and an end. Given the sheer number of reality TV programmes and
the continuing shifts in format styles as producers in various contexts
try to predict and outpace audience tastes, no traditionally chronological history could cover such diversity, nor explain reality TV in
terms of a single origin. Thus, the genealogical method I have selected
seeks to trace multiple origins, intersections and resemblances among
reality TV forms. Adapting Foucault's genealogical method to genre
studies, this book maps structural connections as well as key conceptual shifts by breaking reality television into three 'generations' based
on discursive resemblances, namely, the camcorder generation, the
competition generation and the celebrity generation. To answer the
tricky question 'what is reality TV', the book will work through its
more complex variant: how do we find order in such a diverse, protean
yet omnipresent array of programmes?

## So what is reality television?

If there is a simple definition of reality television then we might say that the term refers to unscripted shows with non-professional actors being observed by cameras in preconfigured environments. The immediate temptation, however, is to think of exceptions to this rule, so the simple definition is quickly revealed to be reductive. A more complex definition might seek to supplement the internal features of reality TV texts with information about the critical discourses and cultural economies in which they are embedded. In this view, reality television is associated with low production values, high emotions, cheap antics and questionable ethics because it is 'an unabashedly commercial' form that mixes the serious traditions of documentary with the entertainment purpose of populist formats (Murray and Ouellette 2004: 2). While this is a more nuanced definition, it has little to say about the appeal of reality TV, or why this genre has had such an impact on the production, distribution and consumption patterns of television itself. Indeed, the cultural devaluation of reality television has more to do with the expectations associated with its genre label than with individual programmes, many of which their detractors will not even have watched. As I indicated above, the actual programmes that fall under the umbrella term 'reality television' are so highly differentiated as to make any definition quite tenuous. This, of course, poses problems for claiming its status as a singular TV genre.

But to what extent is reality television an 'it'? Unlike soap operas, sitcoms or even gameshows, which have a long history establishing their status as recognisable genres, reality TV is a relatively new genre. It can be traced back to the late 1980s, when reality crime shows appeared in the US, or to 1992, when *The Real World* appeared on MTV, or to 1999/2000, when *Big Brother* began to break ratings records. This uncertainty in mapping its origins reminds us that genres do not spring fully formed into cultural consciousness. Rather, there is a period of name-testing, categorising and recategorising before a genre becomes accepted by audiences, critics, programmers and broadcasters. The process has been made more difficult in the case of reality TV, however, because the one defining feature on which critics seem to agree is its generic hybridity, suggesting that reality TV shows have combined aspects of other television genres rather than inventing any of their own. This might lead us to question, as Jason Mittel puts it, whether reality TV can be considered 'a full-fledged television genre' (2004: 197). The *E!* channel, in contrast, has no such concerns. It is so confident that contemporary viewers know what to expect from the term that it now promises 'more reality!', not even needing to specify it as 'reality TV'.

So it seems that we face a quandary that is common to genre studies but is exacerbated in the case of reality TV: programmers and viewers know what reality TV is, while genre theorists encounter difficulties once they scratch the surface. There are no doubt recognisable, repeated cultural practices that have accrued around the term 'reality TV', involving viewing choices, programming schedules, production decisions and format sales. There are also numerous discourses that have become consolidated around these practices, such as the language of promotion and marketing, television reviews, viewer discussion boards and the idioms popularised by the shows themselves (e.g. 'flying under the radar'). At the same time, the theoretical work of defining and grouping these programmes remains contentious. But this does not mean the work is not worth doing. In fact, twenty years on – at least according to my version of the history of reality TV – it may be time to stop and take stock. What do we mean when we call reality TV a genre, or treat it as one? Which shows do we include, and on what basis? And how do we think about the relationship between genre classifications, cultural practices and production histories in this broad group of shows?

## Genre and Genealogy

Historically, the term 'genre' refers to texts which can be grouped together on the basis of shared characteristics. These shared attributes are traditionally considered to be integral to the texts themselves, which in turn provides the basis for defining a text according to its genre (e.g. a novel) and a genre according to its internal features (e.g. a single-authored fictional work of prose organised around characters and events). This notion of genre has been instrumental to the categorisation of texts within a range of established aesthetic forms, such as literature, theatre and film. Most critics now agree, however, that the definitional approach is too limited, since texts always operate within contexts of reception and production. Steve Neale, for instance, in his influential study of film genre, has insisted that the text-based understanding of genre be expanded to include 'specific systems of expectation and hypothesis that spectators bring with them to the cinema' (1990: 46), while Jane Feuer's (1992) approach to the genre of sitcoms introduces historical contextualisation by analysing changing industrial and cultural conditions in the 1970s and 1980s.

In television studies, however, there has been much debate about the applicability of even contextualised notions of genre to the medium. While scholars in film studies have developed a sustained theorisation of genre, their counterparts in television studies have been less willing to do so. Addressing this relative lack, Laura Stempel-Mumford has argued that television's adaptable formats and self-reflexive borrowings make it 'resistant *as a medium* to the rigidity that [genre] categorizations are thought to require' (1995: 20; original emphasis). John Fiske, however, has argued that television is a 'highly generic' medium (1987: 109), with genre classifications informing how television texts are placed in schedules and how they are read by audiences. For Fiske, this is not to deny the adaptability of television formats but to argue that audiences, producers and schedulers incorporate format fluidity into their use of generic designations. Against the backdrop of these debates, reality television has been treated either as the exception to the applicability of genre in television or as the exemplar of television genre itself. Because reality TV self-consciously and self-reflexively mixes generic forms (Holmes and Jermyn 2004: 6–7), this can be read either as its failure to fit the basic criteria of genre or as the grounds for considering it to be the definitive genre within an inherently adaptable medium. Mittel, tending toward the latter position, has noted that television itself 'regularly mixes narrative and nonnarrative formats' (2004: xiii), which would suggest that reality TV is working within the medium's own traditions.

This book will consider reality television to be exemplary of television genre owing to the ease with which it mixes fictional and documentary forms, soap operas and game shows, talkshows and advertising platforms – all without losing its legibility as 'reality TV'. This does not mean, however, that reality television should be treated as a static genre whose features have already been canonised. On the contrary, the interest of this new form lies precisely in the rhythms of its emergence, consolidation and continuing development. Jason Mittel's work on genre and television (2004) provides a helpful theoretical framework for tracing this emergence. For Mittel, television genres are first and foremost cultural constructions, and hence must be studied as 'generic clusters' that emerge through 'discursive practices of definition, interpretation and evaluation' (2004: 196). While these discursive practices appear to reflect on a given genre, as though the genre comes first and the talk about it second, Mittel argues that discourses are in fact 'constitutive of that genre' (2004: xiv). This argument shifts the focus from understanding television genre as a shared set of attributes to understanding it as a form that is 'constantly in flux' and hence always in a state of adapting formats, borrowing material and moving on the next thing. Mittel's approach proves doubly useful for the study of reality television. First, reality TV changes so quickly that flux is one of its key attributes, and hence any attempt to discuss it as a genre must incorporate its mutability rather than sidelining it as incidental to the form. Second, in my earlier musings about how to connect *Cops* with *I Love Money*, I ended up suggesting that there is not a single feature that is shared by all of the programmes which today circulate in the discursive category of 'reality TV'. For a traditional or textual approach to genre, which seeks to distil a shared set of attributes, this would obviously be a problem. With an approach that understands genres to 'operate in an ongoing historical process of category formation' (Mittel 2004: xiv), however, the focus shifts from generic attributes to history.

This book thus addresses reality TV as a genre from a historical perspective. In and of itself, I find this a useful task because the history of reality television has so far been told from partial perspectives, depending on the national viewing contexts of scholars and their chosen time frames as well as criteria. While I cannot make a claim to being able to cover all reality TV shows in every country they have appeared, I do attempt in this book to take a multi-national perspective, with a particular focus on innovations and influences arising in the US, UK, Europe and Australia/New Zealand. Addressing reality TV from a historical perspective, however, also raises a theoretical question about how to do history. Although this sounds like an impossibly grand question, I will again take my lead from Mittel, following his suggestion that Foucault's historical model of genealogy is appropriate to studying genres as discursive formations (2004: 13).

In his celebrated essay 'Nietzsche, Genealogy, History', Foucault argues that telling history should not involve a search for origins, since such a search 'assumes the existence of immobile forms that precede the world of accident and succession' (1984: 78). Although Foucault is talking about the historiography of world events, the method seems peculiarly applicable to television studies. If television genres are always in flux, as has been argued, then any method that assumes 'immobile forms' will fail to capture the conditions for their emergence. Thus, in order to grasp a history that accounts for accidents and detours and multiple origins and broken threads – such as have been the pathways of reality television – Foucault argues that one must take a genealogical approach. Resisting 'ideal signification and indefinite teleologies' (1984: 77), Foucauldian genealogy seeks to 'record the singularity of events outside of any monotonous finality' (1984: 76). Rejecting overarching narratives, it finds history in the twists and turns taken by particular elements rather than in neat arcs with a beginning, middle and end. A genealogy on this model is thus sensitive to ruptures in timelines as well as the co-existence of diverse forms; it looks for commonalities across related strands rather than attempting to map linear routes.

In taking such an approach to reality TV, I will be collecting together the 'micro-instances' that constitute the 'macro-account of a genre's history from the bottom up' (Mittel 2004: 14). The process will involve following different genealogical strands, allowing some continuities to be broken while paying attention to connections and interrelations among others. Rather than looking for a single origin, I will find numerous starting points for reality TV. In place of linear trajectories, I will highlight the socio-political contexts, cultural shifts, technological innovations and industrial practices that have contributed to the formation of reality TV as a genre.

## Chapter Overview

The organising premise of this book is to begin 'before' reality TV, with televisual precedents which later reappear in the discourses of its production and reception. From there, I offer a classification that breaks reality TV down into waves or, more in keeping with geneal-ogy, into *generations*, each with a set of significant discursive charac-teristics connected to a particular historical, national and conceptual context. In doing so, I am aware of producing categories that exist only as a result of my analysis; yet, given that genre distinctions are by definition mobile, the aim of the book is to offer an explanatory paradigm which can be tested against readers' own viewing experi-ences. In my schema, the first generation, or the camcorder genera-tion, encompasses the reality crime programmes of the first half of the 1990s, which had their start in the US, as well as the 'docusoaps' of the second half of the 1990s, which had their start in the UK. The second generation, or the competition generation, begins with *Big Brother*, the ground-breaking show which appeared in 1999 in the Netherlands and introduced game show-type competition under conditions of surveillance in a contrived setting. Within a few years, this developed into interventionist formats predicated on a challenge, in which par-ticipants are given an opportunity for self-transformation. The third generation, although it lacks a major programme that encapsulates its attributes, is concerned with the production of celebrity. At this stage, reality TV disengages from its documentary roots and becomes a self-conscious participant in the rituals of self-commodification and self-legitimation that define contemporary celebrity culture. Although the breaks between these generations cannot be rigidly enforced, they do help to focus our attention not only on historical contexts but also on associated concepts.

To set the scene for the later appearance of reality TV, the first chapter reviews important genealogical antecedents by focusing on two early attempts to capture televisual 'reality': Alan Funt's Cold War-era *Candid Camera* (1947–1970s) and the 1970s documentary series *An American Family* (PBS, 1973). These two programmes are both concerned with the observation of everyday life, but they implement different innovative techniques to do so, namely, the hidden camera in *Candid Camera* and what I call the 'live-in' camera in *An American Family*. The discussion of *Candid Camera* in this chapter draws links with the surveillance culture of the Cold War era as well the growing scientific interest in observing everyday life and behaviours. The discussion of *An American Family* extends beyond the series itself to follow its legacy through the 'family docs' it influenced, from the controversial UK series *The Family* (BBC, 1974), to the even more controversial Australian series *Sylvania Waters* (ABC, 1992/BBC, 1993), and finally to the relatively quiet return of *The Family* in Britain on Channel 4 (2008–10).

The second chapter is devoted to the first generation of reality television, the crime/emergency shows that sprang up in the early 1990s in the US, followed some five years later in the UK by docusoaps. The chapter combines consideration of political climate, conditions in the television industry and the rise of camcorder culture to make a claim for the similar bases of these two new format types while keeping their contexts of emergence distinct. Conceptually, the chapter considers how conservative economic policies of deregulation led to the television industry creating hybrid forms that sought to document 'everyday life' within the framework of entertainment. As these programmes repeatedly show, the everyday is equal parts banality and conflict, a paradox which challenges conventional programming practices in television and leads to what John Corner (2000) has called a 'post-documentary' culture of diversion.

For many television scholars and commentators, reality TV only begins with *Big Brother* in 1999 and *Survivor* in 2000. In Chapter 3, I argue that these two programmes mark the start of the second generation of reality TV by placing surveillance technology within the framework of competition. The idea of putting strangers together in a living situation and filming the results, however, belonged to the producers of *The Real World* (MTV, 1992), so this chapter begins by reaching back to a different 'origin' in order to map the concerns that would become relevant to the second generation. The bulk of the chapter is devoted to the phenomenon of *Big Brother*, considering it as a controversial social experiment, an international new media object and a site for competing discourses about authenticity and performance. In the final section, the chapter focuses on the implications of the competitive framework by using theories of play to analyse *Survivor* in its own discursive terms, as a game.

In Chapter 4 I trace the direct legacy of these two major competitive surveillance formats on the programmes that followed in the first half of the 2000s. In order to map the explosion of reality TV formats in this period, I argue that the competitive focus of *Survivor* becomes redefined more broadly in terms of the personal challenge, which then provides participants with opportunities for self-improvement and self-transformation. The chapter traces the development of reality TV as a transformative opportunity through four programme clusters: post-*Survivor* competition formats, real-love formats such as *The Bachelor*, makeover programmes and 'life intervention' shows (the term comes from Ouellette and Hay 2008). Conceptually, the chapter interrogates the meanings and effects of televisual transformation, laying the groundwork for thinking about reality TV as a mechanism of 'biopolitics', which is a term derived from Michel Foucault to address the way that institutions use political means to regulate how people live and thrive.

The fifth chapter claims that reality television has entered upon a third generation, which marks the shift from a focus on ordinary people to a concern with the mechanisms of celebrity. Tracing the various ways in which reality TV engages with these mechanisms, the discussion moves from a focus on talent formats (e.g. *American Idol*) through no-talent-required formats (as exemplified by reality TV stars who are famous for 'nothing') to those formats which are based on the participation of existing celebrities (e.g. *The Osbournes*, *Strictly Come Dancing*). In its approach, this chapter focuses on celebrity as a commodity which circulates in the economy of reality TV production and consumption. 'Economy' is used here in a broad sense, since celebrity serves a number of purposes in reality TV: as the highly desirable commodity called 'fame', as a form of labour leading to lucrative reward and as a form of capital that can be reinvested to produce greater celebrity. Finally, the book concludes by returning to the vexed question of genre through one of the channels that pioneered reality television, MTV, in order to better understand the contemporary hallmarks and legacies of reality TV. Although I offer some general observations about the generic consistency of reality television, my preferred mode remains at the level of the particular. My investigation of reality TV thus closes with a brief case-study of *Jersey Shore*, a programme which seems to encapsulate the highs, lows and ambiguities of this constantly developing form.

By tracing the generations of reality TV, this book seeks to introduce readers to the key themes that have structured this field of study. It covers central concepts such as authenticity and realism, ordinary life, competition, self-transformation and celebrity culture, while also providing a history of the clustering and consolidation of reality television as a genre. Along with relevant technological and industrial developments, these concepts are considered in the context of specific socio-historical periods and television programming trends to argue that reality television definitely comes from somewhere, even if we may not quite know where it is going.

# 1 Before Reality TV: From *Candid Camera* to *Family* Docs

No genre springs into culture fully formed. Rather, scholars like Steve Neale (2000) and Jason Mittel (2004) stress that genres are always in the process of formation. This is in part because any genre's textual forms and associated industry practices take time to coalesce, and in part because a genre develops through its usage, as it circulates in the discourses of high or popular culture. Reality television is no exception. Its prehistory can be traced back through documentary, quiz shows, talent competitions and talk shows – any television format that over the decades has invited 'real people' before the camera. For this reason, many critics have argued that reality TV offers little that is new. A more careful genealogy, however, must draw attention not simply to the presence of non-actors before the camera but also to the place of the camera itself in relation to 'real people'. This chapter thus reviews the important genealogical antecedents to reality television by focusing on two early modes of capturing reality through television: the hidden camera and what I will call the live-in camera. The former was brought to television and popularised by Allen Funt's *Candid Camera*, which began in 1948 and has continued off and on to the present day. The latter is exemplified by two 1970s documentary experiments in capturing 'real' families, one from each side of the Atlantic: *An American Family* (PBS, Alan and Susan Raymond, 1973) and *The Family* (BBC, Paul Watson, 1974). Although all three of these programmes have been identified by scholars as key sources for the development of reality television (notably McCarthy 2004; Clissold 2004; and Ruoff 2002), they have yet to be considered together as providing a dual legacy – technological and conceptual – for reality TV.

Both kinds of camera, the hidden and the live-in camera, are reliant on technological developments in the mid-twentieth century that led to smaller, portable audio-visual recording devices. Documentary film-makers in the 1940s had been severely restricted by the large and clunky apparatus required to film with synchronised sound; they preferred to film black-and-white images with lighter equipment and add sound in post-production (Ellis and McLane 2005). When Allen Funt began using the innovative wire recorder in the mid-1940s, he became one of numerous documentarists in the post-war period who used its portability to capture real voices – although he was the only one to think of concealing it to produce 'candid' vignettes as a media commodity. By the late 1950s, fuelled by the recording needs of the television news market, technological advances were making it possible to record image and sound synchronously on portable equipment (Neupert 2007). It was the mobile 16 mm cameras and magnetic tape recorders of the 1960s, however, that revolutionised both fiction and documentary film-making. The film-makers of the French New Wave, for instance, made an art form out of the possibilities presented by the new technology, favouring location shooting, natural lighting, short shooting schedules and non-eventful, everyday storylines. The same techniques meant that documentary-makers were discovering that it was 'possible to film everyday events with minimal staging or intervention' (Nichols 2001: 100). The clichéd storylines of traditional fiction film and the didactic narration of conventional documentaries could be traded in for something more real, shot direct from life. As the new equipment became more lightweight, dropping from 200 to 20 lbs in 1960 alone (Ellis and McLane 2005: 210), filming reality without alteration or interruption became more plausible – and more desirable.

The 1960s and 1970s saw the rise of two observational documentary approaches made possible by the technological advances in portable filming equipment: *cinema vérité* in France and direct cinema in the US. Although both sought to capture life on the fly through the synchronous recording of image and sound, the two methods had a different approach to the role of the camera. The term *cinema vérité* was coined by French ethnographic film-maker Jean Rouch, who was himself inspired by pioneer Soviet film-maker Dziga Vertov's *kino pravda* (cinema of truth) from forty years earlier (Ellis and McLane 2005: 216). Borrowing concepts from New Wave film-makers, *cinema vérité* acknowledged the role of the camera as a catalyst to events and the film-maker as an active participant, producing a visual style 'that incorporated informality and spontaneity into its "look", including such unconventional "mistakes" as poor lighting and the optically violent movement of the camera, which was frequently handheld' (Monaco 2001: 203). On the other side of the Atlantic, photojournalist Robert Drew and cinematographer Ricky Leacock joined American documentary makers in creating 'direct cinema', which sought to revolutionise the tradition of didactic documentary film-making by doing away with a narrator and giving viewers a sense of 'being there'. Both of these documentary movements are observational, in the sense that they claim to let the material speak for itself. They are distinguished, however, by their stance on filmic objectivity: whereas *cinema vérité* denied the possibility of objectivity and embraced the subjective involvement of the film-maker, direct cinema placed its faith in an unobtrusive, fly-on-the-wall camera held by an objective observer. Climactic events or tense scenarios provided the best material for both documentary approaches, but Erik Barnouw notes the crucial distinction between the way they approached climaxes: 'The direct cinema documentarist took his camera to a situation of tension and waited hopefully for a crisis; the Rouch version of *cinema-vérité* tried to precipitate one. The direct cinema artist aspired to invisibility; the Rouch *cinema-vérité* artist was often an avowed participant' (Barnouw 1993: 254–5).

This struggle to decide whether the camera should offer reality directly or direct reality remains pertinent for discussions of reality TV. In this chapter we will consider *Candid Camera* as an early televisual form of directing reality, since situations on this programme were constructed in order to elicit humorous behaviour from unknowing participants. In *An American Family* and *The Family*, by contrast, we will find the observational or 'fly-on-the-wall' camera used in these programmes in an attempt to show reality directly and objectively. Both of these approaches to filming reality, the contrived and the observed, become crucial strands of the reality TV genre yet to be developed. Of course, any media form must by definition mediate the reality it seeks to capture, and this inevitably opens the way to accusations of intervention, manipulation, simulation and even deception. Such accusations are exacerbated when the mediated reality intersects with the genres and frameworks of television entertainment. In this chapter we will thus consider the foundational issues for reality TV. Do 'real people' before a camera remain real and under what conditions might this be possible? How much manipulation is permissible, or even necessary, by reality documentarists and at what stage of the process? What is the social value and the ethical cost of putting real people under surveillance? And finally, what are the legacies of the observational style for the development of the reality TV genre?

## *Candid Camera*: History and Format

*Candid Camera* originated in audio format as *Candid Microphone*, broadcast on radio in 1947. Allen Funt, the creator and producer, traces the provenance of the programme to his early beginnings as an 'idea and gimmick man' for radio shows (Zimbardo 1985: 44), which in turn led to his 'show business apprenticeship' in the US Army Signal Corps during World War II (Nadis 2007: 14). Here, he was given the opportunity to create radio shows, including one called 'The Gripe Booth' in which GI's aired their complaints. Whereas Funt began by inviting soldiers to speak into the microphone, he soon discovered that the men would speak more candidly if they did not know they were being recorded; the new wire recorder that was available in the Army, Funt says, 'was a revelation because it was small enough to conceal' (Zimbardo 1985: 44). In the hands of Funt, this revelation was revolutionary: the concept of the hidden microphone, placed in the service of media entertainment, was born.

For Funt, the appeal of covert recording, which he successfully pitched to producers on his return to New York, lay in creating 'a program that would simply record the beauty of everyday conversation' through 'pure eavesdropping' (Funt and Reed 1994, cited in Nadis 2007: 14). In the hands of Funt, eavesdropping became a neutral and even necessary tool of the documentary impulse to capture everyday reality. But Funt also discovered that everyday conversation could be dull if allowed to unfold at its own pace. He thus created scenarios to see how people reacted when they were 'unposed, unrehearsed and completely off-guard' (Funt, cited in Nadis 2007: 18). In an episode of *Candid Microphone*, for instance, one vignette involves the icon of early horror films, Bela Lugosi, posing as a curiosity shop owner and asking an unwitting female customer to admire his shop's collection of shrunken heads, human bones and sundry unpleasantries.[1] While the setting is obviously staged, Funt had already figured out in 1947 that 'everyday conversation' was only truly interesting if people were given something to react to, a strange situation or everyday crisis that would test their responses. The hidden microphone was not just an eavesdropper, but also a stagehand.

In 1948, *Candid Microphone* switched media, from radio to television, and from microphone to camera. The new show *Candid Camera* 'became the first programme to be aired on the new ABC network', as Bradley Clissold points out, thus placing this progenitor of reality TV at the origins of network television itself (2004: 35). Over the next two decades, *Candid Camera* appeared on all three major US networks, in syndication and as part of evening talkshows,[2] eventually achieving prime-time popularity as a weekly series on CBS from 1960 to 1967. During this same period, a UK version was developed which ran for five series. In the early 1970s, Funt made three films on

the model of *Candid Camera* about sex, money and marriage, respectively.[3] Throughout the 1970s and 1980s, *Candid Camera* appeared
sporadically in syndication, as network specials and on cable, including
an adult version produced by Funt for the Playboy Channel. Although
Allen Funt ended his involvement in 1993, his son Peter Funt continued with the programme, co-hosting a weekly show on CBS from 1998
before moving in 2001 to the PAX network and eventually switching
from production to DVD sales. This decades-long output does not
include the numerous other countries that have picked up the format
and adapted it to their own specifications.[4] To say, then, that *Candid
Camera* has enjoyed enduring popularity is an understatement: Funt's
entertainment concept of placing ordinary people in a simulated scenario, unaware that they are being filmed, struck a chord with viewers
that overflows historical and cultural boundaries. Fred Nadis expresses
some surprise that the original show 'pleased audiences even though
it did not fit pre-existing genres or broadcasters' notion of television's
strengths as a medium' (2007: 15). With the advantage of hindsight,
however, it might be more accurate to suggest that Funt was inventing a genre, one that presciently foresaw the possibilities to come of
television as a channel for 'mediatized observation' (Yesil 2001).

The format of *Candid Camera* is disarmingly simple and hence
repeatable with endless variation. The show consists of multiple short
vignettes, each of which involves a preconceived scenario set up in
a public place to lure unwitting participants, whose reactions are
then secretly filmed. After a few minutes, the camera and set-up are
exposed to the participants, providing a dramatic climax which Funt
called 'the reveal'. Although Funt developed numerous categories
from which to generate vignettes – including 'tricks of the trade', 'wish
fulfilment' and 'human frailties' (Nadis 2007: 15) – the mainstay of the
long-running series was the 'small crisis' (ibid.). Whether the 'crisis'
is a mailbox that engages passers-by in conversation, a mimeograph
machine that won't stop spitting out paper or a temporary secretary
ushered into a business office and asked to take a love letter, in all of
these situations people find themselves in familiar, 'normal' settings
that are made somehow strange or abnormal. Repeatedly in these
scenarios, Funt is interested in the interpersonal context, especially
in the way that people respond to authority, whether institutional or
simply social pressure. He thus returned several times to the elevator
gag, where *Candid Camera* operatives face to the side or back of a lift,
forcing the unwitting participant to do the same or stand out as different. Similarly, he tested how motorists would react to a motorway
sign claiming that the state of Delaware is closed for the day (they

obediently turned around and tried another state). Interestingly, despite the fact that the camera is always concealed, most participants respond to abnormality in an everyday situation by looking around to see if they are being observed. This is one reason, perhaps, why the 'reveal' is so often met with smiles and relief, since the camera materialises a gaze that the participant was already expecting.

Although *Candid Camera* is best remembered for creating small crises in everyday scenarios, the 'reveal' is equally pertinent to the success of this reality TV precursor. Crucially, the skits work only because the reveal at the end balances the unequal power relations between duped and duper, bringing the unwitting participants into the circle of the knowing and placing them on an equal footing with the 'ordinary' members of the audience. With the ubiquitous catchphrase 'Smile, you're on *Candid Camera*!', Funt invited the duped participants to laugh at themselves along with the social community of *Candid Camera* crew and viewers at home. In fact, it is in the moment when participants discover the camera – and hence look directly into it – that the connection between the ordinary person on screen and ordinary viewers at home is made most strongly. In the reveal, then, it is not only the duped who become knowing but also the knowing who recognise their affinity with the duped: 'It works when we are essentially laughing at ourselves and our weaknesses, and when it plays up our ability to endure those weaknesses and still get on with the business of living' (Funt, cited in Zimbardo 1985: 47). The contrary is precisely what does not work. Placing people in cruel scenarios or 'show[ing] people at . . . an enormous disadvantage' causes audiences to dissociate themselves from the prank. In these cases, writes Funt, 'one simply starts laughing at [the subjects] with total sympathy and exhibits a total antipathy toward the people who are perpetrating the hoax' (Funt 1971: 254). Such antipathy to the perpetrators, whether on the part of audiences or participants, represents the Achilles heel of a format based on pranks and contrived situations. This is why Funt stresses that 'I am personally supportive, not aloof or condescending . . . Everyone who agrees to let us air their segment gets medals inscribed, "I was on *Candid Camera* and I was big enough to let other people share the experience with me" – and they were' (cited in Zimbardo 1985: 47).

By thus cajoling people into seeing themselves as associates who 'share the experience' with him – and offering a medal as proof of achievement – Funt was able to obtain signed releases from the majority of his subjects. In fact, Funt made a point of obtaining releases from all recognisable participants; if someone refused to sign, then he would not even develop the film (Funt 1971: 258). The release, both a legal document and a statement of acquiescence to 'sharing' the experience, was a guarantee against future lawsuits. But it also granted participants a degree of (retroactive) choice as well as a literal buy-in to the process, thereby redressing the ethical imbalance of power in the prank. As Clissold points out, the release placed participants, who had previously been unwitting dupes, in the position of '"knowledgeable agents" capable of resisting and negotiating the terms of their own surveillance' (2004: 42). Further, the release constituted the basis of an economic exchange. Paid on average $50 for signing the release, participants turned their performance into a commodity, making surveillance, Clissold argues, into 'a business transaction' (ibid.).

## *Candid Camera* as Surveillance

When Funt first began experimenting with the wire recorder, the concept of the hidden microphone already existed, although not yet for purposes of business or entertainment. Rather, it was an important part of surveillance practices being carried out by governmental and military forces, especially in the aftermath of World War II as a political and ideological stand-off escalated between the US and the Soviet Union. From the late 1940s until well into the 1970s – that is, the same period in which the original *Candid Camera* appeared regularly on networks or in syndication – daily life in the US was marked by the Cold War era, a period characterised by threats of nuclear attack, fears of Communist infiltration, domestic vigilance against 'un-American' activities, and the spread of surveillance on both sides of the political divide. Funt himself was well aware that the popularity of *Candid Microphone* had much to do with the cultural context of surveillance:

> In those days, the late forties, the public was fascinated by the idea of recording equipment that was so small it could be hidden. Remember, this was the beginning of the Cold War and fears of the Russians spying on the U.S. were constantly on people's minds. Publicity for *Candid Microphone* always mentioned how the microphone was hidden. (Funt and Reed 1994: 35)

Allen Funt, in other words, was 'the idea and gimmick man' who produced the right idea for the right time.

The initial reviews of *Candid Microphone* archived by Funt suggest a degree of anxiety associated with covert surveillance as well as a fascination with its seemingly unstoppable spread. A *Time* magazine reviewer noted, '[t]he whole country seems likely to be plagued with hidden microphones', while the *New York Herald Tribune* had the prescience to foresee the next move: 'The possibilities are limitless: the prospect is horrifying. Wait till they get the Candid Television Camera. You won't be safe in your own bathtub' (Funt and Reed 1994: 30). As articulated in these reviews, the concern has less to do with Communists or un-American activities than with the violation of privacy implicit in skits which catch people off-guard. Of course, for practical as well as legal reasons, Funt was careful to set up candid scenarios in public places, but the idea of covert surveillance, then as now, inspired anxiety about being caught in one's most private moments (e.g. naked in the bathtub). Bradley Clissold, however, argues that the reviewers mistakenly held Funt's show responsible for the spread of private surveillance:

> *Candid Microphone* wasn't responsible for placing hidden microphones or cameras in suburban backyards and households; they were already there in the eyes and ears of concerned and vigilant citizens encouraged by government propaganda to report any signs of "un-American" activity. (Clissold 2004: 35)

Since a culture of surveillance involving citizens as well as the government had already established itself on American soil, this meant that *Candid Microphone* and later *Candid Camera* found it easy to take root. Clissold goes on to point out, moreover, that this was a two-way relationship. Whereas '[t]he climate of Cold War politics and culture arguably made audiences ideologically receptive' to the hidden-camera show, *Candid Camera* '[i]n turn . . . made surveillance entertaining, less threatening and ideologically acceptable' (ibid.). The show not only asked participants literally to accept surveillance by signing a release but also diluted viewers' surveillance-anxiety with laughter (Clissold 2004: 33).

In this Cold War climate of surveillance, where people watched each other as intently as they watched themselves to make sure their behaviour could not be construed as 'un-American', it is no surprise that authority and conformity are major themes of the *Candid* shows. Indeed the very first skit Funt undertook for *Candid Microphone* signalled the series' interest in institutional authority and obedient citizenship:

> In the first scenario I used, I went up to a New York City policeman and confessed to overparking my car the day before. I asked him to give me a ticket. As he tried to talk me out of it, I became more insistent about the values of citizenship and obeying the law. (Funt, cited in Zimbardo 1985: 44)

Funt's exaggerated obedience to the law as a 'model citizen' in this skit subverts the power of the policeman (to give tickets) and deflates the grand ideologies of citizenship (into paying fines for parking infractions). Thus, in the very act of drawing attention to the 'values of citizenship' and the power of institutional authority, he undermines both. By using a hidden microphone, moreover, Funt inverts the conventional power hierarchy: in place of government authorities using recording equipment for 'espionage and surveillance', Funt uses these 'same recording technologies' to undercut authority for the purposes of entertainment (Clissold 2004: 39). This attitude to institutional authority goes hand in hand with Funt's lifelong crusade against social conformity: 'the worst thing, and I see it over and over, is how easily people can be led by any kind of authority figure, or even the most minimal signs of authority' (cited in Zimbardo 1985: 47). In scenarios like people facing the wrong way in an elevator or a motorway sign that Delaware is closed for the day, viewers are asked to laugh at – and hence to undercut – their own willing conformity to social pressure and minimal degrees of authority. By pressing his subjects to 'Smile!' and be a good sport, however, Funt was himself engaged in modelling a certain kind of citizen, the individual who accepted surveillance with grace. His position as a well-known personality on *Candid Camera* was its own kind of authority, and the laughter his skits evinced was also a means of social regulation. If *Big Brother*-style surveillance, whether institutional or social, can be used to produce the model citizen, then Funt was among the first to use surveillance both to critique authority and to promote a citizenship that accepts surveillance as a useful tool of the modern mediated world. As with reality TV, the ethics are troublingly circular: surveillance is the tool of resistance that provides the means of 'teaching responsible citizenship' (McCarthy 2004: 23), which in turn involves being compliant with (televisual) surveillance.

### *Candid Camera* as Behavioural Science

Allen Funt was not the only one between the 1950s and the 1970s to be using 'covertly filmed behavior [as] a tool for teaching responsible citizenship', as Anna McCarthy points out (2004: 23). This was also a period of social experimentation with human subjects by psychologists and experimental sociologists eager to understand the motivations of human behaviour in a world which had produced fascist and Communist totalitarianism. In this era, which was beginning 'to use *simulation* as a problem-solving tool' and 'as a means for producing new knowledge' (McCarthy 2004: 30; original emphasis), Funt was praised for his ability to elicit the norms of human behaviour from simulated situations. Embracing Funt's work as a popularisation of their own models, social scientists praised *Candid Camera* for the 'educational value' (Funt, cited in Zimbardo 1985: 47) of placing people in an experimental situation to test their responses. Philip Zimbardo, a social psychologist at Stanford University, compared Funt to Sigmund Freud in his preface to a 1985 interview with Funt in *Psychology Today*: 'What Sigmund Freud did for the couch and the study of the abnormal, Allen Funt has done for elevators, street corners, mailboxes and the study of the normal' (Zimbardo 1985: 43). Zimbardo's belief in the scientific importance of Funt's work was echoed by James Maas, a social psychologist at Cornell University who persuaded Funt to donate the *Candid Camera* film records to Cornell for scientific uses (Maas and Toivanen 1978). Funt's work also met with appreciation from Stanley Milgram, a Yale University professor of psychology who co-wrote an article with a graduate student in 1979 pointing to the convergences, as well as divergences, between *Candid Camera* and social scientific techniques. In this article Milgram and Sabini noted the similarities between *Candid Camera* and the ethno-methodological approach of Harold Garfinkel, an experimental sociologist who asked his students to disrupt the habits of their daily interactions in order to prove 'that people continuously construct meanings out of the flux of daily life, even out of incongruity' (Milgram and Sabini 1979: 74). For Milgram and Sabini, *Candid Camera* was to be praised for 'giv[ing] us a new vision through the disruption of the habitual' (1979: 72). In the view of these contemporary social scientists, the candid scenarios are not the settings for pranks, but for serious studies of human behaviour.

In the 1985 interview with Zimbardo, Funt admitted to some ambivalence about the ethical aspects of his show: 'I believe *Candid Camera* has educational value, but I also worry about what happens when the same type of deception or exposé of human frailty is used by the wrong people' (Zimbardo 1985: 47). What Funt has in mind as 'wrong' uses of the hidden camera concept are 'the scams of confidence men, or spying by governments or businesses, or even TV programs that encourage people to make fools of themselves for money' (ibid.). We will return to the suggestion that TV shows subsequent to *Candid Camera* might constitute a wrong or unethical use of surveillance and simulation, but for now it is interesting to note that Funt does not include experimental psychologists in the list, even though a number of these experiments have since become notorious for their unethical treatment of subjects. In the Cold War climate of anxieties about fascist and Communist totalitarianism, many behavioural psychologists and social scientists were concerned, like Funt, to test the human response to authority and social pressure by setting up situations which experimented with human subjects. Two of these experiments, carried out by vocal supporters of Funt, were particularly controversial. In the early 1960s, Stanley Milgram conducted an experiment in which subjects were asked to administer increasing doses of electric shock to a person attached to a machine as part of a putative experiment on aversion tactics in learning. The experiment depended on simulation; the shocks were a fake, the 'learner' was an actor, and the actual purpose of the experiment was to find out how far people would go to obey an authority that commands them to hurt another human being. The experiments found over and over again that subjects were willing to continue administrating increased shocks when told to do so, with the majority carrying on despite hearing cries of pain (which were actually sounds on playback) (McCarthy 2004: 32).

Although no human subjects were physically hurt in the experiment, the psychological community (as represented, for instance, by the American Psychological Association) questioned the ethics of subjecting unwary participants to the distress of causing pain to others. Moreover, as Anna McCarthy makes clear in her choice of words to describe the experiment, there is a blurred line between simulation and outright deception: 'Using actors, props, a script, and an artificial laboratory setting, Milgram *deceived* human subjects into believing that they were administering punitive electric shocks to other participants' (2004: 31; my emphasis). Not surprisingly, perhaps, Milgram's own co-authored article about *Candid Camera* is very careful to use the word 'simulation' with reference to the hidden-camera technique, even though he excuses the ethical dilemma in the interests of scientific purpose: 'Ethically, this aspect of *Candid Camera* [observing behaviour without the awareness of the participants] is problematical; scientifically it is indispensable to a full understanding of human behavior' (Milgram and Sabini 1979: 73).

Philip Zimbardo, who not only interviewed Funt but also collaborated with him on psychology classroom films, created the notorious Stanford Prison Experiment, which remains highly controversial today. In this experiment, carried out in 1971, a group of male volunteers were randomly divided into 'guards' and 'prisoners' and placed in a simulated prison setting, from arrest through booking and incarceration. The point, writes Zimbardo on the dedicated website (www.prisonexp.org), was to ask, 'What happens when you put good people in an evil place? Does humanity win over evil, or does evil triumph?' The answer, it seems, came more quickly than expected when Zimbardo lost control of the two-week experiment and shut it down after six days: 'In only a few days, our guards became sadistic and our prisoners became depressed and showed signs of extreme stress' (www.prisonexp.org). Although this experiment, unlike Milgram's, used volunteers who understood the conditions of their undertaking, the concept of placing people in an extreme situation over whose outcome they have little or no control is highly problematic, especially given that both simulations invite people to do violence to others.

Nonetheless, perhaps because of its ability to address issues of state control in relation to social and psychological violence, the Stanford experiment has had a cultural reawakening. In 2001, a disturbing German film called *Das Experiment* (dir.: Oliver Hirschbiegel) offered a fictional re-enactment of the event, and in 2005 the Polish video artist Artur Zmijewski created a restaging of the experiment with actual volunteers, from which he produced the 20-minute video *Repetition* (see Kavka 2009). Just as Milgram went on to make a documentary based on his experiments called *Obedience* (1965), so the Stanford Prison Experiment has had a media after-life, although not in Zimbardo's own hands. One notable form of this after-life is the discourse of social and psychological experimentation that clings to reality television, especially with *Big Brother* and other programmes that house 'inmates' together to see what will happen over prolonged cohabitation (see Chapter 3). Perhaps not coincidentally, early seasons of *Big Brother* in numerous countries used in-studio psychologists to provide analyses of the dynamics in the *Big Brother* house as well as to lend the gravitas of science to televisual simulation. As Anna McCarthy argues, 'reality TV in the 1950s and today . . . is a place where TV and social and applied psychology come together' (2004: 23).

### Candid Camera as Seen on TV

With the *Candid* series, Allen Funt brought the tools of surveillance to the medium of radio and then television to produce entertainment within 'a psychological or sociological framework' (Funt 1971: 257). Combining art and science, theatre and pedagogy (McCarthy 2004: 27), Funt was able to capitalise on the technological base and cultural context of mass media in the 1950s and 1960s to popularise scientific discourse and assuage surveillance anxiety through documentary tactics. He did this by understanding that the mass media could – and in his mind, should – capture a 'poetics of everyday life' (Nadis 2007: 18) that was more immediate than film and more quotidian than the outdated newsreel. Proud of having recorded an estimated one and a quarter million people in the course of his career (Zimbardo 1985: 45), Funt believed that the technology and reach of broadcast media could be used for the democratic purpose of picking individuals out of the anonymous mechanisms of history (Nadis 2007: 18). In the introduction to his first LP anthology from the *Candid Microphone* series, he celebrated the fact that 'the plain everyday kind of people you never see in the headlines or in the movies or on the stage . . . make themselves heard here as individuals' (cited in Nadis 2007: 18). In a sense, Funt implemented the utopian promise of mechanical reproduction that the cultural theorist Walter Benjamin had foreseen in the 1930s. Prior to the twentieth century, argues Benjamin, people could be recorded for posterity only by becoming a work of art in the literal sense of having their portrait painted. With the arrival of recording technology, however, it became possible to document countless people, hence 'offer[ing] everyone the opportunity to rise from passerby to movie extra. In this way any man might even find himself part of a work of art' (Benjamin 2006: 27). While Benjamin had in mind the newsreel, Funt's *Candid* vignettes go one better than offering everyone a part as an extra; they offer everyone the opportunity to appear as *themselves* in the mass media. This is the first legacy of *Candid Camera* to subsequent generations of reality TV.

Once the *Candid* format moved from radio to television, the camera increased the individualisation of the 'everyday kind of people' who passed before the lens. Beyond simply being heard, people could be *seen*, expressing their particularity through a whole range of actions and non-verbal expressions, even if – or precisely because – they did so unknowingly. It is in this potential of the television medium to capture an individual's particularities that Funt found his medium: 'Most of all, I wanted to go beyond what people merely said, to record what they did – their gestures, facial expression, confusions and delights' (cited in Zimbardo 1985: 45). When asked by Zimbardo to reflect on what made *Candid Camera* work, Funt did not emphasise the hidden recording, which he saw as little more than a red herring (Funt 1971: 259). Rather, he drew attention to the medium itself: 'We used the medium of TV well. There were close-ups of people in action. The audience saw ordinary people, like themselves, and the reality of events as they were unfolding' (cited in Zimbardo 1985: 46). This insightful combination of 'ordinary people' with an immediate 'reality of events' unfolding before the viewer lies at the core of *Candid Camera*'s success. This is its second legacy to reality television.

I suggested earlier, in response to Fred Nadis's bemusement that

*Candid Camera* was popular 'even though it did not fit pre-existing genres', that Funt was in the process of creating a genre. More accurately, since a genre is not made out of just one programme, he was laying the groundwork for what might later become a genre, creating an outline in the cultural imaginary where a particular set of techniques and terms might eventually coalesce into a recognisable generic form. Interestingly, *Candid Camera* remained a unique format from the late 1940s until the late 1980s, arguably until the appearance *America's Funniest Home Videos* discovered that the humorous-situation clip could be self-made. Although the format was sold to other countries and has recently spawned a subgenre of reality-prank programmes (e.g. *Punk'd* (MTV, 2003–7); *Prank'd* (MTV, 2010–)), the show had no US competitors and hence little generic recognisability in its 1960s heyday. This is evident from an episode of the popular quiz show *What's My Line* (CBS, 1950–67) in which Allen Funt appears as the 'mystery challenger' (TX, 15 September 1963).[5] Facing a blindfolded celebrity panel that must guess who he is or what he does, Funt disguises his voice and succeeds in flummoxing the panel. They discover early on in the questioning that he is on a TV show but they cannot figure out which one because they try to narrow it down by genre: panel show, situation comedy, drama, variety show? Even Arlene Francis's question about whether the show is based on comedy meets with the ambiguous response, 'sometimes yes and sometimes otherwise'. Had the panel, of course, asked whether this was a hidden-camera programme which captured ordinary people's reactions to small crises in everyday settings, the answer would have been obvious. But no one thought to use any of those terms – hidden camera, ordinary people, contrived situations – because at the time the show was unique. Setting out the terms around which a genre could coalesce around these terms is the third legacy of *Candid Camera* to reality television.

## Observing Ordinary People

At the same time as Allen Funt and his camera crews were taking advantage of portable – and concealable – sync-sound equipment for CBS in the 1960s, another team of American film-makers was taking candid recording for film and television in a different direction. Drew Associates was founded by Robert Drew in the late 1950s and consisted of a group of young documentarists whose names would soon become synonymous with direct cinema: Drew himself, Richard Leacock, D. A. Pennebaker, Albert and David Maysles and others.

In 1960, with Robert Drew as writer and director, Drew Associates made the landmark film *Primary*, which chronicled the battle between Democratic presidential nominees John F. Kennedy and Hubert Humphrey on the campaign trail before the Wisconsin primary election. Using hand-held cameras, long takes and no interviews or narration, the film literally follows the two candidates and observes them from an insider position, shooting them in their hotel rooms as well as in town halls. This up-close, fly-on-the-wall style represented the direct cinema documentarists' commitment to recording actuality 'without script, without direction, with scarcely any editing' (Ellis and McLane 2005: 218). The documentary subjects were left to direct themselves, and the stories told themselves in the pictorial style Drew called 'candid photography', which he had learned as a photojournalist at *LIFE* magazine in the 1950s.

The observational style of direct cinema became the mark of cutting-edge documentary film-making in the 1960s. Seeking to show rather than tell, documentary makers such as the Maysles brothers, D. A. Pennebaker and even the artist Andy Warhol experimented with placing an objective camera in intimate relation to the unfolding of everyday life. Perhaps the best-known film is D. A. Pennebaker's portrait of Bob Dylan on tour, *Don't Look Back* (1967), but not all direct cinema required famous subjects from politics or culture. On the contrary, the observational style lent itself to up-close portraits of ordinary people as a way of addressing social issues. In the UK, John Boorman produced a five-part series for the BBC called *Citizen 63* (1963), which made use of extensive mobile observational footage, combined with narration, to focus on one ordinary person per episode as 'part of our society' (cited in BFI Screenonline). In 1964, the investigative current affairs show *World in Action* (ITV, 1963–98) launched the experimental *Up* series with *Seven Up!*, a documentary which selected fourteen British schoolchildren from a range of socio-economic backgrounds for a project which would film them every seven years to show how social class determines future status. In the US, independent film-maker Frederick Wiseman documented unnamed individuals in American social institutions, such as *High School* (1969) and *Hospital* (1970). And in 1969, Allan King extended the same logic by applying the observational style to the most intimate of social institutions – marriage. His film about ten critical weeks in a marriage, called simply *A Married Couple*, directly inspired Craig Gilbert, producer of *An American Family*, to apply the observational style to tracking an ordinary family (Ruoff 2002: 12–13). The result, much to producer Craig Gilbert's surprise, was a media and cultural event, which would influence future televisual representation of real families and (eventually) spawn the 24/7 reality TV form.

## An American Family: The Original Family Doc

On 11 January 1973 the Public Broadcasting Service (PBS) aired the first episode of a twelve-part unscripted series devoted to the everyday life of the Loud family in Santa Barbara, California. Over the ensuing three months, it became one of the most watched and talked-about non-fiction programmes in the history of US television, with an estimated 10 million viewers tuning in per episode (Ruoff 2002: xv). It was widely, if not necessarily positively, reviewed in respected newspapers and magazines. The members of the Loud family themselves wrote articles, gave interviews and appeared on all three of the major issue-oriented talkshows of the early 1970s: *The Phil Donahue Show*, *The Mike Douglas Show* and, most memorably, *The Dick Cavett Show*. Producer Craig Gilbert made it clear that this was intended as a sociological programme about the issues affecting – and irretrievably changing – family life in 1970s' America: divorce rates, the women's movement, the generation gap, and new attitudes to sex, sexuality and drugs (Rupert and Puckett 2010). The Louds may not have been the 'average or typical' American family, as Gilbert's introductory narration to the first episode insisted, but they were certainly *an* American family. Hence, they were worth watching as individuals undergoing many of the daily strains and crises that plagued other families. Critics and viewers alike, however, tended to overlook the sociological aspects of *An American Family* for the far more fascinating spectacle of real people living out their lives on television,[6] especially when it came to the on-screen break-up of Pat and Bill Loud's twenty-year marriage or the revelation that eldest son Lance was gay. As Gail Rock contended in a review for *Ms.* magazine, the show was 'more candid than Allen Funt's wildest dreams' (cited in Ruoff 2002: 102).

The Louds were an affluent and attractive nuclear family, but they were not the idealised family of sitcoms. Craig Gilbert had selected them in part because they lived in California, which Gilbert thought was at the cutting-edge of American culture (Ruoff 2002: 17), and in part because they were educated and promised to be articulate about the social pressures on family life. To some extent the pressures on this nuclear family were standard: with five children aged between thirteen and twenty, the family was prone to disruption by teenage rebellion and the older children's bids for independence. The pressures were also, however, specific to the changing social mores of the 1970s: while father Bill, who owned a concrete company, preached the values of hard work to his long-haired, less-than-motivated sons, mother Pat was the educated but bored housewife targeted by the women's movement. Lance Loud, the eldest and most opinionated of the children, had already left the family for New York, where he was unemployed and living at the Chelsea Hotel, famed as a centre for artistic and bohemian life. When, in the second episode of the series, Lance 'came out' to TV audiences by speaking openly with his mother about being gay, the revelation sent shock waves through viewers. And when, in the ninth episode, Pat asked Bill for a divorce, it became clear that Gilbert had found a family who radically subverted the traditional representations of family life on television while reflecting the shifting family demographics of the early 1970s.

Although the series aired in 1973, filming took place two years earlier, for seven months from May to December 1971. This was the first time that a television production team had placed ordinary people under such close scrutiny for such an extended period of time. To capture the lived reality of the family, Gilbert hired husband-and-wife team Susan and Alan Raymond as the film crew, with Susan recording sound and Alan behind the camera. The Raymonds shot the Louds continuously over the seven-month period, producing over 300 hours of film (including the footage from a second camera crew with Lance). Between the hours of 8 am and 10 pm, the Raymonds had uninterrupted access to the Louds, becoming in effect a part of the family. For all intents and purposes, then, the Louds were monitored by a *live-in camera* whose presence became an accepted part of their intimate domestic space. In keeping with the observational style, Craig Gilbert had counselled the Louds 'to live their lives as if there were no camera present', and had told the Raymonds not to intrude, alter or in any way direct events (cited in Ruoff 2002: 27). The crew, in other words, was to be omnipresent but invisible, an expected but ignorable element in the Louds' daily lives. Bill Loud, appearing with the family on *The Dick Cavett Show*, said approvingly that the presence of the crew was like having 'a maid in the house' (cited in Ruoff 2002: 34), while Pat Loud noted about the Raymonds that '[w]e really liked and cared about each other' (cited in Ruoff 2002: 29). Trust was thus a necessary part of the relationship between subjects and film-makers, as other direct cinema documentarists had found (Ruoff 2002: 29; Ellis and McLane 2005: 215–16), but the depth of the relationship between the Raymonds and the Louds also meant that the crew was unlikely to be invisible. This was to some extent offset by a sense of contractual obligation on the part of the Louds. Even though the family by common consent was not being paid (Ruoff 2002: 27), Pat Loud reflected in her subsequent autobiography on the sense of obligation 'to live up to our part of the bargain, which was, of course, to try to be as honest and candid as we normally would be had the cameras *not* been there' (cited in Ruoff 2002: 35; original emphasis). As Jeffrey Ruoff succinctly notes, the Louds' job was to live their lives and the Raymonds' job was to film it (2002: 35).

The 'missing' year between filming in 1971 and screening in early 1973 was devoted entirely to editing. Although the long takes and wide shots of the observational style allowed the action to unfold 'without script, without direction', there was no hope of producing the series 'with scarcely any editing' (Ellis and McLane 2005: 218). On the contrary, the editors had to reduce over 300 hours of film into 12 hours of screen time, which meant deciding not only what to cut but also how to arrange the little material that made it to air. Since the family had been filmed over such a long period, numerous events had occurred in causal and seasonal relation to one another, so the editors opted to arrange material chronologically. They thus organised scenes around incidents rather than characters. The result was a multiple-focus and multiple-character narrative that told a coherent story, even if this remained open-ended. The only exception to this editing strategy occurred in the first episode, which opened with on-camera narration by Craig Gilbert describing not only the history of the William C. Loud family and their settlement in Santa Barbara, but also admitting upfront, 'There is no question that the presence of our camera crews and their equipment had an effect on the Louds, one which is impossible to evaluate' (TX, 11 January 1973). More striking in the first episode, however, is the editors' decision to start the story with the last day of shooting. Over the family's preparations for that evening's New Year's Eve party, Gilbert intones, 'This New Year's will be unlike any other . . . for the first time, the family will not be spending it together' – before the camera cuts to a shot of Bill alone in his office. The entire narrative is thus framed by the break-up of the marriage and the rupture of the family. Everything that unfolds thereafter is organised around this climactic moment to come, and the family is represented from the start as a broken family. Even Gilbert's chirpy voice-over saying 'our story begins seven months earlier at 6.30 on a late spring morning' signals the beginning of a story of decline.

The decision to book-end the chronological framework with footage of the ruptured family invites comparison with the structure of fictional narratives. Indeed, *An American Family* is a heterogeneous combination of non-fiction and fiction formats: it is shot in an observational style without direction or script but adapted in post-production to television as a storytelling medium. Given that there was no pre-set genre for this kind of programme, the producer and editors borrowed from existing TV genres in order to make the show more recognisable to viewers. As Ruoff notes, the opening credits sequence for each episode emphasises the series' connection to television sitcoms by introducing each of the family members to an upbeat theme song and then boxing them into their own space on screen, recalling the openings of *The Brady Bunch* and *The Partridge Family* (2002: 67) but also prefiguring the tongue-in-cheek credits of *The Osbournes* (MTV, 2002–5). Unlike the idealised sitcoms of the 1970s, however, the word 'family' cracks at the end of the *American Family* title sequence, signalling that the family itself is broken. The ongoing disagreements between Bill and his sons about the importance of work, Pat's morose and sometimes jealous responses to her husband, Lance's bohemian lifestyle and homosexuality, not to mention the break-up of the parents' marriage on air – for viewers, this material was recognisable from soap operas, not sitcoms or documentaries. Indeed, the multiple-character narrative and division of the programme into episodes copied the format of soaps, keeping viewers tuning in to see what will happen 'next time'. The fact that this was a real-life soap, however, shot using the conventions of observational realism, meant that viewers were also reminded they were watching non-fiction. This generic instability led reviewers to compare it to 'home movies, television commercials, talk shows, variety shows, situation comedies, soap operas, novels, plays, sociological studies and documentaries' (Ruoff 2002: 108). No one could quite figure out what they were watching, but everyone tuned in to watch.

The post-production decisions about editing, screen credits and publicity impacted strongly on how the series was received. By and large, *An American Family* met with highly critical reviews and negative publicity (although Pat Loud stresses in her autobiography that she received many letters of support from viewers as well). If there was genre confusion among reviewers, there was even greater confusion about where to draw the line between reality and mediated fiction. On the one hand, '[t]he open-ended episodic structure of the program, broadcast weekly, accentuated similarities with everyday life and promoted strong identification with the Louds' (Ruoff 2002: 105). Audiences accepted the Louds as ordinary people like themselves, so much so that 'most reviewers . . . talked about the Louds as if they were their next-door neighbours' (Ruoff 2002: 102). On the other hand, the very fact that the Louds were on television raised questions – and invited condemnation – about the effect of the camera on their

behaviour. It became a common refrain in reviews and later criticism
that the series had caused the Louds to break up, even though Pat Loud
asserted in her autobiography that the filming had probably extended
the life of the marriage (cited in Ruoff 2002: 111). Similarly Lance
Loud was deemed to have come out on TV, as though the presence
of the camera had forced the dramatic event, even though Lance's
family had already known for some time he was homosexual. As an
anonymous reviewer wrote in *America*, 'As this journal of deteriora-
tion unfolds . . . might it have been otherwise if there were no camera
and no microphone?' (cited in Ruoff 2002: 117). The suggestion here
is clear: the camera is not an observer but an intruder into the family
home, *causing* dramatic ruptures by its very presence. As Ruoff points
out, '*An American Family* may best be remembered as a nonfiction
program haunted by the presence of the camera' (2002: 117). More
to the point, it is the first non-fiction programme to be haunted by
the presence of the live-in camera, which holds out the promise of a
more intimate portrait of everyday life while it threatens to distort that
everyday life by intervening in it. This tension between reality and
mediation is unresolved in the responses to *An American Family*. Roger
Rosenblatt wrote in *The New Republic*, 'never was there greater realism
on television except in the murders of Oswald and Robert Kennedy'
(cited in Ruoff 2002: 102), while S. I. Hayakama claimed in the *Chicago
Tribune* that the series was 'a most artificial situation' (cited in Ruoff
2002: 117). Both responses, of course, were equally true – a paradox
that would only be exacerbated as later generations came to 'live their
lives' on TV.

### *The Family*: Realism and Social Class

In 1974, influenced by *An American Family*, producer Paul Watson
made the twelve-part series *The Family* for the BBC in Britain. The
series, which screened from early April to late June, brought the
live-in camera to the home of the extended Wilkins family in Reading,
England. Despite the similarity in episodic structure and observational
style to *An American Family*, there were some notable differences
between the two programmes. Most importantly, there was a difference in social class. Whereas the Louds were an affluent family with
a sprawling eight-room ranch house and four vehicles in suburban
southern California, the Wilkins were a working-class family of nine
people living in a small six-room flat above a greengrocer's shop in
an industrial town. Like the Louds, Terry and Margaret Wilkins had
children spread across a range of ages, from nine to nineteen, but their

flat was also home to the elder two children's partners and one grand-child: eighteen-year-old Paul had married his pregnant girlfriend at sixteen, with his small family occupying a room of the Wilkins's flat, while nineteen-year-old Marion was sharing her bedroom with her boyfriend Tom. Like *An American Family*, this programme raised con-troversial social issues, such as pre-marital sex and interracial relation-ships (fifteen-year-old Heather had a mixed-race boyfriend, Melvin), but the series took a more didactic approach, adding voice-over nar-ration and directorial engagement to the fly-on-the-wall observational style. Moreover, the series began screening during the fourth week of filming, which allowed later episodes to incorporate self-reflexivity about the reception of the programme. Despite these differences, however, the impact of *The Family* was much the same as that of *An American Family*: the series was 'one of the most talked-about docu-mentaries ever shown on television',[7] and the Wilkins became celebri-ties surrounded by negative publicity. They were vilified in the local, tabloid and broadsheet press for being immoral, immodest and, ulti-mately, both too real and not real enough. Unlike the Louds's recep-tion in the US, the mediation of the Wilkins's lives cast doubt among the British public about the value of the observational domestic gaze.

Just as the Louds had been explicitly selected for *An American Family* because of their social class, the Wilkins were intended to provide an individualised portrait of class-based life in Britain. The difference between the two approaches to class, however, could not be more striking, first, because of the stark difference between the socio-economic status of the two families and, second, because the issue of class is masked by the myth of self-invention in the American context, whereas in the British context it remains central to social identity. The Louds were chosen primarily because they represented the American dream (Rupert and Puckett 2010); as the pre-screening publicity emphasised, they had a large house, numerous cars, experience as international travellers and a poolside lifestyle in the sunny paradise of southern California. In other words, their affluence and lifestyle were the central components of the dream to which it was presumed all Americans aspired, a dream which had been regularly depicted in idealised family representations on sitcoms since the 1960s. Their class status, as is still the case in American culture, was deemed to be secondary to their material success, although the desirability of their possessions did not prevent the Louds from being demonised in the press as 'affluent zombies' (cited in Ruoff 2002: 103).

The Wilkins, by contrast, were positioned as 'ordinary people' precisely by dint of being working class. This emphasis on class looks forward to reality TV, but it harks back to the British documentary tradition of social realism, which since the 1930s had 'privilege[d] actuality and verisimilitude as a mode and working-class lives and social change as its subject matter' (Biressi and Nunn 2005: 36). In the UK, the working classes have long served as a cultural signifier of authenticity, and social realist film-makers since John Grierson – often called the father of British documentary film – sought to educate the public about the harsh realities of working-class life so as to bring about social change. *The Family* adopts a less expository mode than the Griersonian documentaries of the 1930s and 1940s but its implicit claim to the authentic representation of family life has as much to do with the Wilkins's working-class status as with the fly-on-the-wall technique. In fact, producer Paul Watson was aiming to correct the tendency of television to give airtime only to people who were already 'somebody' (Young 1974: 208) by placing on screen the kind of people who were not usually represented (Corner 2004) – the 'nobodies' who were authentic because they were ordinary workers. The footage shot for *The Family* is carefully organised in the early episodes so as to high-light the socio-political themes of everyday working-class life: housing shortages, pregnancy and marriage, schooling, work and income, parenting and domestic responsibilities, and racial tensions. The dif-ference from previous representations of working-class life in Britain, however, lies with the live-in camera, which offers a protracted gaze on the private lives of a family that speaks for and about itself. As Mrs Wilkins makes clear in the first episode about her motivation for taking part in the series: 'All right, so we get paid . . . but it gives us a chance to portray ordinary people' (TX, 3 April 1974). Of course, once they appear on television, they become 'somebodies' and far from ordinary people, which we now understand to be the contradictory, and often disturbing, effect of television cameras that seek out ordinariness. But already in the 1970s, as Su Holmes argues, 'Watson was as much inter-ested in how the family would respond to being mediated as he was in reflecting aspects of social life in Britain' (Holmes 2008b: 202).

As in *An American Family*, the camera (and crew) did not literally live in the house, but it seemed that way: the family was filmed for some sixteen hours a day for three months largely in the confines of their six-room flat. The initial description of the show in *The Radio Times* did not mince words about the novelty of the programme: 'The ups and downs of a real life family are captured week by week in this twelve-part documentary serial. The Wilkins family of Reading have a BBC crew living with them' (cited in Holmes 2008b: 198). This is accentuated in the first episode of the series, when Watson, sitting with the family at the kitchen table but remaining off-screen, warns them that 'we are here all the time, and we can film you anywhere, anytime' (TX, 3 April 1974). The live-in camera thus promised viewers unparalleled accessibility to and intimacy with everyday life, but this required finding 'a family prepared to tolerate the intrusion of a film crew into their every private moment' (opening voice-over, episode 1). In such a small house, the intrusion is palpable; the frame and the space are literally crammed with people. Unlike the 'human' point of view favoured by realist documentary, camera angles are often rakishly low or high with people pushed to the sides of the frame as the unseen camera crew presses into what little space is available. The *mise-en-scène* registers the vibrant but claustrophobic atmosphere of this overcrowded flat, especially in the kitchen, where cooking, eating, dishwashing, hairwashing and laundering compete for space alongside extended conversations and altercations.

The notion of intrusiveness as a tool of accessibility and intimacy is accentuated by the opening credits to each episode. The camera moves through a series of dissolves as it swoops from high above the city, across rooftops and chimneys, before entering a window and moving through the lounge to seek out picture frames positioned on the mantelpiece. The pictures consist of black-and-white family shots but the camera then intrudes into the frame itself, animating the subjects into motion in colour, before zooming back out to the family posed for a portrait in the lounge. This title sequence not only promises full revelation as layer after layer of wall, curtain and frame are peeled back but also offers to animate the family for the viewers' gaze. It is small wonder, then, that the series met with outcries about voyeurism and intrusions on privacy from viewers who felt uncomfortably placed by the promise of live-in access. As Colin Young stated in a contemporary overview of the responses to *The Family*, 'There is nothing necessarily subversive about observational cinema. But in the present case it has clearly made people consider where they personally would draw a line between observing and snooping' (Young 1974: 209). The subject matter of the observational gaze may be authentic but, when the camera lives in, viewers in the 1970s begin to feel uncomfortable about 'prying into the private lives' of a family (letter to the editor, cited in Young 1974: 206).

To offset this discomfort, the early episodes of the series are organised thematically to introduce each family member as a character with particular concerns that reflect larger social patterns. The second episode, for instance, presents a still of the lodger Tom who, the voice-over informs us, 'has finally told Margaret that he is not marrying her daughter [Marion] on April 27', while the third episode starts with a still of daughter Heather, who 'is 15 and hates school', and the fourth episode introduces a photo of daughter-in-law Karen and baby Scott accompanied by the information that she was sixteen and pregnant when she married Gary Wilkins. This pattern not only extends the metaphor of the family portrait visualised by the opening credits but also indicates the logic of the edit: the series will be organised according to character rather than event, with the lively but repetitive kitchen conversations given structure by intermittent narration. The narration, in keeping with the didactic documentary style of the era, is both omniscient and at times patronising, especially with regard to the young women's prospects (such as noting that, as a young mother, Karen is 'ensnared in the trap of low wages, inadequate education and early marriage' (TX, 24 April 1973)). From the fourth episode, however, another level of voicing enters the series, for the overlap of filming and screening means that the family have begun to watch themselves on air. Although Paul Watson wanted to film the family watching themselves on TV, this footage ended up on the cutting-room floor. What proved interesting, however, was the Wilkins's ability to respond on air to what people had written about them in the press after seeing them the previous week on television. Although this roundabout communication between press and television did not make the criticism any less vitriolic, it did set up an innovative feedback loop between one medium of popular culture and another, culminating in the last episode, when the Wilkins were shown being interviewed on Jimmy Savile's radio show. The trans-media potential of the programme had already been demonstrated earlier, when Mrs Wilkins was given her own column in the *Evening News* (Holmes 2008b: 204).

In one important sense, this trans-media reflexivity had a different outcome than the one that Watson had intended. While it certainly accentuated the presence and voice of a working-class family in the British media, it also turned them into celebrities, which radically called into question their position as an ordinary, typical or even particularly private family. Letters to the press protested that there was nothing typical about a family in which the elder daughter cohabited with her boyfriend, the elder son had had a child at sixteen, the younger daughter had a black boyfriend and the younger son was fathered by someone else during a brief hiatus in the marriage (as Mrs Wilkins revealed in the first episode). As 'Disgusted' wrote in the *Reading Family Post*, 'I can only say that if the Wilkins are an average family, Heaven help the community' (cited in Young 1974: 206). Critics also argued that there was nothing typical, or any longer private, about a family whose activities were under the scrutiny of a camera. Philip

Purser, writing in *Sight and Sound*, chided the Wilkins not only for being 'too wrapped up in their own affairs' to care about matters of socio-political import but also for engaging in role-playing for the sake of the camera (Purser 1974/5: 48–9). While this may indicate that British reviewers had a keener sense of the mediation involved than American critics reviewing *An American Family*, they were also more intent on casting the programme as a fiction so as to disparage the Wilkinses and discredit *The Family* as documentary (Purser 1974/5). The family was vilified for literally making a spectacle of themselves, lurching between washing their dirty laundry in public and acting 'as they felt behoved them as public [figures]' (Purser 1974/5: 49). They were thus too ordinary and not ordinary enough, a paradox which came to a head at the long-awaited wedding of Tom and Marion when they were mobbed by guests, fans and press photographers alike. Chosen precisely because they were working-class and hence not special, the Wilkins courted vitriol from middle-class writers for seeming to leave their 'proper' place in the class hierarchy through celebrity (Holmes 2008b: 205). Paul Watson had hoped to bring the camera into the private lives of real people to give them a voice which had been under-represented in the media. But the live-in camera, as we now know all too well, has spectacularising effects.

The lessons to be learned from the 1970s' observational family docs are thus twofold. On the one hand, the intimate, live-in camera creates a filming situation that invites viewers into the family space, offering to present reality directly. On the other hand, the presence of the camera crew and the screening of the resulting programme threaten to change this space as well as the family in it, which suggests that presenting reality directly also means directing that reality. Moreover, the greater the intimacy offered to viewers by the live-in camera, the more the subjects lose their recognisability as ordinary people, first, because the camera spectacularises the family's private space, and, second, because the screening of the footage on television turns these once ordinary people into celebrities. By the time Paul Watson made his second family documentary in the early 1990s, this time with an Australian family living in Sydney, the spectacularising effects of the live-in camera had become more pressing, exacerbated by viewers' willingness to accept the hybridisation of documentary with soap opera.

## Aftershocks: *Sylvania Waters* and the Return of *The Family*

Two decades after *The Family*, in 1992, Paul Watson returned to the live-in camera – and to controversy – as the executive producer of *Sylvania Waters*, a co-production between the BBC and ABC (the Australian Broadcasting Corporation). The format was very similar to the earlier family doc – a twelve-part documentary series focusing on the everyday lives of an extended family in a suburb of Sydney – and once again it proved to be a media event that subjected the family to fierce press scrutiny and vitriol. Shot over a five-month period from December 1991 to May 1992 by a small camera crew that had access to the family from morning till night, *Sylvania Waters* aired on ABC from July to October 1992 and on the BBC in spring of the following year. Three aspects of the programme, however, made it markedly different from *The Family*. First, the Baker-Donahers of *Sylvania Waters* were an 'exploded' rather than a nuclear family (Stratton and Ang 1994). Noeline Baker and Laurie Donaher, both middle-aged divorcés, were in a fifteen-year de facto partnership and shared the series with two of Noeline's children – fifteen-year-old Michael and twenty-six-year-old Paul – and one of Laurie's sons – twenty-one-year-old Mick – as well as Paul's pregnant fiancée Dione and Mick's wife Yvette and their two children (Noeline's daughter had declined to take part in the series (Donaher 1993)). Second, as a co-production initially pitched by Watson to the BBC, the programme positioned Australia as 'an antipodean, exotic Other' for British audiences (Stratton and Ang 1994: 5) as well as an object of self-identification for Australian audiences. Strung between two countries with a complex postcolonial relationship, the series became much more about representations of nation than class. Third, although it was shot in an observational style and promised viewers fly-on-the-wall access to the Baker-Donahers, *Sylvania Waters* was publicised, edited and viewed as a generic hybrid of documentary and soap opera, or a 'docusoap' (Biressi and Nunn 2005: 67). The advertisement seeking a family for the programme described the show as '[b]etter than a soapie, this is real life', a slogan which was continued in the show's publicity and repeated in various guises throughout the Australian press. These three aspects – family, nation and genre – set out the terms in which the programme was understood, and provided the basis for much of the media vilification and celebritisation of the central figure, Noeline Baker.

As Stratton and Ang argue in their comprehensive article about *Sylvania Waters*, the show hit a chord with audiences precisely because of the way that issues of family, nation and (television) genre resonate together in the programme. Family has long been central to television as both its subject matter and its viewer base, as can be seen from the historical importance of the family sitcom and family melodrama in soap operas (Stratton and Ang 1994: 1–4). By positioning itself as a

'real-life soapie', *Sylvania Waters* thus drew on established intersecting discourses of family, television and soap opera. Notably, by 1992
the omniscient narration from *The Family* had disappeared in favour
of a self-reflexive voice-over provided by fifteen-year-old Michael,
who sends up soap conventions by teasing viewers with questions
and urging them to 'tune in next week to find out'. Although there
is far greater use of to-camera interviews in *Sylvania Waters* than in
*The Family*, parallel editing is used to intercut interview segments
with contrasting action to suggest forthcoming drama between family
members. At the same time, the interviews and observational presence
of the live-in camera explicitly recall the documentary basis of the
earlier series. Ironically, in terms of the relation between documentary and the family, Stratton and Ang point out that 'documentaries
aimed at scrutinizing and displaying – rather than explicitly com-
menting on – family life began just as the nuclear family form went
into its period of steep decline' (1994: 12). This occurred, of course,
in the 1970s, as the Louds's marriage was breaking up on camera and
the Wilkins embraced pre-marital cohabitation and a child from an
adulterous relationship, before themselves divorcing in 1978. The
Baker-Donahers, then, simply bring this already exploding family up
to date: of the three cohabiting couples in the programme, only Mick
and Yvette are married at the start of the series. Admittedly, there is
an impetus to 'proper' marriage in the show, with Paul and Dione
getting married in the penultimate episode (as did Tom and Marion
in *The Family*) and Noeline and Laurie tying the knot after filming
finished, but in the 1990s having a baby precedes Paul and Dione's
marriage, while both Noeline and Laurie are on their second marriage. More importantly, the blended Baker-Donohue clan involves
ongoing tension (read: screaming matches) between Noeline and her
sons about their relationship with Laurie, her partner but not their
biological father, as well as endless battles about who receives financial
support from whom.

This is the point at which the exploded family overlaps with class
considerations, which in turn become conflated with representations of
nation. Noeline and Laurie could well be called the working class made
good: they run a contract-hire company and live in a nouveau-riche
suburb of Sydney, Sylvania Waters, in a million-dollar home with a
boat moored at the back and multiple cars in the garage. Although
affluent, like the Louds, they come from working-class roots (Noeline
is from rural New Zealand and Laurie was a butcher before they met),
a fact which then-Deputy Prime Minister Brian Howe accentuated
by attributing their 'unhealthy' lifestyle (smoking, alcohol and eating

habits) to their 'disadvantaged backgrounds' (cited in Donaher 1993: 129).[8] Concerns about money, which are rarely articulated on *An American Family* but repeatedly voiced in *The Family*, form the bread-and-butter subject matter of *Sylvania Waters*, with every possession priced and constant money battles raging between family members. Unlike the utopian representation of nation in the Australian soap operas *Neighbours* and *Home and Away*, this 'real-life soapie' presented Australian viewers with a representation of a family that they were unwilling to accept as 'average' or typical of their nation. Seen as materialistic, drunken and argumentative, Noeline was constructed by the press as the soap villain at the centre of a dystopian version of excessive, out-of-control Australian life (Stratton and Ang 1994: 8, 18). Worse, as the programme had been made for a British audience but was watched by Australians first, Australian audiences and reviewers anxiously rejected the Baker-Donahers not only as a national *self*-representation but also as a representation of Australianness for British viewers to poke fun at (Stratton and Ang 1994: 5).

From this explosive configuration of family, nation and soap opera as framed by the live-in camera, a media frenzy was all but inevitable. In the process, the Baker-Donahers became *more* mediated. Reporters mobbed their house (Donaher 1993: 67–9), articles in the mainstream press accompanied every new episode, viewers called in to talkback radio to express their opinions, and back-story exposés of the Baker-Donahers appeared in newspapers alongside gleeful character assassinations. Interestingly, the question of what was real and what was not barely arose. Seamlessly, Australian reviewers treated the Baker-Donahers as a combination of people-next-door and soap opera characters. This is what Stratton and Ang, following French theorist Jean Baudrillard, refer to as the 'simulacrum' of family representation in *Sylvania Waters*. With real people living their lives on TV as if the camera were not there, 'it becomes impossible to distinguish acting from natural, daily life, the representation from the real' (Stratton and Ang 1994: 13). As Baudrillard has theorised, the representation absorbs reality and the real family members *become* their TV characters, a simulacrum of themselves. Ruoff had already noticed this effect in the critical responses to *An American Family*: 'One striking development – the climax of the reality effect – was the belief that the Louds had lived their lives on television and that television was absorbing the real' (Ruoff 2002: 102–3). Anticipating postmodern theories such as Baudrillard's, the live-in camera's framing of family life seemed to toll the death knell of the family by collapsing the distance between documentary and fictional representations (Stratton and Ang 1994: 13).

Nonetheless, there is a difference between soap operas, sitcoms and family docs, if only in terms of the level of investment and response from viewers. No sitcom family had ever instigated the kind of media attention that resulted from the screening of *An American Family*, *The Family* and *Sylvania Waters*. The fact that these were real people, however much they may have been mediated through recognisable genres of television fiction, meant that viewers felt they had a far greater reason to care, especially when these television 'characters' turned up in other media formats as themselves (e.g. the Louds on talkshows, Mrs Wilkins's column, Noeline Donaher's autobiography). It should be noted, however, that these three family documentary series were one-offs, as though the emotional investment of an entire nation into one televised family had exhausted the broadcaster's and nation's reserves – and possibly put off other families who might have volunteered for the role. It is also important to consider that these family observational series are precursors to reality television; the pressing issues raised about reality, ordinariness, mediation and celebrity in these observational series were as yet unfamiliar and hence attracted a level of debate that would not be likely now, when we take the paradoxical cohabitation of real life and performance, ordinariness and celebrity much more for granted.

Despite the barrage of criticism aimed at Paul Watson and the Baker-Donahers, *Sylvania Waters* did not spell the death of the family doc, even though it went into hibernation. The observational family doc was revived in 2008 on Channel 4 in the UK with a series that acknowledged its pedigree with the simple title, *The Family*. To date, there have been three seasons of the recent *The Family* (2008–10), all of which have applied the same basic selection criteria as *The Family* of 1974: the family must have at least three children of varying ages under one roof and be preparing for some major event for the sake of narrative interest, often a wedding. There are two differences, however, from the previous family documentaries of the 1970s/1990s. First, although Channel 4 advertises *The Family* as 'a unique observational series that documents the universal themes of family life', the emphasis on 'universal themes' does not translate into an attempt to portray a 'universal' family. While the Hugheses of 2008 were a white, middle-class, single-breadwinner family who could have been considered normative, if not universal, in 2009 the producers chose the Grewals, a British-Asian family with grown children negotiating conflicting sets of cultural expectations, and in 2010 it was the Adesinas, a Nigerian immigrant family with British-born children who experience cultural difference through cross-generational conflict. This multi-cultural perspective fits, on the one hand, with Channel 4's remit as a public service broadcaster to appeal 'to the tastes and interests of a culturally diverse society' (Communications Act 2003). On the other hand, the emphasis on cultural diversity, made rich with the minutiae of everyday life, is subsumed within an overall narrative arc that stresses family unity. Unlike *Sylvania Waters*, then, the family in this later series is represented not as 'exploded' but rather as the site where cultural differences at the level of the nation-state can be resolved through the audiences' recognition of their own and the participants' shared family values.

The second major difference from the previous family series is that the 2008–10 *Family* is a serial documentary self-consciously produced in the era of reality TV. It has thus traded in the technology of observational documentary for surveillance tactics modelled on *Big Brother*. Instead of filming the family with a fly-on-the-wall camera team, the houses of each of the families were outfitted with twenty-eight mounted and mobile cameras, the same number as in the *Big Brother* house. This affects the aesthetics of the programmes, since many shots are captured from low-gauge, immobile video cameras to reinforce authenticity, but it also positions the series firmly in relation to the genre of reality TV. As Stephen Armstrong of *The Guardian* asked, 'So does *The Family* represent a return to public service values after a decade of extraordinary exploits, or the final genre-crushing victory by the panzer tank of reality TV?' (2008). By and large, in all three series reviewers praised the documentary impulse of *The Family*. As Armstrong wrote with relief, in answer to his own question, 'reality TV has returned to its non-fiction birthplace – documentary' (2008). Compared with the vociferous negative responses generated by the earlier family docs, however, the positive response to Channel 4's *The Family* – including enthusiastic engagement with the second and third series on internet discussion forums – suggests less that the programmes have changed than that the cultural terrain for their reception has radically shifted over twenty years. In the chapters to come, we will investigate the variables of this shift in the way that ordinary people and family life are perceived on the small screen.

## Conclusion

The aim of this chapter has been to provide a historical background for the study of reality TV by looking closely at two of its antecedents, *Candid Camera* and observational documentaries of the family. The key concepts discussed have been actuality, surveillance, ordinariness and the implications of mediating privacy. Although *Candid Camera* and the family docs represent very different kinds of television programmes, both fall under the heading of what Bilge Yesil has called 'technologised or mediatised observation' (2001: n.p.). Both, in other words, stress the importance of the *camera* to the observation of reality, and both forms found a new use for the camera in everyday life: the hidden camera was Allen Funt's breakthrough, while what I have called the 'live-in camera' was the breakthrough of *An American Family* producer Craig Gilbert. *Candid Camera* and the family docs should thus be recognised as influential sources for the core business of reality TV: placing ordinary people under observation in a mediated situation.

While the chapter has outlined a number of legacies that reality television has inherited from *Candid Camera*, the programme's greatest influence lies in the way it combined actuality with contrivance to evoke an unpredictable reality. For Funt, the surprise element was crucial to *Candid Camera*, for his interest lay in actuality rather than staging: 'When you work with actuality, you work with your wits because you are being constantly confronted with the unexpected and the unpredictable and the uncontrollable' (Funt 1971: 260). The insight gained by Funt in his early years, arguably from the scientific climate of his era, was that it is possible to combine surveillance and simulation to produce real effects. More radically, the longevity and success of *Candid Camera* suggests that it might be *necessary* to combine surveillance and simulation in order to capture reality through the television medium. The problematic ethics associated with both terms – surveillance and simulation – was something that Funt ultimately shrugged off: 'There will always be a large segment of the public that is uncomfortable about the whole idea of hidden cameras and microphones and will interpret it in fifty different prejudices and points of view' (Funt 1971: 263). But, as we shall see in later chapters, these ethical questions do not go away so easily.

Ethical issues also frame the representation of families in observational documentary series. In all three of the family docs considered in this chapter, a new threshold of privacy was crossed, which made the programmes as controversial as they were popular. Many critics held the intrusiveness of the live-in camera responsible for the various family break-ups and breakdowns, such as the Louds's marriage in *An American Family*, while Noeline Donaher of *Sylvania Waters* openly accused the producers of exploiting her family for the purposes of gaining good footage (Donaher 1993). The participants in these family docs, moreover, found themselves caught between being 'too real' and 'not real enough': on the one hand, they bared all for the camera, whether family secrets or ongoing battles, while on the other hand their scandalous revelations and behaviours edged the programmes closer to soap opera than documentary. The intense media interest generated by these three series, each in a different country, also led to an unexpected, often negative celebrity. For viewers, such celebrity only compounded the suspicion that these families were more exhibitionist than ordinary, and thus had little information to share about 'normal' family life. It was not until the return of *The Family* on Channel 4 in 2008 that the conditions of mediatised observation could be broadly accepted by audiences, and then only because audiences were already nostalgic for the media innocence that had caused such consternation twenty and thirty years previously (Cooke 2008).

The live-in camera went into hibernation after 1992, not to be reawakened until the arrival of the *Big Brother* juggernaut at the end of the decade. In the interim, Allen Funt proved prescient again, this time with his interest in authority figures and institutions of law and order. As we will see in the next chapter, these institutions underpin the programmes that herald the first generation of reality TV. Although television documentary persists throughout this period, especially in the British context, it undergoes reconfiguration in the second half of the 1990s as observation techniques are increasingly placed in the service of popular entertainment.

## Notes

1. Available at <http://www.youtube.com/watch?v=MmGTwbOmPX8> (accessed 20 December 2009).
2. Clissold provides a useful overview of *Candid Camera*'s early broadcast history: ABC (August–December 1948), NBC (May–August 1949), CBS (September 1949–September 1950), ABC (August 1951–May 1952), NBC (June–August 1953) (Clissold 2004: 51, fn 1). Later in the decade, it was a regular feature on NBC's *Tonight Show* (1958) and CBS's *Garry Moore Show* (1959).
3. *What Do You Say to a Naked Lady?* (1970) about sex and sexuality; *Money Talks* (1972) about money, livelihood and poverty; and *Smile When You Say I Do* (1973) about marriage.
4. The simplicity of the *Candid Camera* format makes it particularly well suited to adaptation to local cultures and their humour traditions. In a recent *Candid Camera* vignette made in Italy, for instance, a young woman carrying heavy bags and listening to music on earphones walks through the streets of an Italian city asking male

passers-by to help her by adjusting the sound on the iPod that lies nestled between her ample breasts (most of the men are keen to help) (available at <http://www.youtube.com/watch?v=29k98C9Y-Mg&feature=related> (accessed 10 January 2010)). In a Russian skit, by contrast, we see men lying down on low massage tables in preparation for a woman to walk on their backs, but the masseuse who arrives turns out to a shot-putter type who cracks her knuckles and flexes her pecs before trying to step on their backs (all of the men run away) (available at <http://www.youtube.com/watch?v=ynSvYNJYTpY> (accessed 10 January 2010)). Neither one of these skits, presumably, would be possible on US television, where a different moral sensibility and different gender relations prevail.

5. Available at <http://www.youtube.com/watch?v=_e5TXWCzJXw> (accessed 9 August 2011) also available at <http://www.youremberthat.com/media/11223/Allen_Funt_on_Whats_My_Line/> (accessed 9 August 2011).

6. The first review of the programme in the *New York Times*, in fact, was entitled '*An American Family* Lives Its Life on TV' (Ruoff 2002: 103).

7. Ros Cranston, notes to Episode 1 of *The Family* held in the Mediatheque, BFI Southbank, London.

8. Brian Howe's remark caused a media outcry, with most media outlets siding with the Baker-Donahers and supporting Noeline's demand for a personal apology. As Howe explained in the letter eventually sent to Noeline, he had intended 'to use the program . . . as a means of making a general point about the relationship between social background and the health of groups of people in Australia' (reprinted in Donaher 1993: 130). He had obviously failed to accurately gauge the response to his 'outing' of the Baker-Donahers as working class, since it was at this late point in the screening of *Sylvania Waters* that public sympathy began to turn their way (Donaher 1993: 131).

# 2 First-Generation Reality TV (1989–99): The Camcorder Era

In the preceding chapter, we considered two important precursors to the development of reality television, *Candid Camera* from the 1950s and the family observational documentary from the 1970s. Keeping in mind the themes of surveillance and ordinariness raised by these antecedents, we will turn our attention in this chapter to the real-crime shows that were the first to be grouped together under the 'reality television' label in the late 1980s/early 1990s. This first wave of reality TV, which peaked in the mid-1990s, arose from a distinct political, economic and industrial context. In the US, this was the era of deregulation, tabloid television and law-and-order culture. In the UK, where the documentary tradition had a much stronger footing, factual programming became integrated with the purposes of popular entertainment to produce a 'post-documentary' culture (Corner 2000). To understand both of these shifts, we need to investigate the socio-political and industrial conditions of the 1980s that led to the emergence of reality TV.

The 1980s was a decade marked by shifts in the Western political landscape, which in turn had far-reaching implications for the television landscape. Under the conservative policies of Ronald Reagan (US president, 1980–8) and Margaret Thatcher (British Prime Minister, 1979–90), social and political institutions were overhauled according to the principles of a market economy, leading to deregulation in the US (that is, decrease of governmental control) and privatisation in the UK (that is, the selling off of state-owned assets). Alongside a return to anti-Communist Cold War policies, the Reagan and Thatcher governments were characterised by a focus on security, both at the national level of militarisation and the domestic level of law and order. On the home front, family values became a moral byword, encompassing such disparate discourses as the propagation of the nuclear family, law-and-order ideology and the 'war on drugs'. Liberal individualism joined with economic deregulation to shore up the conservative populism of Reagan, the ex-Hollywood actor, and Thatcher, the greengrocer's daughter. This was the era of 'real people', defined in the narrow sense of law-abiding, middle-class individuals doing their best for their families and businesses. It was also the era of 'getting real', although there were competing discourses about what this might entail.

In the US, the network television industry found itself in a changing marketplace of viewing habits and tastes. The Reagan administration's deregulation policies had made it easier for competitors of network television to enter the broadcasting market. While overall viewer numbers stayed the same, audiences were beginning to be fragmented by a growing number of independent stations, cable and satellite providers, as well as the widespread availability of VCRs. The launch of major cable stations – that is, HBO in the 1970s, CNN in 1980 and MTV in 1981 – represented the first serious inroads on the networks' audience share. Adding to their woes, the three major networks (CBS, NBC and ABC) faced direct competition from the 1986 launch of the FOX television network by media mogul Rupert Murdoch. The deregulation of the industry in the US forced producers and distributors to diversify their appeal to audiences. As Kevin Glynn observes in his expansive study *Tabloid Culture*, 'the medium developed strategies for catering to a wider variety of social taste formations than it once could' (2000: 161). Of course, the economic stranglehold of advertising on commercial television meant that producers still measured their success in terms of ratings, so in a climate of shrinking viewership they sought to broaden the possible audiences for their programmes by expanding the range of 'taste formations' that might attract them. Television programming thus remained mainstream but the 'mainstream . . . moved downmarket' (Glynn 2000: 162), toward what both Kilborn (1994) and Dauncey (1994) have called 'lowest common denominator TV'.

Greater competition among channels as a result of deregulation also resulted in declining advertising revenue, since there were now more providers and distributors sharing the same pie (Raphael 2004: 121–2). Faced with rising production costs as well as diminishing returns, producers looked for cost-cutting alternatives. Amongst the more promising options, broadcasters experimented with what Chad Raphael calls 'non-traditional labor . . . and production inputs' (2004: 120), which is a euphemism for 'cheap' programming. Capitalising on the spread of camcorders and a growing public interest in actuality footage, broadcasters in the late 1980s found an audience for programmes that consisted of few or no actors, few or no writers, low production values and the use of existing amateur and surveillance video footage.

These were the first 'reality' shows. Conservative estimates suggest that such programmes could be made for half the cost of fictional programming (Raphael 2004: 137) and up to as much as a tenth of the cost of primetime television dramas or sitcoms (Fishman 1998: 67).[1] Interestingly, the initial push for these cost-saving initiatives came not from the major networks, whose deep pockets were better able to withstand the economic pinch, but from the newest network, FOX. Rather than seeking broad audiences to offset high production costs, FOX's market-entry strategy was to embrace niche audiences with programmes made on a low budget. Out of invention and necessity, reality TV was born.

Although the British television industry underwent deregulation, too, it did so a few years later and from the very different television tradition of public service broadcasting. The UK Broadcasting Act of 1990, which legislated changes to deregulate the industry, opened the floodgates for copycat 'reality' programmes, originating in the US, to appear on British television in the early 1990s. While these shows also spread elsewhere in Europe (especially to France and Italy (see Dauncey 1994)), another development was occurring in British television which came to be known as the remarkable boom in 'docusoaps'. Arising from a new wave of audience interest in lifestyle programming in the mid-1990s, docusoaps like *Airport* (BBC, 1996–2005, 2008) and *Driving School* (BBC, 1997) took the documentary camera into institutions of daily life and leisure. Although the camerawork and interview tactics of docusoaps were reminiscent of the long tradition of television documentary in the UK, the narrative structure and characterisation of these programmes borrowed heavily from fictional programmes, especially from the multiple plotlines of the soap opera. Although the televisual hybridisation of fact and fiction can be traced back to *An American Family* and its offshoots (see Chapter 1), it was not until the docusoaps of the 1990s that the hybridisation of documentary and soap opera became an established television format.

The first generation of reality TV thus breaks into two parts: reality crime programmes, or 'flashing blue light TV' (Dovey 2000), in the first half of the 1990s and British docusoaps in the second half of the 1990s. Together, these forms shift audience expectations of how reality can or should be mediated on television. Characterised by low-gauge visuals and everyday subject matter, these early reality TV shows sought to produce entertainment from the trivia of reality. The grainy and seemingly spontaneous aesthetic, which relied on actuality footage captured on CCTV and camcorders, lent these programmes a privileged relation to reality that broke with earlier documentary traditions (Jermyn 2004: 73). As we shall see, the real-crime shows and docusoaps announced a new 'appeal of the real' (Andrejevic 2004: 8), which melded a growing accessibility of surveillance and camcorder technology with a populist interest in individual, everyday lives. The first signs of this intersection, however, came from a trend not usually associated with reality, namely, the 1980s' tabloidisation of factual programming.

## Tabloid Culture

In a bid to offset their declining audience share in the 1980s, US broadcasters moved to capitalise on popular taste by 'softening' elite forms of programming, especially factual programmes such as news and current affairs. While the major broadcasters had long been showing 'respectable' current affairs programmes (e.g. *60 Minutes* on CBS from 1968), in the late 1980s this format went 'tabloid', borrowing the strategies of the sensationalist press to create television shows that eschewed the highbrow knowledge economy and sought to appeal to the 'common man'. Tabloid television shows of this era reconfigured news sources for entertainment purposes (Langer 1998), shifting the focus to human interest stories, sensational events, emotional reactions and a combination of scandal and spectacle. Although John Fiske emphasises the difficulty of providing a single definition of tabloid news, he does list certain broad characteristics of the genre, such as sensationalist style, a populist tone, subject matter 'produced at the intersection between public and private life' and a modality that moved fluidly 'between fiction and documentary' (cited in Glynn 2000: 7). This tabloidisation of factual programming provided a springboard for what would become the main hybrid features of reality TV – the blurring between fact and fiction, information and entertainment, public and private lives.

In the US, the first dedicated tabloid news show was *A Current Affair* (1986–96), which aired on FOX and its affiliates. Within a few years, it was joined by *Hard Copy* (1989–99) and *Inside Edition* (1989–), both syndicated programmes. Like its successors, *A Current Affair* – colourfully dubbed 'the *60 Minutes* of slime' by a TV critic (cited in Glynn 2000: 101) – took its material from the scandalous, gossipy, indecent underside of the news. Presented in the first two seasons by seasoned journalist Maury Povich, *A Current Affair* was initially intended as a tongue-in-cheek local broadcast. It then expanded to include factual material that was largely ignored by conventional news formats, focusing on all kinds of 'abnormality' and social non-conformity (see Glynn 2000: 114–42). For Kevin Glynn, this made the show not only populist, in the sense that it appealed to popular tastes, but also politically progressive, since it featured stories about people whose experiences were well out of the mainstream. As a nominal newscast that focused on non-normative events and people in the real world, *A Current Affair* can be seen as an antecedent to other programming forms that sprang up at the end of the 1980s and charted the eruption of sensational events within ordinary life: programmes about real courts, real crimes, real disasters and real emergencies. What connects US tabloid television to early reality programmes is thus their similar approach to pitching content. All of these shows used the appeal of ordinary people involved in sensational events to gain viewers on a low production budget. Indeed, Bethany Ogdon traces the start of reality TV to the debut night of *A Current Affair*, claiming this was the 'exact moment that what would come to be ... referred to a "reality TV" emerged onto the popular cultural landscape' (2006: 29).

This is probably a rash statement, not to mention an American-centric one, since it is difficult to map a direct connection between *A Current Affair* and the real-crime programmes that would soon become internationally synonymous with reality television. Nonetheless, *A Current Affair* helped to establish the discursive conditions under which subsequent reality shows could attain visibility as a new 'generic cluster' (Mittel 2004). In addition to tabloid news shows, other tabloid genres that started in the same period on network and local channels include occult shows like *Unsolved Mysteries* (NBC 1987–97/CBS 1997–9/Lifetime 2001–2, 2010–), amateur clip shows like *America's Funniest Home Videos* (ABC, 1989–), sensationalist talk-shows like *The Jerry Springer Show* (synd., 1991–), and crime-appeal programmes like *America's Most Wanted* (FOX, 1988–) – all of which are still, or are once again, on air two decades later. What these programmes have in common is populist rhetoric, non-normative subject matter and an appeal to 'social tastes' that had not been served under the hegemony of the national network system. Though populism means that many of these shows are about the experiences of ordinary people, we should note that there is no particular interest in documentary traditions in the context of US network television. Aside from PBS, the Public Broadcasting Service which screened *An American Family* in the 1970s (see Chapter 1), television programming in the US has always been commercial and entertainment-driven. Documentary, and attendant concerns about authenticity, belong more strongly to the British televisual context, as we will see in the second part of the chapter on docusoaps.

## Camcorders and 'First-Person Media'

The new 'real-life' programming (Goodwin 1993: 26), as it was called in the late 1980s/early 1990s, relied on two camera technologies that were undergoing parallel development: CCTV (closed-circuit television) and the video camcorder. Just as *Candid Microphone* had been made possible in the 1940s by the wire recorder and *Candid Camera* in the 1950s by the lightweight synch-sound camera (Chapter 1), so the technologies that were spreading in the 1980s had direct repercussions for television content. Although CCTV and the video camcorder were developed for very different purposes, they both represented a move toward personalisation, either in the form of picking a face out of crowd or bringing video recording technology within the reach of ordinary people.

CCTV, or mounted surveillance cameras, had already been in use for decades by government agencies, banks and private institutions, but in the 1980s the technology became more widely available. Small store and business owners began installing mounted cameras to secure their premises at the same time as CCTV camera trials were launched in public spaces in the UK and the US as part of crime-prevention programmes in the new law-and-order political climate (Jermyn 2007: 114). In the 1990s, CCTV systems spread through city and town centres at a rapid pace (Norris and Armstrong 1999), with Britain leading the field for sheer number of public CCTV systems in operation by the mid-1990s (Fyfe and Bannister, cited in Jermyn 2004: 76). In the US, video surveillance cameras became a commonplace of shopping malls, car parks and 24/7 stores, while police cruisers were routinely outfitted with CCTV cameras. At around the same time, video camcorders for personal use became available on the mass market, with Sony and JVC releasing the first consumer camcorders in 1983.[2]

Despite relying on the same technologies of videotape and miniaturisation, camcorders and CCTV cameras in some sense fall at opposite ends of the spectrum of recording technologies. After all, CCTV surveillance footage comes from mounted, impersonal cameras, usually not monitored by the human eye unless an event has already happened. The images are static, and even if the camera is motion-activated the framing is unresponsive to whatever is captured in the visual field. Camcorder footage, on the other hand, bears the personal, indexical traces of the (usually amateur) wielder of the camera. The footage is often unsteady or wildly mobile, reflecting the response to events of the body that holds the camera (West 2005). Crucially, however, both technologies suggest a privileged relation to reality, since CCTV as well as camcorder footage appears to bypass the professional production mechanisms of media institutions. Either there is no one operating the camera at all, as with surveillance footage, or the person behind the camera him/herself is part of the scene, relegated behind the viewfinder only for the moment. Either way, whether the camera represents human or inhuman mediation, 'first person' (Dovey 2000) or 'no person' media, it seems to offer direct access to the reality of events unfolding before the lens. In the late 1980s, this special access meant that footage shot on camcorders joined CCTV footage as a treasure trove for low-cost programming with a high reality effect.

This is not to say, however, that the technology alone determined the television content of the era. Jon Dovey cautions against such a technologically deterministic account, arguing that 'the spread of low gauge video-based forms of programming' required a particular cultural context to determine 'the ends to which technology w[ould] be put' (2000: 56). In the cultural and political climate of the Reagan/ Thatcher era, television viewers found themselves in a security-conscious, crime-focused society where the need for law and order was propelled equally by government rhetoric and social paranoia. In this context, CCTV footage of criminals caught in the act helped raise the profile of tabloid news and reality shows, at the same time as these programmes fed the flames of a growing consciousness of crime. The other contributing factor in the late 1980s was a shift away from elite, institutional discourses to discourses of the self. The 'truth' seemed to be spoken no longer by those in power, but by ordinary people speaking in the 'first person'. Dovey argues that in the 1990s such 'expressions of subjectivity' were to be found across all media forms and hence were not specific to television (2000: 57). Rather, they were part of 'the regime of truth generated by and for contemporary western culture [that] *requires* subjective, intimate, exposing expression as dominant form' (ibid.; original emphasis). This regime of truth made avid use of the technological availability of camcorders but was not caused by it; rather, the camcorder represented 'the emergence of a medium whose time ha[d] come' (Dovey 2000: 57). Similarly, the use of CCTV footage resonated with television audiences who were increasingly aware of the existence of public surveillance technology and incorporated it into their self-positioning within law-and-order culture.

## Cops and Crimes

The discourse of 'real-life' programming (Goodwin 1993) coalesces around two shows that appeared in the 1988/1989 television season in the US: *America's Most Wanted* and *Cops*. This is the point at which a number of factors – the deregulation of the television industry, tabloidisation, 'law and order' politics, and camcorder availability – intersected to create the framework of what industry professionals and later academics would begin to call 'reality TV' (e.g. Goodwin 1993; Kilborn 1994; Dauncey 1994; Nichols 1994). The fledgling FOX network had begun showing *America's Most Wanted* in the spring of 1988, while *Cops* had its first screening on FOX stations in the spring of 1989. Both of these programmes focused on the capture of criminals, were relatively inexpensive to produce and made heavy use of CCTV and/or camcorder footage. Neither economic nor techno-logical arguments alone, however, can explain the snowball effect that resulted from this Saturday-night pairing of these two related formats. In addition to spawning numerous national spin-offs and international format adaptations, *America's Most Wanted* and *Cops* have proven to be surprisingly resilient. The two shows still command the Saturday night slot on FOX affiliates more than twenty years later, marking the most stable programming line-up in the history of US prime time.

As FOX's first hit series, *America's Most Wanted* (*AMW*) was not a format innovation. It was modelled on the mid-1980s British pro-gramme *Crimewatch UK* (BBC, 1984–), which was itself adapted from a long-running German programme called *Aktenzeichen XY – Ungelöst* (*File Number XY – Unsolved*, ZDF, 1967–). Categorised by some critics as tabloid TV (Glynn 2000) and by others as reality TV (Kilborn 1994), *AMW* crystallised the 'crime appeal' format (Jermyn 2004, 2007), which uses dramatic reconstruction of crimes in combination with CCTV footage, interviews with police, victims and families, and direct appeals to TV viewers for information and tip-offs. Aaron Doyle refers to this format as the 'video wanted poster' (2003: 66), a phrase which captures the particular combination of collective crime fighting and vigilante sensationalism that is significant to *AMW*. At least one earlier show, *Unsolved Mysteries*, was already using dramatic reconstruction combined with participant interviews to highlight the sensational aspects of actuality, but in that case the themes were more broadly construed as paranormal events, criminal activities and alternative histories. *America's Most Wanted*, however, positioned itself as more urgent and more 'real' by accentuating the pressing need for social justice for victims of unsolved crimes and then offering a televisual solution. To this day, *AMW* uses the discursive technique of direct appeal to viewers, grounding its claim to reality as well as its sentimental morality in the fact that the presenter, John Walsh, is himself the father-turned-advocate of a young son who was abducted

and murdered in 1981 (Glynn 2000: 35). Like its predecessors
*Aktenzeichen* and *Crimewatch*, *AMW* makes much of the effective collaboration between television, police and viewers, with police taking
phone calls on the *AMW* set, John Walsh reminding viewers that '*you
can make a difference*' and a recursive structure allowing later episodes to follow up on the results of earlier appeals. The crime-appeal
format also heavily publicises its successes, with *Aktenzeichen* boasting a 42 per cent success rate[3] and *AMW* celebrating its thousandth
fugitive capture in 2008. Soon after the initial success of *AMW*, the
eyewitness-reconstruction format was extended to emergency call-
out situations on *Rescue 911* (CBS, 1989–96). The popularity of this
latter show, hosted by William Shatner, led to book spin-offs[4] and
international adaptations, including the UK's *999* (BBC, 1992–2002),
Germany's *Notruf* (RTL, 1992–2006) and New Zealand's *Rescue 111*
(1991–6).

The other half of the real-crime pairing pioneered by FOX in
1988/9 was *Cops*, which boasted an innovative format. Rather than
using CCTV footage to add actuality to reconstructions, as on *AMW*,
*Cops* is based solely on camcorder footage gathered by video crews who
'ride along' with the police on call-outs. The effect of this 'ultra-verité'
technique (Corner 1996: 183) is to intensify values of immediacy and
decrease the appearance of mediation, offering viewers a seemingly
direct, 'you are there' relation to reality. Producer John Langley has
described *Cops* as 'raw reality' (cited in Doyle 2003: 34), thereby accentuating not only the appeal of the show but also the promotional value
of using 'raw reality' to appeal to viewers. Of course, highly selective
editing and to-camera narration (by the cops) are nonetheless necessary to the success of the programme. Through this combination of
seeming raw footage and narration, *Cops* sets the style and conventions
for ride-along crime programming: mixing low-gauge video footage
with framing voice-overs, the aesthetic elides the camera operator
while foregrounding the on-site presence of the camera itself. The
show thus engages in what Bill Nichols has called the 'spectacular
oscillation between the sensational and the banal' (1994: 45). By
shaping actuality footage to produce the feel of immediacy – that is,
by generating reality *effects* rather than framing reality naturalistically
– actuality becomes 'reality' and reality becomes the source of viewer
engagement. The success of *Cops* spawned numerous spin-off shows,
such as *American Detective* (ABC, 1991–3), *I Witness Video* (NBC,
1992–4) and *Real Stories of the Highway Patrol* (synd., 1993–9) in the
US and *Police, Camera, Action* (ITV, 1994–2002, 2007/8), *Crime Beat*
(BBC, 1996–7) and *X-Cars* (BBC, 1996) in the UK. By the mid-1990s,

'reality TV' had become synonymous with reality crime programming, which in turn was understood on the model of *Cops*.

The importance of *Cops* also lies in the fact that it was not simply a television programme but an innovative extension of the collaboration between producers, police and the public that had begun with crime appeal formats. It is of course in the interests of the police that their work be represented as effective and their methods as justified, so in the law-and-order culture of the 1980s the police began to forge new relationships with the media. In both the US and the UK, the police had suffered a fall-off in public confidence, because of the memory of police brutality in response to 1960s/1970s civil rights and Vietnam War protests in the US and 1980s industrial unrest in the UK (Palmer 1998). As a corrective, police forces offered to cooperate with the media, appearing in segments on the British crime appeal formats *Crimestoppers* (ITV, 1988–95), *Crime Monthly* (LWT, 1989–96), and *Britain's Most Wanted* (ITV, 1998–2000) as well as more extensively on *Crimewatch UK* and *America's Most Wanted* (Jermyn 2007: 30–4). Deborah Jermyn argues that in the UK programmes like *Crimestoppers* 'fostered a new kind of relationship between the public and police that aimed to ease the process of "informing"' on any criminal activity (2007: 27). The public were thus invited to be vigilant and share in police work, at the same time as the police were invited to join in television production and even appear as regular presenters on *Crimewatch UK* (Jermyn 2007: 30–1). It was not until *Cops* producers John Langley and Malcolm Barbour struck a deal with the sheriff's department in Broward County, Florida, however, that the police and media reached a fully collaborative arrangement on the former's own turf: video crews would ride along in police cruisers while in return the police would have full edit control before footage went to air (Doyle 2003: 51). The programme producers were nonetheless careful to follow principles of crime selection that were equally good for the demands of television as well as the representation of the police. While the crime-appeal shows concentrated on brutal crimes such as murder, rape and child abuse, often drawing on aesthetics familiar to audiences from fictional crime programmes (Jermyn 2007: 62–79), the ride-along shows focused on the more quotidian fare familiar from local news: street crime, prostitution, domestic violence and, above all, the pursuit (see Friend 2006). In all of these programmes, television placed the techniques of storytelling at the disposal of the positive representation of the police, figuring them as public servants, heroes and citizens (Palmer 1998: 16) who need only viewers' help to hold back the tide of deviancy in an inherently dangerous world.

## Law-and-Order Ideology

Most scholars of reality crime programming agree that its emergence was directly related to the political climate of the 1980s. Gareth Palmer, for instance, does not mince words: 'I see these programs as the logical result of a series of impulses which right-wing governments in Britain since the early 1980s have engineered in broadcasting' (1998: 12). Alongside broadcasting deregulation, the Reagan/Thatcher decade produced a 'law-and-order' approach to crime that was sustained and exacerbated by media portrayals of criminal justice (Doyle 2003: 38). Kevin Glynn claims that the Reagan administration's war on drugs 'saturated U.S. media with images of an urban battleground steeped in violent criminality that struck all too often at innocent (white) victims' (2000: 31). Indeed, the war on drugs was regarded by many as a covert 'war on race', which specifically targeted people of colour (Glynn 2000: 32; see also Austin and McVey 1989). This perception was corroborated by the racial bias in programmes like *Cops*, in which, as studies have revealed, people of colour were more likely to be portrayed as suspects, while white participants were more likely to be portrayed as police officers (Oliver 1994).

  The widespread 'drug and crime crisis' in this period, however, had less to do with actual increases in crime than with heightened discourses of criminalisation and the adoption of greater punitive measures. Projections made by the US National Council on Crime and Delinquency (NCCD) in 1989 anticipated a 68 per cent rise in prison populations by 1994 because of the war on drugs rather than any increase in violent crime (Austin and McVey 1989). Pamela Donovan goes so far as to claim that crime rates in the US were actually in decline in this period, while voter anxiety about crime was paradoxically on the rise: 'A kind of panic about crime and punishment emerged in the early nineties that engaged the attention of politicians and the mass media, despite stable rates and recent declines' (Donovan 1998: 121).[5] A similar ideology held sway in the UK, where *Crimewatch UK* 'chim[ed] in with the mood of law-and-order politics and fear of crime that characterised the 1980s in Britain' (Schlesinger et al. 1991: 408), while legislative measures introduced in the late 1980s placed more control in the hands of the police (Palmer 1998: 14). Reflecting such policies and political discourses, reality crime programming thus depicted a world which was more violent than in actuality, while portraying the police as far more effective than statistics showed (Eschholz et al. 2002: 328). This led, according to Andrew Goodwin, to a dramatic shift in the function of television 'from truth to use'

(2003: 27), that is, from documentation to active complicity with the goals of the law-and-order regime. As Pamela Donovan notes, reality crime programming 'implicates itself in the prowess and dedication of law enforcement, in its recent successes, and consistently reminds the viewer that it is *really* involved in catching criminals' (1998: 125). No longer limited to providing information about the world, television positioned itself 'centrally as the new authority figure in a frightened, atomised society' (Goodwin 1993: 27).

We must no doubt be cautious about suggesting that a single entity called 'the media' or even 'television' engages in a common discourse about criminal justice, or even that the message received by audiences from reality crime programming is 'merely cautionary and censorious' (Jermyn 2007: 133). These programmes, after all, entertain through spectacle as much as they caution through their content, and it is possible for audiences to read oppositionally and admire some of the criminals (Jermyn 2007: 144). Taking the ideological context into consideration, however, Aaron Doyle convincingly argues that the television industry was part of 'a wider system of meaning about criminal justice' during this period (2003: 38). Doyle refers to the dominant discourse of the time as 'law and order ideology' which understands society 'to be in a state of decline or crisis' (ibid.) because of an increasing threat of violence from the underclasses. This threat is represented as the inevitable result of previous Democrat (US) or Labour (UK) governments of the 1970s having been soft on crime and drugs, allowing street crime to go unchecked and putting domestic security in grave danger. Against this governmental ineptitude, the police are figured by law-and-order ideology as highly effective crime fighters whose hands are tied by desk-bound bureaucrats with no understanding of the frontline. Indeed, in the law-and-order system, as in reality crime programming, the police are characterised as the heroic 'thin blue line' between Us (right-thinking citizens) and Them (psychopathic criminals).

The Us-and-Them mentality (Doyle 2003: 38) promoted by law-and-order ideology sustains the emotional force and narrative appeal of reality crime programming. Overlapping neatly with media templates of heroes and villains, this mentality individualises criminals as social deviants rather than presenting any structural causes for crime (Donovan 1998: 125). Violence on the part of the police is condoned and authorised, adding to their symbolic power (Doyle 2003: 39) and to the pleasure of viewer identification with cops as heroes. Violence on the part of 'Them', on the other hand, is attributed to evil or deviant characters, like those familiar from fictional programmes, while the solution is to give the police broader powers to restrain and immobilise aberrant individuals, thus supporting their authority with televisual authority. This narrative is driven by the affective force of the Us-and-Them mentality. In a climate of increasing concerns about personal and domestic security, law-and-order ideology generates a paranoid fear of 'Them', suggesting that everyone on the side of 'Us' is vulnerable to attack anytime and anywhere: 'In paranoid, post-imperial America, the family has retreated to the home, where it nests comfortably in front of the television set . . . only to find that here, too, there are dark threats in every nook and cranny' (Goodwin 1993: 27). Television is adept at exploiting the ambivalent pleasures of fear, particularly in tabloid culture, but in real-crime programming it also offers viewers something they can do to mitigate their fear: either they can call in directly with information or they can learn to be more vigilant at home by watching and learning from the shows. Indeed, Deborah Jermyn argues that being able to mitigate the fear of crime aroused by these programmes is particularly important for the many female viewers, who are able to *manage* their fear by engaging with the formulaic structure of these shows (2007: 166–9).

Reality crime programmes do not, then, simply justify surveillance by CCTV and video cameras in the name of law and order. Rather, they claim to position audiences as participants in these surveillance mechanisms for the sake of better citizenship. Effective citizenship is modelled not by the cops but rather by the programme's address – 'your call counts!' (*Crimewatch UK*) and '*you* can make a difference!' (*AMW*) – to the viewers who engage in the televisual spectacle or 'surplus visibility' of law enforcement (Donovan 1998: 122). In keeping with law-and-order ideology, reality crime programming thus 'construes the reconstruction of citizenship and the public sphere through the categories of law and order' (Donovan 1998: 132), suggesting to viewers that they are performing citizenship by vicariously following the police as they fight crime and make society secure. These programmes thus turn citizens into viewers and viewers into citizens, redefining citizenship 'from below' on the affective grounds of fear, anger and excitement (Jermyn 2004; Doyle 2003: 39). In doing so, they mix models of public service with commercial entertainment.

## *Cops*: Narration and Affect

Although the low-gauge aesthetic of video footage in these shows signals authenticity, the narrative framing follows rules of fiction, aiming for hero/villain characterisation, sensational climaxes and moral closure. Each episode of *Cops*, for instance, is divided into three call-out vignettes per half-hour show, with each vignette introduced by a 'host cop' who talks directly to the camera before the action (Doyle 2003: 37). Each episode also ends with a closing statement from the host cop, usually in voice-over with a fade to the *Cops* logo, thus emphasising the joint purpose of law enforcement and real-crime television. A structural tension is set up, however, between the narrative function of the opening and closing messages on the one hand and the footage of the cops performing police work on the other. Not surprisingly, the footage of the actual police work is far less coherent in its aesthetics and message than the host cop's voice-overs would suggest. The suspects are often angry or abject, yelling or cursing or mumbling as they attempt to come to grips with the situation, and there is rarely any moral lesson or social gain evident in footage of police bursting into prostitutes' houses or stopping someone for a traffic violation who is then revealed to have syringes in his/her pocket. Nonetheless, the tension between the putative social purpose of the show and the minutiae of the actuality footage is resolved by the continuity of the host cop's voice and the fact that the storyline in each case achieves – or, more accurately, ascribes – closure.

The disappearance of this tension, which is in effect a disavowal of narrative mediation in the programme, works in the same way as the elision of the camera through the invisibility of the camera operator. Even though viewers know that the camera is there, it presents itself simply as a transparent eye, becoming a portal between television viewers and the peopled, kinetic world on screen. The camera is both not there, accentuating immediacy, and palpably present, since it is a material stand-in for the cameraman's body that is bounced or pushed around in the fast-paced world of police pursuits and confrontations (see West 2005). The reality promoted by this televisual style draws viewers into a space that offers greater affective appeal than interpretive significance (see Jermyn 2004).

The reality effect of ride-along programming is thus produced for viewers as a felt experience through first-person, on-the-fly techniques of capture. These techniques include narration, the use of the camera as witness, tight framing and a range of indexical camera and recording techniques. In a standard vehicular pursuit from Season 8 (TX, 18 May 1996), for example, the object of the chase is a (black) youth on a stolen moped. This surely counts as a non-event in the annals of violent crime, yet the immediacy and excitement are generated by the fact that the camera works to embed the viewer in the space of the action. Disorientatingly quick zooms, out-of-focus shots, wild dips

of the camera, tight shots of the car interior and even a close-up of a
suburban hedge – all of these techniques evacuate the fleeing criminal
of interest and place the focus on the experience of riding along with
the pursuit. For this reason, the numerous filming 'mistakes' are not
edited out of the footage, since they serve the purpose of heighten-
ing sensation and 'super-enhanced realism' for the television viewer
(Jermyn 2004: 84). Pamela Donovan extends the point by arguing that
even instances of police brutality are not edited out of *Cops* or *American
Detective* because they serve 'to add more personalism and hypercom-
petence of the cops in action' (1998: 132). Here the editing – or lack
of editing where it might be expected – does not compensate for 'poor'
camera technique or brutal police behaviour but rather *increases* the
effect. Such techniques are used purposefully in order to generate
reality as the zone of the unshaped, the unscripted, the banal. In this
border zone of law and order peopled by prostitutes, small-time drug
dealers, aggressive boyfriends and street crazies, sensationalism of
technique and banality of content work hand in hand to produce the
affect of the real in the service of citizenship.

   As we will see in Chapter 4, concerns about television's role in promoting citizenship return in the second generation of reality TV in
the form of 'life intervention' formats that radically extend the appeal
of television as 'use' rather than 'truth' (Goodwin 1993). For the
moment, however, we will turn our attention to another first-generation form of 'real-life programming' that uses low-gauge video footage
set within a narrative framework. While associated with a public
interest in lifestyle and leisure rather than law-and-order ideology,
the British docusoap of the late 1990s had certain characteristics in
common with real-crime programming. Both formats were propelled
to dominance by the effects of broadcasting deregulation; both strove
to gain audiences with populist subject matter; and both deliberately
blurred the difference between fact and fiction in their structure and
address. Both, moreover, were heavily criticised for focusing on the
individual at the expense of representing the structural causes that
affect 'the social body' (Dovey 2000: 138).

## The Rise of the Docusoap

Although *Crimewatch UK* provided the model for *America's Most
Wanted*, real-crime programming was rooted in American soil. The
raft of flashing blue light programmes that appeared on British and
European television channels in the first half of the 1990s (Dauncey
1994) were offshoots or format replicas of American shows rather than

a homegrown phenomenon. In the second half of the 1990s, however, a particular form of locally derived factual programming swept across UK evening schedules. Referred to by journalists as 'the docusoap' for its open mixing of factual and fictional styles, this form of programming drew heavily on the tradition of observational documentary characteristic of the British public service broadcasting model and propelled it toward what John Corner has called 'post-documentary culture' (Corner 2000). Unlike the traditional documentary's imperative to inform and interrogate, the docusoap made no secret of its purpose to entertain viewers with a focus on personalities, storylines and interpersonal conflicts. Criticised by journalists and traditional documentary-makers alike for soap-bubble appeal and 'unabashed populism', the programmes *Airport* (BBC) and *Vet School* (BBC) surprised broadcasters in 1996 by drawing audiences of 10 million during peak time (Dovey 2000: 134), while *Driving School* drew over 12 million viewers per episode in 1997 (ibid.: 135). Combining high ratings with relatively inexpensive production costs, the docusoap spread with startling speed, and by 1998 there were twelve new docusoap series on air, among them *The Cruise*, set on a cruise liner, *Premier Passions*, about the Sunderland Football Club, *Clampers*, about traffic wardens, and *The Store*, set in Selfridge's department store (Dovey 2000: 139). After three or four years as a mainstay of the peak time schedules, the docusoap receded in the late 1990s almost as quickly as it had come, but the rise and fall of this programme form had lasting effects.

Producer and scholar Jon Dovey calls the docusoap '*the* phenomenon in the UK factual TV industry of this period' (2000: 133; original emphasis). To appreciate this claim requires understanding 'factual TV' as a term with a potential double meaning, referring either to documentary or to reality TV. According to historians of documentary like John Ellis and Stella Bruzzi, the arrival of the docusoap represented an extension of the observational documentary (Ellis 2005: 346), which – seen in a positive light – 'addressed some of the deficiencies and inaccessibilities of more earnest predecessors' (Bruzzi 2000: 86). Whereas televised documentary had previously offered big-picture views of the social world, the docusoap strove for little more than a 'backstage' view of ordinary individuals going about their business. This would suggest that the docusoap belongs to the other arm of 'factual TV', to the genre of reality television, since in 'reality programming . . . the available maps of meaning are predominantly framed by categories which almost always privilege the personal and the impersonal, rarely the social, the historical or the political' (Langer

1998: 164). Indeed, Annette Hill categorises docusoaps, along with lifestyle shows, as 'the second wave of reality programming', following on from emergency-services programming as the first wave (Hill 2005: 24).

In my schema, I position the docusoap within the first generation of reality TV because, on the one hand, it is the first isolatable home-grown reality TV trend in Britain and, on the other, it shares features of form and function with reality crime/emergency programming. While the boom period of the docusoap, from 1996 to 1999, is concurrent with a growing interest in 'lifestyle programming' (Brunsdon 2004) such as cooking, decorating and makeover shows, it also maintains characteristics of (digital) camcorder culture that differentiate it from formats like *Ready Steady Cook* (BBC, 1994–) and *Changing Rooms* (BBC, 1996–2004). Since a genealogy must be sensitive to ruptures in timelines as well as commonalities across related strands, understanding the emergence and import of the docusoap means interweaving it with emergency services as well as lifestyle programming. Like emergency services programming, the docusoap uses relatively inexpensive production techniques to focus on the particularities of ordinary people. Like lifestyle shows and other forms of reality TV to follow, the docusoap introduces quotidian life as entertainment and in the process discovers the seed of celebrity within the ordinary person. Despite its short period of efflorescence, the docusoap illuminates changes in UK television culture in the early 1990s, technological innovations in the mid-1990s and what John Ellis (2005) has called the 'crisis of documentary' in the late 1990s.

## Before the Boom

Although law-and-order ideology and related real-crime programmes had begun to ebb in importance by the mid-1990s, other influences from Thatcher's period as British prime minister were only just beginning to affect the British television industry. The deregulation of commercial enterprises during the 1980s was extended to the British broadcasting industry with the Broadcasting Act of 1990. As with the deregulation of the US television industry in the 1980s, the intention of the Act was to promote competition for the sake of 'choice' and greater free-market revenues. Among other mandates, the 1990 Broadcasting Act created a fifth terrestrial channel (Channel 5), sponsored the growth of multi-channel satellite television, put up ITV (Independent Television) franchises for auction, and required that 25 per cent of television output be commissioned from independent production companies. This last requirement had the greatest impact on the BBC, which up until then had produced the majority of its programming in-house, determining budgets and schedules. The emphasis on 'producer-choice', in the language of deregulation advocates, meant that the BBC was now placed under pressure to deliver cheaper programming (Hill 2005: 18). It subsequently introduced 'cost-control measures which many in the industry felt were antithetical to creative work' (Palmer 1998: 14) as well as to the socio-political reach of the serious documentary.

By the mid-1990s, these conditions were causing sharp decreases in production budgets and timelines, especially in documentaries, which were a lynchpin in the BBC's function as a public service broadcaster. With less money spent on documentary-making and fewer documentaries being made, audience interest in the documentary was also waning, to the extent that 'no documentary of any kind . . . made it into the top 100 programmes of 1993' (Winston 2000: 54). At the same time, other evening genres such as comedy and light entertainment were not faring much better, leading to 'a crisis in early evening programming' (Coles 2000: 27). The BBC met the challenge of competing with commercial channels in peak time by revitalising its documentary stronghold but in a new form – increasing its popularity, in effect, by making it more populist. As a result, the documentary underwent 'a decisive shift towards diversion' (Corner 2000: n.p.). That this shift was spearheaded by the BBC, a public service broadcaster committed to making documentary as a 'duty-genre' to the public (Winston 2000: 45), was an ironic outcome of the commercialisation of public broadcasting in the early 1990s.

There had, of course, been predecessors on British television to the populist documentary, especially in the observational or 'fly-on-the-wall' tradition. Paul Watson's 1974 series *The Family* (see Chapter 1) is often cited as a precursor to the docusoap (cf. Biressi and Nunn 2005: 64) because of the way it combines social actors and observational conventions with the personal conflicts of family life.[6] The more self-reflexively melodramatic *Sylvania Waters*, produced by Watson in 1992 (also discussed in Chapter 1), was called a 'docu-soap' by contemporary journalists who were searching for a term to describe the multiple-character storylines structured around inter-generational turmoil in this observational series. The new era of docusoaps, however, did not focus on family life as their setting or subject matter: in fact, none of the docusoaps in the boom period 1996–9 were set within families. While the 'soap' component of 'docusoap' might suggest a domestic setting, the mid-1990s docusoap invariably investigated personal lives within the setting of social institutions (Biressi and Nunn 2005: 63). In the boom period of the docusoap, institutional environments such as hospitals, airports, department stores, or a cruise ship allowed a documentary interest in socially regulated structures to be telescoped through a soap-operatic focus on individuals. This trend had begun in the early 1990s, with fly-on-the-wall programmes that offered viewers a behind-the-scenes look at institutions that dealt with the suffering and welfare of 'innocent' creatures. According to Annette Hill, *Children's Hospital* (BBC, 1993), an eight-part fly-on-the-wall series about staff and patients at Liverpool's Alder Hey Hospital, 'had all the hallmarks of a docu-soap' (2005: 28), while *Animal Hospital* (BBC, 1994–2004), set in an RSPCA hospital in north London, delivered surprisingly good ratings for the BBC in 1994 (Ellis 2005: 343).

The model provided by heart-warming series about animal and human welfare, however, was given a surprise twist with the ratings success in 1995 of *The House*. This observational series revealed the backstage goings-on at the Royal Opera House in a period of transition, revelling in the squabbles, preening and wild over-expenditures of an institution under threat. As Stella Bruzzi argues in her extensive analysis of the programme, *The House* had a 'direct stylistic influence on docusoaps with its use of ironic, pointed narration, its confrontational editing and its pursuit of crises and star performers' (2000: 83). Indeed, the only major difference between *The House* and the docusoaps that followed was that the former had a much larger production budget. Shot for £150,000 per episode over a nine-month period, this was a BBC documentary financed on the old model (Bruzzi 2001: 84), involving a substantial investment of time and money. Nonetheless, its peering interest in strong personalities and dramatic conflicts (Bruzzi 2001: 132) was in step with the new remit of commissioning editors for 'observational narrative that is character-led with a strong story' (Dovey 2000: 134). This 'observational-character-story' formula, as Jon Dovey calls it, was the key to popularising the traditional documentary form, shifting its emphasis from social interrogation to narrative diversion and flaunting the unstable distinction between fictional and factual tactics. In 1996, with the BBC series *Airport* and *Vet School*, the 'observational-character-story' formula was joined to a serial format, low production values and populist content. The surprisingly high ratings for *Airport* and *Vet School* announced the arrival of a hybrid format which would soon be extended and copied across all the channels. In the deregulated broadcasting climate of 'producer choice', with the traditionally serious and expensive documentary facing competition from commercial broadcasters, the docusoap found its niche:

'it was an idea whose time had come' (Dovey 2000: 134; Ellis 2005: 345–6).

## Hybridising Fact and Fiction

The docusoap boom was part of a larger cultural shift in 1990s Britain toward a fascination with the televisation of everyday life. Whereas emergency services programming had highlighted the sensational within the banal, the tragic within the ordinary, the docusoap embraced ordinary people in everyday settings, providing 'extensive coverage of relatively mundane lives' (Ellis 2005: 343). In this 'popular ethnography of the everyday' (Dovey 2000: 138), ordinary people become extraordinary just by virtue of being the objects of the televisual gaze, rather than the subjects of socially meaningful or extraordinary events. The version of everyday life in the docusoap is rife with low-level interpersonal conflicts but, like emergency services programming, it does not address the sociological reasons which might cause such conflicts. This refusal of a larger perspective translates stylistically into a character-focused repertoire of medium shots and close-ups that engages with the minor scraps, obstacles and resistances of everyday life. Buoyed by the mixing of factual and fictional forms, the unordered, unpredictable minutiae of mundane life are magnified by the dramatic conventions of the soap opera such as multiple-character storylines, single-setting location, musical accompaniment and fast-paced editing. These 'dynamics of diversion' (Corner 2000) signalled a shift in the aesthetics and function of documentary, away from the marginal appeal of serious documentaries (Winston 2000: 40–5) to 'a new popularity [achieved] by exploring the mundane' (Ellis 2005: 344).

As we have seen, adjustments in television's relation to the real are frequently associated with technological developments, and the arrival of the docusoap was no exception. In the early 1990s, observational documentaries were still largely shot on 16 mm film, which was a relatively expensive undertaking because of the high shooting ratio (Bruzzi 2001: 132). This changed quite drastically when Sony introduced the first lightweight DV camera to the consumer market in late 1995 (Ellis 2005: 345). Within a year, it became possible to feed digital footage directly into non-linear edit suites, which made cutting faster and more flexible. By 1997, producers were taking advantage of digital camera and editing technology to enable 'a more intimate style and longer shooting schedules' without greater expense (Ellis 2005: 344). By 1998, docusoaps could be produced as much as three times more cheaply than other light entertainment, according to the head of BBC Documentary Features (cited in Bruzzi 2001: 132). Although the digital camera was put to many other uses, including experimental production, its compact size, light weight and expanded recording capacity made it particularly suited to observational shooting. The camera could more easily 'follow' subjects and be tucked away into smaller spaces (such as under the steering wheel of a learner car in *Driving School*). With digital technology making the fly-on-the-wall perspective more mobile, cheaper to produce and faster to post-produce, a minor revolution thus occurred in peak-time schedules and audience viewing habits. While *Airport* and *Vets in Practice* were the surprise hits of 1996, in 1997 *Driving School*, which followed a handful of instructors and their hapless clients, and *The Cruise*, set on a luxury Caribbean ocean liner, drew audiences of up to 12.5 and 11 million, respectively (Bruzzi 2001: 132). A host of other programmes also appeared, such as those which followed the fortunes of models (*Babewatch*), footballers (*Premier Passions*) and traffic wardens (*Clampers*); programmes that followed staff and visitors in theme parks (*Pleasure Beach*), department stores (*The Store*) and shopping malls (*Lakesiders*); and a programme that in 1997 turned the Adelphi Hotel in Liverpool into a national institution (*Hotel*) (Dovey 2000: 139).

While the low-gauge observational style of these shows indicates the documentary parentage of docusoaps, they also owe a clear debt to soap operas in their narrative emphasis on character, story and drama. Like the classic soap opera, the docusoap foregrounds a recurring set of multiple characters, each with a recognisable personality and an immediate goal. A limited number of stories is interwoven in each episode through the use of quick cross-cutting, sometimes indicating thematic juxtaposition but more often setting up temporal coherence. As with sitcoms and serial dramas, docusoap episodes are cyclical in structure, meaning that the permanent characters remain unaffected by the events of an episode so that by the end they have returned more or less to the same point at which they started. Any dramatic, life-changing events are left for the transient characters who appear in one episode only, providing narrative diversity and drama through their encounters with the lead characters.

The institutional setting of docusoaps, whether airport, hotel, shop or hospital, is well suited to the demands of cyclical narrative, since such places are managed by permanent staff but have porous boundaries which are crossed daily by travellers, customers and patients. These settings are thus closed ecologies with internal regulations for their staff but they remain open for traversal by fee-paying customers, such as the travellers on board the ocean liner in *The Cruise*. Closed ecologies allow for intimate relations to build, interpersonal conflicts to develop and some degree of psychological characterisation to be attained – all necessary to fictional structure – while the porous boundaries allow for new encounters and narrative trajectories to be introduced. This similarity to the narrative structure of sitcoms and soaps is openly, even reflexively, embraced by the credit sequences of docusoaps, which use stylised graphics to introduce the lead characters by first name over jaunty theme music. In *Airport*, for instance, the title sequence uses the lines of a lit runway to create angular graphics that group the permanent cast two by two, according to their roles, for example Sara and Peter, El Al customer relations; Kevin and Barry, Heathrow fire service; Eric and Caroline, immigration. Each person is dramatically caught in slow motion midway through a representative action, reminding us of his/her documentary presence as a social actor while the graphics emphasise his/her character role. Marked as entertainment, 'the programme's introduction invites the audience to *enjoy* the self-conscious hybridisation of fact and fiction' (Dovey 2000: 141; original emphasis).

Documentary has long borrowed from the tactics of fiction in order to contain and mould the intractable elements of everyday life. What makes the docusoap a novel form, however, is precisely the self-consciousness with which it combines the strategies of factual and fictional programming, mixing theme music with authoritative voice-over, narrative arcs with interviews, performance with observation. Along the way, the fly-on-the-wall style alternates with seemingly unprompted interviews, usually delivered by the permanent characters as they go about their work. The disparate storylines emphasise the diversity yet iterability of everyday life in an institutional setting like the airport. The proximity of the observational camera to unfolding events thus promotes a documentary 'sense of life captured as it is lived' (Coles 2000: 35), yet at the same time it offers audiences a diverse set of narrative identifications with characters to whom they can relate. Similarly, the diversity of stories and characters is smoothed out by quick editing patterns borrowed from fictional programming, yet the whole is stitched together by sombre voice-over narration borrowed from the documentary tradition. The voice-over – usually male, authoritative and unmarked by regional accent – speaks from a position of 'panoptic authority' (Dovey 2000: 142), appearing to provide full access to information but actually delivering a scripted 'just so' narration which treats all information as equally important. The result of this repertoire of interviews, camera proximity and authoritative voice-over is what Dovey calls the 'illusion of complete accessibility' (2000: 143) but it occurs at the expense of any discrimination among documented events: 'everything is equally visible, all material is of equal import' (Dovey 2000: 144). The structural tactics borrowed from fictional programming override traditional documentary standards of selection, so that on *Airport*, for instance, the fates of Columbian asylum-seekers, painted bullfrogs and passengers without seats are all treated as equivalent drama arcs in the chronology of day-to-day airport life.

For the many detractors who inveigh against the docusoap for being trivial and shallow (see Winston 2000: 45), the docusoap's hybridisation of fact and fiction ends up being the worst of both worlds. In this perspective, the ability, indeed purpose, of documentary to make serious claims about the world is overridden by the story-character formula, while the ability of fiction to imagine alternate universes is swamped by the minutiae of everyday life. The result of 'the illusion of complete accessibility', according to Dovey, is that viewers are not allowed to come to their own conclusions; they are positioned as 'participants in a process of narrative storytelling' (Dovey 2000: 148) rather than as participants in potential processes of social change. Pitched as documentary diversion, the docusoap turns inward to the personal rather than outward to the social, taking consumerism as its subject – focusing on the consumerist behaviours of travellers, shoppers, holiday-makers – as well as its object, since it is meant to be consumed as evening fare by audiences seeking entertainment. Dovey is surely right when he points out that the topics and settings of the docusoap suggest 'a portrait of the operations of the new service economy, a new ethnography of consumerism' (2000: 140). The regime of law-and-order ideology evident in the first half of the 1990s is thus replaced in the second half of the decade by the service-industry regime of consumption: the 'soft' social institutions of shop, ship and theme park that serve as settings for the docusoap leave aside the legal and juridical contexts of *Cops* in favour of privatised sites of 'leisure and aspirational desire' (Dovey 2000: 140; see also King 2006).

For defenders of the documentary tradition, the failure of the docusoap to make arguments about the social world (Nichols 1994) was part of a broader concern about the 'dumbing down' of British television in the 1990s (Winston 2000: 45). Nonetheless, even though the docusoap does not interrogate the development of the new service economy or the circulation of leisure capital, it does *portray* such an economy, in minute detail. It captures the affective weight of people's daily struggles and aspirations, using the techniques of ethnographic portrayal to make 'these people more complex and knowable than

mere comic stereotypes', while offering diverse points of identification for viewers (Coles 2000: 37–8). Brian Winston also points out
that the popularity of docusoaps, the very willingness of 40 per cent
or 50 per cent of viewers to tune in to a form that had traditionally
attracted small, elite audiences, must indicate some positive attributes.
For instance, docusoaps do not treat their subjects as social victims;
they regularly inject humour into the representation of everyday life;
they attract large audiences to documentary on cost-effective budgets.
They could be seen, says Winston, as the price of the survival of
documentary (2000: 55), or even as an improvement necessitated
by the deficiencies of the documentary (Bruzzi 2000: 86). But even
these more positive views continue to look at the docusoap from the
perspective of the documentary tradition. If we shift our perspective
and see it as part of the first generation of reality TV, it becomes a
cutting-edge form that introduces elements which will soon be very
familiar in the television landscape: performance, celebrity and contrivance, or what might be called the potential for finding actuality
within artifice.

## Performance, Celebrity and Artifice: The End of the Docusoap Boom

A less noticeable but directly related counterpart to the generic
hybridisation of the docusoap is its capacity for harnessing the celebrity apparatus of light entertainment programming. Prior to the
docusoap, celebrity mechanisms on real-crime and emergency services
shows had been limited to highlighting the visibility of presenters,
such as John Walsh of *America's Most Wanted*, or recycling newsread-
ers as narrators to lend prestige to a show, such as Martyn Lewis front-
ing *Crime Beat* and *X Cars* (Palmer 1998: 15). The innovative celebrity
mechanism at work in docusoaps, however, involves not the mobilisa-
tion but rather the production of celebrity by transforming 'ordinary
people' into stars (see Chapter 5). The docusoap can thus fittingly be
called the first celebrity-making strand of reality TV, for it offers a
ready overlap between the consumption of the shows as entertainment product, their settings in leisure/consumer institutions and their
emphasis on how workers perform within such settings. In some cases,
this performance is literal, as when Jane McDonald, cabaret singer on
board the ship in *The Cruise*, attracted considerable press attention and
went on to become a recording artist. In other cases, the emphasis lies
on how well people negotiate the contradiction between their roles as
docusoap characters and as performer in an institutional setting. For

instance, the sharp-tongued and strong-willed, if exam-challenged, driving pupil Maureen Rees from *Driving School* became an unlikely star, as did the campily attentive Aeroflot worker Jeremy Spake from *Airport*. All of these 'starring' characters, once they received exposure in the press, attempted to make the transition from their 'ordinary' occupations to media personality, hence capitalising on as well as trying to sustain their celebrity. As has become common for reality TV celebrities, however, most experienced the limitations of their so-called fifteen minutes of fame, enduring a fall from celebrity into obscurity, while a few managed to parlay their docusoap role into a more extended media career (such as Jane McDonald, who went on to co-present the daytime talkshow *Loose Women* (ITV, 1999–) from 2004 to 2010 as well as appearing as a celebrity guest or panellist on various other TV programmes).

The fates of these docusoap stars make it clear that reality TV celebrity is inherently but paradoxically dependent on ordinariness. To push the point, as *Big Brother* soon would, this is to say that performance on reality television is integral to an authentic projection of the self. As both social actors and characters, the subjects of docusoaps are required both to retain their ordinariness and to perform it; on the one hand they operate within the 'natural' situation of the setting, while on the other hand they are perfectly aware of the cameras that follow them. As Bignell observes, Jane McDonald's celebrity was positively construed because she could be figured as 'a plucky show performer . . . praised for her dedication and achievement as an ordinary person' (2005: 112). Docusoap participants are thus 'famous just for performing themselves' (Dovey 2000: 136). Rather than being constructed as ordinary people to whom extraordinary events occur, as on real-crime and emergency services programmes, the stars of docusoaps are 'hyperordinary people', required to go beyond the character role to achieve celebrity yet also required to retain the character that propelled them to celebrity (Bruzzi 2001: 134). To lose the character of ordinariness, as many try-hard reality TV participants have since learned, means becoming full of oneself and not knowing when to recede from the limelight (Palmer 2005).

This does not mean, however, that the docusoap seeks to elide performance. Rather, it embraces ordinariness as a performative construct within the artificiality of any filming situation. What sets it apart from both documentary and soap opera, as Stella Bruzzi argues, is its 'open acknowledgement of the importance of performance to factual *as well as* fictional programmes' (2001: 134; my emphasis). The observational technique of docusoaps neither draws attention to nor tries to hide the cameras; they are simply there, and the fact that the subjects carry out their tasks before (and to some extent for) the camera is an accepted part of the production process. Bruzzi, in fact, goes so far as to argue that docusoaps

> assume that a reality unaffected by the filming process is an impossibility, concluding that what they are able to achieve is the negotiation of a different understanding of truth – one that accepts the filmmaking process and one that acknowledges the essential artificiality of any filming set-up. (Bruzzi 2000: 98)

In this view, the docusoap marks an important period of transition from documentary to post-documentary, or from what we might call a reality unaffected by filming to an affected reality. As with any transition, however, the boom period in docusoaps created instability in the contemporary understandings of genre. Acknowledging its own 'essential artificiality' left the docusoap open to critical derision and even accusations of fakery.

Far less accepting of artificiality than Stella Bruzzi, Jon Dovey argues that the self-consciously nonchalant performances in docusoaps invest the form with 'an air of knowing camp' in place of educational or critical potential (2000: 139). Dovey's concern about the 'knowing' air of docusoaps is in keeping with a growing public suspicion of artifice in factual programming that arose in the late 1990s. John Ellis explains this suspicion by arguing that problems inevitably arise when the degree of fiction in factual material exceeds whatever level 'current generic understandings' allow (2005: 352). The hybridity of docusoaps precisely tests the elasticity of these 'generic understandings' by importing the discourse and structure of fictional narration without giving up the discursive claim to presenting 'real life'. This requires a balancing act, which is judged by audiences on a show-by-show basis. From docusoaps to *Big Brother* and beyond, one aspect of the balancing act remains crucial, namely that the audience maintains its belief that whatever situation plays out in front of the cameras, however self-reflexively, would *have occurred anyway* had the camera not been present. The camera in docusoaps, in other words, is allowed to affect the performance but not the event.

*Driving School* and *Clampers* found themselves at the heart of mini-scandals in 1998 when they seemed to break the 'natural event' rule. First, it was revealed that Maureen Rees of *Driving School* did not really wake at 4am to study for her driving exam, as the programme suggested that she did, and then came the claim that the most stringent patroller on *Clampers* was in fact no longer a traffic warden but a manager who had returned to the street so as to appear on camera. These two seemingly trivial revelations drastically undercut the popularity of docusoaps, not strictly on their own but because they occurred against the backdrop of a far greater threat to generic understandings, which John Ellis calls the documentary 'crisis of 1998–1999' (2005: 346). This crisis began when *The Connection*, an hour-long documentary produced by Carlton TV about the process of smuggling cocaine from Colombia to Britain, was accused by *The Guardian* of being 'an elaborate fake' (cited in Ellis 2005: 346). The immediate uproar in the press was exacerbated by an investigation on the part of the Independent Television Commission, which agreed with *The Guardian*'s findings and fined Carlton £2 million. Other similar revelations followed, ranging from fakery on the part of documentary-makers to documentary/talkshow subjects who had successfully hoodwinked producers (Ellis 2005: 347–8). The press kept the controversy alive, with the *Daily Mail* asking readers whether they could any longer believe anything they saw on TV (cited in Ellis 2005: 343). The television documentary genre was thrown into crisis precisely at the point where generic divisions between factual and fictional discourses were beginning to give.

John Ellis, who was working in documentary production at the time, draws a direct link between the broadcasters' need to exert damage control and the end of the docusoap boom in 1999 (2005: 354). Although we might expect that the response to a blurring of the divide between factual and fictional discourses would be the consolidation of the documentary genre around conservative understandings of 'authenticity', Ellis argues that the response went the other way. The television industry's answer, he claims, was to show *more* of the filming process. Authenticity, it turned out, could only be guaranteed by greater transparency of artificiality, since no one could be accused of fakery if filmic constructions were apparent and the set-up was part of the format. This nod to 'the connoisseurship of the camcorder generation' (Ellis 2005: 355) served to spur the development of post-docusoap formats.

## Conclusion

This chapter has provided a detailed investigation of the two major trends in first-generation reality TV: reality crime programmes and docusoaps. Both of these programme types have strong links to traditions of documentary and observational filmmaking. Both use low-gauge video technology, made available in the 1980s/1990s by the growth of camcorder and surveillance culture, to provide viewers with 'ride-along' and 'behind-the-scenes' access to social institutions, whether of police work or everyday life. Although the crime appeal format dates back to the 1960s, real-crime shows became a recognisable and repeatable format only in the political climate of law-and-order ideology, which configured society as a collection of right-minded people ('Us') against dangerous criminals ('Them'). In such a climate, these programmes prospered because they positioned viewers as engaged citizens who could help the police – and themselves – by watching television. While crime/emergency programmes exploited the camcorder aesthetic in order to claim a privileged relation to a dangerous reality, docusoaps in the UK combined this aesthetic of authenticity with narrative structures reminiscent of soap opera, producing a hybrid of fictional and factual programming styles that revived audience interest in television documentary.

As we have seen, different traditions of television production pertain on each side of the Atlantic, but both strands of first-generation reality TV serve as programmes arising in a climate of deregulation, individualisation and a growing public fascination with the 'appeal of the real' (Andrejevic 2004: 8). Since the 1990s, the real-crime programmes that initially gave a boost to the nascent FOX channel have developed into lasting international formats, while the shorter-lived docusoap boom is widely recognised as being responsible for the shift from documentary to 'post-documentary' culture in the UK and elsewhere (Corner 2000). Both of these programmes also have in common the fact that they observe participants in their 'natural' or found environments, a documentary characteristic which would soon change with the onset of second-generation reality TV.

The 'crisis' in documentary, which John Ellis locates in 1999, did not sound the death knell for reality TV in Britain. On the contrary, factual programming in the peak time schedule developed rapidly in the direction of 'formats which used explicitly manufactured rather than found situations' (Ellis 2005: 355). Whether this meant setting up situations for purposes of public education, such as the history series *1900 House* (Channel 4 1999), or for the sake of the personal challenge, such as the role-swapping programme *Faking It* (Channel 4, 2000–), or for the sake of manufacturing music consumables, like *Popstars* (ITV, 2001), artifice was now explicit. Television's relation to the real had shifted again: now events as well as performances could – and, according to viewers' expectations, should – be affected by producers. The idea that something real could be gained from watching people labour under artificial constraints ushers in the second generation of reality

TV, beginning with the seismographic shift in the televisual landscape brought about by *Big Brother*.

## Notes

1. Mark Fishman, writing in 1998 about the US television industry, estimates that drama and comedy series cost between $1 and $3 million per episode, quoting $1.5 to $1.7 million for an hour-long episode of *Star Trek: Next Generation* and $2 to $3 million for a half-hour episode of the sitcom *Roseanne*. Against this, he claims that tabloid newsmagazine programmes, running five half-hour shows per week, cost between $250,000 and $600,000 per week to produce, whereas reality programmes cost between $150,000 and $250,000 per week (Fishman 1998: 67). We should note, however, that these costs apply specifically to real-crime programmes; such costs would skyrocket from 2000 onward with the appearance of shows that spend large on sets and crew (e.g. *Survivor* or *The Apprentice*, which *The Wall Street Journal* estimated in 2004 to cost just under $2 million per episode (<http://www.realityblurred.com/realitytv/archives/related_news/2004_Jul_28_costs_rising> (accessed 1 February 2011)).
2. In 1983, Sony released the Betamovie BMC-100P, which used Betamax cassettes. In the same year, JVC released the first consumer model that used VHS tape.
3. See the *Aktenzeichen XY Ungelöst* webpage called 'Zahlen, Zahlen, Zahlen' (Figures, Figures, Figures): <http://aktenzeichenxy.zdf.de/ZDFde/inhalt/13/0,1872,5276621,00.html> (accessed 1 February 2011).
4. E.g. Hendrie 1993; Maron 1993.
5. As evidence, Donovan cites the election of Rudolph Giuliani as mayor of New York City in 1993 on a platform that promised to be tough on crime and public disorder, despite the fact that federal reports after Guiliani's victory showed that crime rates in New York had in fact decreased by 6 per cent during his predecessor David Dinkins' administration (1998: 122).
6. Watson himself, however, has repeatedly derided docusoaps, insisting that *The Family* has nothing to do with the docusoaps of the later 1990s (see Dovey 2000: 137).

# **3** Second-Generation Reality TV (1999–2000): Surveillance and Competition in *Big Brother* and *Survivor*

The year 2000 marked the much anticipated 'Y2K' onset of the new millennium, but it also brought reality TV onto the popular global stage. This was the watershed year when reality TV went from cheap programming apparently aimed at the 'lowest common denominator' to headline-hogging shows watched and discussed by everyone, even its many detractors. In a short space of time, the discursive uses of 'reality TV' were redefined and substantially widened; from having served as a generic tag for emergency and real-crime programming, it quickly became synonymous with *Big Brother* (in Europe and the UK) and *Survivor* (in the US). Richard M. Huff calls the first chapter of his book on reality television '*Survivor*: The Start of It All', claiming that *Survivor* 'launched the reality revolution in the United States' (2006: ix). A special issue of *Television and New Media* devoted to *Big Brother UK* (Hill and Palmer 2002) chronicles the similarly revolutionary impact of *Big Brother* in Britain, where 9 million viewers tuned in to the first series finale in September 2000 (Hill 2004: 27).

As we have seen from the previous chapter, however, it is not quite the case that either of these programmes represents the 'start' of reality television. Methodologically, the problem with such a claim is that it attempts to map reality TV history in terms of a single point of origin, thereby ignoring the complexity of its discursive contexts and generic strands. While it is too simple to speak in terms of a single starting point, the genealogical approach must nonetheless recognise the crucial role played by *Big Brother* and *Survivor* in consolidating reality TV as a genre. Together, these two shows constituted a kind of evolutionary leap that repositioned reality television as a high-rating component of prime time programming. It is only in retrospect, however, that we can see this as a break between first- and second-generation reality TV. Whereas the development of reality TV during the first generation was highly reliant on external factors – socio-political, cultural, economic – the second generation embedded reality television into cultural discourses as a genre with its own format rules, production practices and audience expectations. Second-generation reality TV found its place in the millennial cultural imaginary by openly combining actuality and artifice in ways that broke ratings records and caused wide-scale debate.

The most important feature that distinguishes second- from first-generation reality programming is the introduction of *competition* under conditions of *comprehensive surveillance*. Whereas first-generation programmes are satisfied to observe ordinary people in the environments in which they are found, second-generation programmes fabricate competitive environments and subject participants' behaviour to full-scale scrutiny by a panoply of mounted and mobile cameras. Competition for the purpose of entertainment, of course, has had a long history on television in the form of quiz or game shows (see Holmes 2008a), but the game show underwent a dramatic revival in the late 1990s with the sudden popularity of *Who Wants to Be a Millionaire?*, an original British format (ITV, 1998–) which exploded into the prime time in the US (ABC, 1999–2002; synd. 2002–) before going global. Like *Big Brother*, *Who Wants to be a Millionaire?* tapped into the renewed 'appeal of the real' (Andrejevic 2004) that placed ordinary individuals in a competitive environment so as to heighten the drama of their ordinariness.[1] *Big Brother*, however, took this appeal further than the studio-based *Millionaire* by turning contestants' day-to-day behaviour in a shared house into the content of the game itself. With the competitive rhythm of *Big Brother* and *Survivor* defined by losing one contestant at regular intervals, reality TV became synonymous in the popular imagination with elimination, eviction and 'voting off' – a phrase that encapsulates the marriage of gameshow entertainment, political metaphor and the sociology of group organisation. Since 1999, countless reality TV programmes have followed the basic model put forward by *Big Brother*: start with a group of people in a constructed environment and whittle them down until only one winner is left. Because of the competitive format, *Big Brother* and *Survivor* are sometimes called 'gamedocs' by academics (cf. Hill 2002; Kilborn 2006), in recognition of their common purpose with gameshows.

What differentiates reality television 'gamedocs' from gameshows, however, is the way that second-generation reality TV settings simulate the lived landscapes of social reality. Even though the environments of these programmes are constructed, the fact that the game involves comprehensive, twenty-four-hour surveillance of participants' activities blurs the line between on- and off-screen worlds. As a result, the interest of these shows lies not simply in the strategy or popularity of a winner, but rather in the way they undermine discursive distinctions between reality and fiction, private and public identities, authenticity and performance. Sociologist Erving Goffman posited in the late 1950s that we perform ourselves even in our ordinary lives; for Goffman, 'ordinary social discourse' is put together out of what he calls 'legitimate performances of everyday life' (1959: 72, 73). Applied to television, this suggests that programmes which place participants in the conditions of everyday life, however constructed, end up eliciting performances that are difficult to separate from those of 'ordinary social discourse'. Jon Dovey takes this insight further by arguing that the constructed transparency of *Big Brother* produces a 'simulation' of social life, not in the sense of something false but in the sense of a model (such as a computer model) that 'produces real knowledge about real things in the real world and has real effects upon real lives' (Dovey 2004: 233). The claim to the real thus expands from the first to the second generation of reality television, as the dividing line between reality TV participants and viewers, between the on-screen world and the social world, becomes more permeable.

There are two further effects of comprehensive surveillance that will be taken up in this chapter. Ethically, the comprehensive surveillance of participants in the *Big Brother* house or on the *Survivor* island threatens long-held ideas about privacy and seems to promote voyeurism; technologically, however, it provides a basis for expanding the role of television in the digital, multi-media age. On *Survivor*, participants are constantly surrounded by camera teams, and regularly break off activities to conduct to-camera interviews. On *Big Brother* participants strapped to microphones cohabit in a house monitored 24/7 by cameras linked to live television and internet feeds. Since there is nothing that participants say or do that is not privy to capture by the camera, critics have railed against the inhumane conditions of this lack of privacy and accused the programmes of appealing to viewers' basest voyeuristic instincts. At the same time, *Big Brother* shows have used the surplus material of comprehensive surveillance to mobilise a highly successful convergence with other media platforms and increase the interactive potential of television. The official website of the first Dutch series allowed visitors real-time access to the *Big Brother* house, a popular feature that became a standard part of the *Big Brother* format, while television audiences were invited to decide who would be evicted by phoning in their votes. Interactivity via the website and voting via telephony provided audiences with a compelling, if limited, 'modicum of participation' in the production process (Andrejevic 2004: 108), as countless later *Big Brother* series and offshoots like the *Idol* franchise and *The X-Factor* would attest.

This chapter will address this range of social, formal and technological issues by focusing on *Big Brother* as an international franchise and new media object framed by critical discourses of experimentation, disciplinary mechanisms, voyeurism and genre hybridity. Further, we will investigate the way in which *Big Brother*'s purpose-built environment of twenty-four-hour surveillance challenges audience expectations about the correlation between authenticity and on-screen performance, privacy and publicity, television and everyday life. Although the *Big Brother* format depends on competition among participants, the observational focus of *Big Brother* means that the competitive element is relatively weak when compared to a programme like *Survivor*. In the final section, the chapter thus investigates the function of competition in second-generation reality TV by discussing the complexities of *Survivor* within the context of game theory. In order to understand the legacies inherited by *Big Brother* and *Survivor*, however, we need to start by backing up – to *The Real World*, an MTV precursor that is often credited, along a very different genealogical strand than *Cops*, with 'usher[ing] in the age of reality television' (Eby 2010: n.p.). Beginning with *The Real World* will allow us to interrogate the role of casting and editing in reality TV, as well as trace the roots of the second generation to constructed dramas of intimacy between strangers.

## Intimate Strangers: *The Real World* and the Politics of Casting

As I have noted, there is more than one way to tell the history of a genre, and more than one starting point. In 1992, while reality programming on US networks and local stations ran the gamut of real-crime shows, disaster-clip programmes and tabloid current affairs, MTV adopted a very different approach to putting ordinary people on camera. Launched in 1981 with the express purpose of showcasing music videos, the cable station decided a decade later to expand into serial programming to promote regular viewing among its target youth demographic (Kraszweski 2004: 184). Seeking something other than conventional soaps or sitcoms, MTV contracted soap opera producer Mary Ellis Bunim and documentary-maker Jon Murray to combine their expertise to make a thirty-minute weekly show, *The Real World*. While the creators of *Big Brother* (Jon de Mol) and *Survivor* (Charlie Parsons) introduced competitive elimination to reality TV in the late 1990s, the basic idea of placing a handful of strangers together in a living situation for a set period and filming the results belongs to Bunim and Murray.[2] As with every claim of origin, however, this too is disputed, in this case by Erik Latour, a Dutch producer who created *Nummer 28*, a 1991 show on the Dutch network KRO that placed seven young strangers together in a student house in Amsterdam and followed them over several months. The similarity to *The Real World* may seem striking, but Jon Murray insists on the debt *The Real World* owes to the serialised observational documentary *An American Family*. With *The Real World*, however, Bunim and Murray gave an important twist to the premise of *An American Family*: rather than having the live-in camera (see Chapter 1) come to the family, the 'family' was created for the sake of – and literally in front of – the live-in camera. Given MTV's youth demographic, this new 'nuclear family' – as Murray himself described it (Museum for Television and Radio 1994) – was built not on the biological model but on the model of house-sharing, an experience presumed to be familiar to MTV's viewers. Accordingly, in 1992 seven people in their early twenties were selected to live in a loft in New York for three months, with two camera crews tracking their interactions while the producers 's[a]t back and wait[ed] for things to happen – sometimes nervously' (Murray, Museum of Television and Radio 2001).

In its mode of production, *The Real World* broke the mould of both the televised drama series and the fly-on-the-wall documentary. Without a script to work from, producers in effect shared control of the production with the cast members, whose actions and interactions made up the content of the show. Members of the production staff and camera crews were forbidden to have contact with the cast to prevent undue influence, and events the camera crew might have missed were not restaged. In keeping with the MTV aesthetic of stylised cinematography and fast-paced editing, *The Real World* nonetheless was and continues to be a highly produced programme, with none of observational documentary's attempt to render the presence of the camera invisible. Tilt shots, quick zooms and head-spinning pans from one person to another are not uncommon, and the editing pace combines the choppiness of MTV music videos with the rhythm of emotional climaxes familiar from soap opera. Jon Murray acknowledges the genre-mixing impulse that led to what he calls this 'commercialised documentary filmmaking' (Museum of Television and Radio 2001):

We looked at all the things that people did in scripted TV and why people watch that and then we set up our premise. Each episode has an A and a B story. It's a three-act structure: hook 'em in the first

act, pay it off in the third act. There are so many stories you don't
see on *The Real World* because there's no finish to the story, so we
don't play it.

Unlike fictional programmes that rely on a script, the narrative arcs
of *The Real World*'s three-act structure are created through producers' choices of what to film and how to edit the footage. With
mounted cameras in the house and two camera crews following the
cast members for up to twenty hours a day over sixteen weeks, this
programme promises full access to participants' lives *at the same time*
as admitting that this is a highly mediated version of events. Only a
tiny fraction of the footage shot ever makes it to air. According to staff
producer George Vershoor, twenty-two minutes (a half-hour episode
minus advertising breaks) represents seventy hours of raw footage,
which means that the editors are highly selective (and subjective) when
they impose shape on what Vershoor calls 'the chaos of this television'
(Museum of Television and Radio 1994). Of course, exerting control
over the presentation of real events through editing is a common
practice in reality TV, necessitated on the one hand by the very high
shooting ratio and on the other by 'the chaos' of filming non-actors.
While such control in post-production has ethical implications, in *The
Real World* Jon Murray sees the relation of editing to shooting simply
as a trade-off of power between producers and participants: 'We don't
have a lot of control during the production process, what we have is
the control to make choices during the editing' (cited in Andrejevic
2004: 103).

Before there is even any footage to edit, however, the casting
process itself is the primary site of control, especially given the lack
of scripts or competition-based story arcs in this hybrid format.
Murray has stated that 'for a show like *The Real World*, when you
don't have a game format, we live or die by our casting' (cited in Eby
2010: n.p.). What is surprising here is less the importance attributed
to the selection process than the fact that Bunim and Murray repeatedly refer to the participants as a 'cast', which openly recognises the
influence of scripted programming on *The Real World*. The common
practice of casting for a scripted series takes on added importance
in this case, however, because the people selected to be on camera
*create* the content of the programme. The criteria for cast selection
highlight the fact that reality television sits at the point of tension
between documentary 'reality' and the narrative demands of scripted
television. The producers of *The Real World*, not to mention later
second-generation shows, attempt to cast equally for authenticity

and narrative consistency. On the one hand, applicants undergo an extended period of interviews and test footage 'to find out if they really are the person they're presenting' to the producers (Murray, Museum of Television and Radio 2001); on the other hand, over the course of six or seven interviews during three months the producers 'look for a consistency in character' (ibid.), which reflects their concerns with narrative coherence as borrowed from fiction. Further, participants are selected according to what are at times the contradictory criteria of social representativity and personal charisma. The selected seven (or eight in some seasons) participants represent a diverse range of social identities as well as religious and political beliefs, yet at the same time they are selected on the basis of their idiosyncrasies, for their potential to create the dramatic tensions that are the mainstay of scripted television. Reconciling these contradictory impulses suggests that, in the casting process as developed on *The Real World*, real people are chosen to 'play' themselves. Highly selective casting, like judicious editing, thus gives producers control over the production before shooting has even begun. Casting for authenticity permits producers to increase the reality effect of the programme, while casting for character consistency lays the groundwork for narratives and characterisation to be strengthened in post-production (Kraszewski 2004: 194).

Like its successors *Big Brother* and *Survivor*, *The Real World* has been criticised for casting participants explicitly for the sake of conflict. When asked at a symposium whether this is the case, Murray offered a politic but evasive response: 'the nature of the show is to bring seven *different* people together' (Museum of Television and Radio 1994; original emphasis). There is no doubt that casting for 'difference' fulfils a number of goals for second-generation programmes: social diversity (so as to avoid accusations of racism, homophobia, etc.); wider appeal to the target viewers (who are presumed to want to see 'themselves' on screen); and a narratological basis for story arcs to come. Since dramatic arcs can be shaped in post-production but not scripted into the programme, they are in an important sense pre-coded by casting. These pre-coded conflicts are first and foremost social: when participants of different genders, races, classes, sexualities and/or regional backgrounds are placed in close proximity, dramatic encounters arising from ideological differences can be expected. While the age range (eighteen to twenty-five) and career aspirations (especially music) of the participants tend to be similar, since many of them are hoping to ignite careers in the culture industries, their conflicting views regarding race, sexuality and religious/political issues offer ongoing points of volatility. For instance, in the first season, which set the pattern for seasons to come, the group consisted of three women and four men, of whom two were African-American (a poet and a rapper), one was gay (a painter), one was a Southerner from Alabama (an aspiring dancer), and all were between nineteen and twenty-five heading toward careers in art or media. In this first season, racial conflicts and debates were a common source of interpersonal strife, usually sparked by Kevin Powell, a highly politicised African American writer from urban New Jersey. Indeed, the dramatic highlight of the season, for viewers as well as the producers, was the eleventh episode fight between Kevin and Julie, the girl from Alabama, who accused Kevin of throwing a candleholder at her during an argument – an accusation that caused the roommates to take passionate sides, since none of them, not even the camera crew, had witnessed the actual argument. What resulted in this particular episode was extensive footage of heated debates as the housemates attempted to work through this rupture to their social microcosm. At the same time, the lack of footage of the argument itself serves as a reminder that a *Real World* house does not constitute the kind of comprehensive surveillance space that would later become a defining feature of *Big Brother*.

This raises ethical as well as political considerations, since the production method of *The Real World*, like *Big Brother* and *Survivor* to follow, is to set up racial, sexual and sociopolitical flash-points by casting participants as the raw material for dramatic narratives. Implicitly, the intimate setting of *The Real World* offers participants the opportunity to resolve such differences through conversation and cohabitation. Jon Kraszewski (2004), however, argues that the show conceals the structural aspects of racism by repeatedly portraying as racist only individuals from conservative rural areas, such as Julie from Alabama, as though racism in the US were simply a regional problem. Mark Andrejevic and Dean Colby (2006) similarly claim that *Road Rules* (MTV, 1995–2007), a Bunim/Murray spin-off of *The Real World* in which five strangers travel together in an RV (recreational vehicle), places the brunt of American racial history onto the individual of colour rather than framing its persistence in terms of social structures. A more optimistic reading of either programme's dynamic, however, might suggest that its social value lies in making manifest the tender spots of the American body politic, by drawing attention to individual narratives of prejudice and struggle so as to show how individuals act out certain approved social scripts. In this light, the tendency of *The Real World* to attribute racism to rural Americans, as Kraszewski argues, or of *Road Rules* to lay the negotiation of race at the feet of the 'ghetto-girl', as Andrejevic and Colby argue, is itself part of the larger social script of American life that rises to the surface in the absence of an actual script written for the programme. This is not to say that *The Real World* is directly critical of society; on the contrary, it is often complicit with the unequal social structures from which it draws its cast. The point is, however, that it can provide the material for viewers themselves to critique these structures. This might explain why *The Real World* – especially the earlier seasons that highlight issues like homosexuality, AIDS, abortion and racism – tends to have a place on many media studies viewing lists at universities.

Whether setting up participants to fight or have sex, *The Real World* is ultimately about *interpersonal* relationships developed in an intimate setting. In this sense, the show is the first example of what I call the 'intimate strangers' subgenre of reality TV (Kavka 2008), which makes it both a progenitor of *Big Brother* and a second-generation programme well before its time. Although the casting process and narrative impetus of the programme mean that participants are treated as individuals, they are of interest to viewers (and producers) because of how they *interact* with others under conditions of *intimacy*. The legacy of *The Real World* for second-generation programmes like *Big Brother* thus lies in the way it builds a ready-made 'nuclear family' from a selection of strangers, none of whom know each other until the moment they meet in their new space of cohabitation. Placing cast members in close proximity with one another is key to the arrangement: no matter how luxuriously sprawling the house or loft in these shows, it is notable that there are never enough bedrooms for each participant to have his/her own room. Rather, sharing the highly intimate space of a bedroom is a format tool of the 'intimate strangers' configuration. The specific content of programmes in this subgenre thus consists of tracking the rhythms that develop when people are thrown together in a close living arrangement. Moreover, it is this promise of intimate interaction – whether positive or negative or merely banal – that underlies the shows' claims to the real.

This intimacy occurs not just between the participants but also between participants and viewers. In another innovation that would remain with reality TV for decades to come, the *Real World* producers introduced what they called a weekly 'confessional' during which participants are asked to reflect on the week's events while speaking directly to camera. Confessional footage, in *The Real World* as well as its successors, is intercut with the footage of participants' day-to-day lives, thereby creating two layers of intimacy: intimacy between participants, to which the viewers are witnesses, and intimacy between participants and viewers, produced by having participants 'confess' directly, as it were, to viewers themselves. *The Real World* thus created a new model for television by casting real people to live in a contrived setting where their unpredictable intimate interactions would constitute the content of the programme. It is this relation between strangers, intimacy and life lived on screen that lays the groundwork for second-generation reality TV. It is the success of this formula, too, that explains the longevity of *The Real World*, which at the time of writing has been renewed by MTV to stretch at least into its twenty-sixth season, making it the second longest-running reality TV show behind *Cops*.

### *Big Brother* as International New Media Object

While there is no direct link between *The Real World* and the launch of *Big Brother* seven years later, *Big Brother* undoubtedly adopts the 'intimate strangers' logic of *The Real World* as its key premise. Nonetheless, the later show also makes four important changes to the earlier format: it introduces a competitive framework, enforces total surveillance of the participants, operates on a very short edit-to-air timeframe and woos viewers across multiple media platforms. These changes strip away the last vestiges of privacy from reality TV participants, creating a manufactured environment of 'scopic comprehensiveness' where the social world has been created explicitly for the purpose of revealing personal 'truths' (Corner 2002: 257). With *Big Brother*, then, the promise of full-scale visibility replaces the naturalism of *The Real World* as the basis of the shows' claims to reality: while *The Real World* offers to show what happens when people 'start being real' (opening credits), *Big Brother* is 'real' because it promises to show *everything*. The reality guaranteed by full-scale surveillance overrides the contrivance of the purpose-built house in which the participants are enclosed. In place of *The Real World*'s two or three camera crews following selected cast members around a big city, the *Big Brother* house has mounted cameras in every room (including the bathroom in most versions) and mobile camera crews gliding up and down corridors behind one-way glass. With the surveillance footage from some thirty or forty cameras edited on a twenty-four-hour turnaround into daily shows and weekly live studio shows, *Big Brother*'s production tactics fully exploit the appeal of 'liveness' (Feuer 1983; Roscoe 2004: 187). What is lost in slickness and aesthetics to such a fast-paced production and editing schedule is more than made up for by the effects of immediacy and authenticity, as viewers check in daily to see what the participants are up to. *Big Brother* thus changes the 'relationship between television and everyday life' (Corner 2002: 255), turning television into an apparatus for the production of everyday life itself. At the same time, *Big Brother* effortlessly, if paradoxically, grounds its claims to the real in a highly manufactured situation. The idea that television can *produce* the real rather than simply *represent* or reflect it was to have profound implications for the relationship of the media to social life.

The first *Big Brother* series screened in the Netherlands from September to December 1999, a harbinger of the changes the new millennium, and new media, would bring to broadcast television. It was produced by Endemol, a Dutch production company co-founded in 1994 by Jon de Mol and Joop van den Ende. Whereas Endemol's previous productions had slipped easily into the mainstream of television programming, the concept and format of *Big Brother* quickly redefined how reality TV programmes were produced, marketed and consumed by audiences. The most important breakthrough, in terms of the economic and technological organisation of television, was that *Big Brother* was not confined to one medium or one nation. From the start, the programme leveraged its association with the internet to draw vast audiences, which turned the format itself into a commodity package that could be bought and sold globally. Arguably 'the first grand-scale confluence of television and Internet entertainment', according to an article published in *The New York Times Magazine* prior to the launch of the first US *Big Brother* (Sella 2000), the broadcast show was accompanied by a website that did much more than simply advertise the programme. The website posted background information (photos and profiles of the housemates), offered an interactive platform for viewers (polls, chat and forums) and, most importantly, provided live streams for round-the-clock viewing access to the house. Although the website was not the central means of delivering the show's content, neither was it simply supplemental, since more information could be gained via the website's live streams than was available on the television programme (Roscoe 2004: 190).

The website was not the only point of media convergence, for *Big Brother* also increased viewer interactivity by inviting the audience to decide the fate of the week's nominees for eviction. Voting was carried out by telephone, first landline calls and then with mobile phone texting, so that telephony became a companion medium and source of revenue for the show. *Big Brother* also made the leap from terrestrial to digital television; in the UK, the *Big Brother* broadcaster Channel 4 used the highly popular programme to launch its digital channel, E4, which from 2001 showed eighteen hours of daily coverage from the *Big Brother* house. With later series, E4 added *Big*

*Brother* spin-off shows such as *Big Brother's Little Brother* and offered interactive features that gave access to additional camera angles as well as voting options. This *Big Brother*-verse was supported by a glut of articles in the print media, from the official *Big Brother* magazine to the often rabid press interest in housemates from the broadsheet, tabloid and magazine press. By combining free-to-air and digital television platforms with live streaming to the internet, phone-in voting and constant attention in the print media, *Big Brother* drastically expanded interactive opportunities for audiences as well as marketing partnerships with other media organisations. Within a few short years after the first series screened in the Netherlands, the multi-platform format had been sold to countries across the globe. In this respect, *Big Brother* is arguably the first television-based 'new media object in so far as it is an international brand that exists as a multi-platform hybrid of traditional and new media' (Dovey 2004: 233).

Although American reality formats of the first generation had been sold and copied in the early 1990s, *Big Brother* was the first reality TV format to go truly global, for it was the first format with the elasticity to be localised to the cultural conditions of each broadcast setting (Roscoe 2004: 183). By 2008 it had appeared in over forty countries, making it one of the most successful franchises in television history (Hill and Palmer 2002: 251). Within a year of its 1999 launch in the Netherlands, the format had been sold to seven broadcasters on the European continent[3] as well as to Channel 4 (UK) and CBS (US). By 2001 the global franchise had been extended to Argentina, Australia and South Africa, not to mention five further continental European countries. Pan-regional versions of *Big Brother*, such as *Big Brother Africa* (M-Net, 2003–9) and *Big Brother Al-Rais* of the Arab world (MBC 2, 2004), appeared in areas joined by a common identity and transnational television networks. In most countries, *Big Brother* followed a similar distribution and reception pattern: licensed by Endemol to a minor private broadcaster, which had itself arisen from the deregulation of television industries in the late 1980s (see Chapter 2), the show caused controversy but also delivered a meteoric rise in ratings.[4] Within a decade of its industry-redefining appearance in many countries, however, audience interest in *Big Brother* had flagged and it was taken off air (e.g. by 2006 in the Netherlands, 2008 in Australia and 2010 in the UK, where it went to twelve seasons). Nonetheless, in many other countries, the show – with format modifications over the years – remains on air at the time of writing; in Germany, Italy, Spain and the US, for instance, it has been running continuously since 2000, while other countries (e.g. Argentina,

Greece, Mexico, Norway and Sweden) have witnessed a recent *Big Brother* revival after many years in hiatus.

## The Gaze of Big Brother: Experimentation, Surveillance and Controversy

At the start, *Big Brother* functioned as both television experiment and social experiment. The element of competition, devised as a knock-out tournament structure familiar from sports, was added to principles associated with scientific investigation: isolation, highly controlled conditions and full-scale visibility. Although the title recalls George Orwell's dystopian novel *Nineteen Eighty-Four* (1949), in which a total-itarian society is ruled by an invisible dictator called 'Big Brother',[5] the concept's creator Jon de Mol has claimed that the inspiration for *Big Brother* came from the Biosphere 2 project (Brenton and Cohen 2003: 59–60). This was an artificial ecological system, built in Arizona in the early 1990s, which ran a two-year closure experiment that locked a crew of eight people inside to test the complex interactions among human, biological and chemical elements. While *Big Brother* cannot make any claim to lofty scientific aims, the appeal of the programme, like later reality TV shows, draws on the 'what would happen if' rheto-ric of experimentation; rather than 'what would happen if mankind had to live in a geodesic dome', the question became 'what would happen if 12 people were locked into a house together for three months?' Unlike participants on *The Real World*, who are encouraged to interact with the social world, the format of *Big Brother* insists on controlled conditions of isolation: participants are locked into a purpose-built house set within a high-walled garden; they are forbidden watches and are subjected to a media blackout; and they are subject to producer intervention in the form of set tasks and the sporadic voice of 'Big Brother' himself. This is life in a petri dish, stripped bare of luxuries (at least in the early series) and peeled back to the essentials of social interaction. The 'back-to-basics' theme, which appears in the opening graphics of the early Dutch and German series, recalls both the show's eco-environmentalism (participants had to tend chickens and grow vegetables) and the conditions of life stripped to bare essentials.

*Big Brother* makes no apology for the artifice of the environment or for yoking together discourses of experimentation and entertainment. Rather than making a documentary claim to naturalism or 'real' life, which as we have seen is the basis of first-generation reality TV, *Big Brother* simulates life as it would be lived under conditions of an exper-iment, in sociality and in television form. Like the Stanford prison experiment (see Chapter 1), however, *Big Brother* also tests human responses to imprisonment and surveillance; media scholar Paddy Scannell, among many others, refers to the participants as 'inmates' (2002). With the unblinking eyes of twenty-eight to forty cameras spread through every room of the house, *Big Brother* recalls the asylum as much as the human zoo, both of which were popularised in the nineteenth century. Similar to the zoos that exhibited exotic human 'others' to a curiosity-seeking public (Bancel and Boëtsch 2008), the pseudo-scientific isolation of the *Big Brother* cast becomes a sellable commodity in entertainment culture. In *Big Brother* participants voluntarily give up their privacy in exchange for money, fame and/or a 'challenge'; producers sell this privacy to viewers; and viewers, through whatever media platform, pay to be entertained by seeing private selves of real people. It is this convergence of confinement, surveillance and entertainment that made *Big Brother* such a controversial programme in its initial series.

The controversy caused by the first series of *Big Brother*, initially in continental Europe, spread well beyond television culture to public debates and even governmental intervention. The publicity for the show's first series repeatedly unleashed a degree of outrage that Daniël Biltereyst has characterised as 'moral panics' (Biltereyst 2004). Most of the commentators who were appalled by the idea of the programme cited concerns about voyeurism, lack of privacy and offences to human dignity. In the Netherlands, for example, journalists, psychologists and media commentators condemned *Big Brother* as an 'inhumane experiment', while an editorial on Spanish *Big Brother* in the newspaper *El Pais* called the show as an 'audiovisual Auschwitz' (Meijer and Reesink 2000, cited in Mathijs 2002: 311, 312) – a reference to Nazi concentration camps which found an uncomfortable echo in the German reception of *Big Brother*. In Germany, the head of the media regulatory commission in Hessen accused the programme of representing 'a serious affront to the intimate sphere'[6] and joined with other regulatory commissions to have *Big Brother* taken off the air (in the end the joint commissions were able only to bend the rules of the format, providing participants with one hour per day when the cameras were turned off). Similarly, the French broadcasting watchdog, Conseil supérieur de l'audiovisuel (CSA), commanded France's version of *Big Brother*, called *Loft Story*, to turn off the cameras for two hours a day, although this was not enough to prevent violent protests against 'trash TV' from taking place outside the BB house.[7] International format sales of *Big Brother* to non-Western countries met with popular appeal tempered by moral and political outrage. On its launch in 2003, the widely watched *Big Brother Africa* quickly became the fulcrum of loud debate between those who praised the show for supporting pan-regional unity (including Nelson Mandela) and those who condemned it for promoting immorality (Biltereyst 2004: 10). In the Arab world the controversy caused by cultural and religious sensitivity to the mixing of genders in the house led to *Big Brother Al-Rais* (MBC2 2004) being cancelled after eleven days. A Chinese attempt to emulate the *Big Brother* format, called *Perfect Holiday* (HNSTV & VHand 2002), was banned halfway through the first season by government media censors concerned that this 'disgusting life farce' would undermine socialist values (Xie and Chen 2007, cited in Luo 2010: 36). In the West, comparisons between *Big Brother* and the Roman gladiatorial arena (von Braun 2000) raised a different spectre of immorality: they suggested that the offence of *Big Brother* lay less with the indignity of surveillance than with the voyeuristic impulse of audiences who would flock to watch a fight to the 'death' for their own entertainment.

The spectre of the gladiatorial arena dramatises the two main concerns raised when the minutiae of private, intimate interactions become the subject of the camera's gaze, namely, accusations of panoptic surveillance and voyeurism. With its panoply of mounted cameras and mobile camera crews, *Big Brother* introduced a scale of surveillance that far outstripped the amateur or ride-along camera operators of first-generation reality TV. Many commentators have noted that in the *Big Brother* house surveillance functions on the model of Jeremy Bentham's eighteenth-century panopticon (McGrath 2004: 7), which Bentham envisioned as a circular building of multi-story cells surrounding a central watchtower. With large windows in the exterior and interior walls of each cell lighting up the inmates, prisoners become fully visible to the guard in the watchtower without the guard himself being seen. For Michel Foucault, who discusses the panopticon at length in his book *Discipline and Punish*, this model of comprehensive surveillance defines the era of the 'discipline society' because it exerts an institutional power over subjects (here the inmates) which is at once visible and unverifiable (1979: 201). The watchtower of Bentham's panopticon is a visible manifestation of power, since the prisoners know they are under surveillance, but this power is also unverifiable because the prisoners cannot tell at what point and for how long they are being watched. Knowing only that they are under full surveillance, they internalise the *condition* of being watched and discipline their own behaviour accordingly, without the need for repressive controls (Foucault 1979: 202). The *Big Brother* house, decked out with many cameras but no visible operators or viewers, translates the physical architecture of the prison into its media equivalent. Like the panopticon, the surveillance system of the house allows the 'inmates' to see the manifestations of the media gaze (the mounted cameras) but without being able to verify whether anyone is in fact watching. Like Bentham's prisoners, *Big Brother* participants can be said to internalise the condition of being watched, disciplining themselves into behaving as though they are being watched at all time – which, given the web links, is likely to be the case.

Of course, Foucault's discussion of the panopticon has little to say about why anyone would watch *Big Brother* participants, other than to maintain the 'automatic functioning' of institutional power (Foucault 1979: 201). While producers or camera operators may be comparable with the guard in the panoptical watchtower, for viewers the model of the panopticon seems to have less explanatory value. To explain the position of viewers, critics have instead turned to the discourse of voyeurism. The moral implication of this turn is clear: to say that viewers follow their voyeuristic impulses suggests that *Big Brother* appeals to the base instincts of audiences who seek sexual arousal through watching others. The applicability of voyeurism to reality TV viewing, however, is less clear, since in the classical Freudian scenario the voyeur's pleasure resides precisely in the object of the gaze *not* knowing that she is being watched (in the classical scenario, the object of the gaze is a 'she'). To take this one step further, Slavoj Žižek points out that the scenario depends on the voyeur *fantasising* that the object does not know she is being watched, because the actual excitement for the voyeur comes in the delicious possibility of being caught, of having the gaze suddenly returned (cited in Buchanan 2001). In *Big Brother*, of course, these conditions do not apply. Participants come into the house in full knowledge that they are being watched, and viewers know that they know. In fact, many participants, especially in later series of *Big Brother*, sign up for the programme in order to be watched, hoping to turn their time on camera into the launch of a media career – a fact which in the UK, for instance, led to a backlash against the programme amid increasing derision for the 'Z-listers' produced by the show (see Chapter 5). The envelope of fantasised privacy that is necessary to voyeuristic pleasure is thus missing in *Big Brother*. Rather, the house, like the panopticon, is built to maximise intrusiveness and minimise privacy (Sella 2000), with the effect that what would conventionally be regarded as private behaviour is voluntarily brought from behind closed doors into the public space of the media gaze. Whatever the initial panics about the inhumane surveillance tactics and base appeal of *Big Brother*, it soon became clear that viewers were not in fact engaging in a voyeuristic scenario. Rather, they had entered into an implicit contract, facilitated by the transparent architecture of the house, between participants' exhibitionism and viewers' will to *see* (which is, after all, what defines the viewer). This shift from an exploitative to a contractual relation perhaps explains why the controversies swirling around *Big Brother* lost their power.

As Ernst Mathijs has shown, there was a marked shift in the European reception of *Big Brother* between the first and second series. Whereas the first *Big Brother* series initially met with 'extrinsic' criticism – that is, concerns about human rights measured within a larger socio-political context – media reporting soon shifted to 'intrinsic' criticism or commentary about the internal features of the programme (Mathijs 2002: 319). Indeed, in the UK and US, where *Big Brother* met with little early controversy, critics skipped the 'extrinsic' response and went straight to discussing the 'intrinsic' aspects of the show, including format, participants' interactions and particularly genre.[8] Was this, asked commentators, a gameshow, a documentary, a soap opera, or 'just' reality TV? The category 'reality TV', which had already attained some cultural currency, now leapt to the forefront of debates about the status of reality presented 'within a fully managed artificiality, in which almost everything that might be deemed to be true about what people do and say is necessarily and obviously predicated on the larger contrivance of them being there in front of the camera in the first place' (Corner 2000: 256). The change of tone from socio-political controversy to genre debate, from extrinsic to intrinsic criticism, can be described as a re-evaluation of how to judge the programme's relation to reality: *Big Brother* went from offering *too much* reality (you can't do that to real people!) to offering *too little* reality (it's not actually reality but a semi-fictionalised 'reality soap' (Meijer and Reesink 2000)).

*Big Brother* no doubt succeeded with audiences by exploiting a mix of genres recognisable from TV's back-catalogue: elements of the gameshow in the eviction rounds, the documentary in the cameras trained on ordinary people, the talkshow in the regular confessionals in the 'diary room' and the soap opera in the dramatic twists of allegiances and intimacies. But the initial controversy and debates in the press indicate the extent to which the programme overlapped with and itself became the subject of real-world concerns. *Big Brother* was a marked event for the history of reality TV less because it blurred genre categories than because it blurred the distinction between real and media worlds by dragging the rhythms of daily life, performed by ordinary people, into the screen frame. This was the crux of the television experiment, to create a space of 'pure sociability' (Scannell 2002: 277), distilled but not demarcated from the world, which could be produced through the intervention of the media apparatus. This in turn began to raise questions about the authenticity of participants' performances in a space created by media intervention.

## Performance and Authenticity

Just as artifice is not opposed to actuality in the second generation of reality television so performance is not opposed to authenticity. Unlike *An American Family*, for instance, there is no attempt to erase the presence of cameras from the visual and ideological field. On the contrary, as the number of cameras increases from one *Big Brother* series to the next so does the publicity for the house as a multi-camera environment; in fact, many *Big Brother* series use the camera or the eye as the central visual element of the opening credits. The multiple cameras ensure the full-scale visibility of personal life in this mediated social space and, since there is no place for the subjects to hide, the cameras seem to promise authenticity: the more we see, the more we know. In this ideological matrix, concealment is the opposite of revelation, and revelation is synonymous with authenticity. At the same time, however, the sheer number of cameras turns the entire Big Brother house into a stage where every act, by virtue of being recorded, is also performed. As John Corner points out, comparing *Big Brother* to the tradition of observational documentary, 'the circumstances are not so much those of observation as those of *display*; living space is also performance space' (2002: 257; original emphasis). But performance, of course, is associated with acting, with playing a role that is different from the 'self'; hence, performance carries overtones of duplicitousness. How is it, then, that authenticity and performance can co-exist within the same framework? The answer lies in recognising *Big Brother* as the pop culture manifestation of a shift that is commonly linked to postmodernism: from a notion of performance that is dependent on a distinction between artificial and true identity, to a notion of performativity that is defined as the self coming into being through the act of performance (see Chapter 4, n. 9). In this sense, we can see why Lothar Mikos categorises *Big Brother* as 'performative reality TV'; rather than a real-life soap, it is 'a carefully produced drama of authenticity' (2004: 96).

The question of authenticity matters for audiences because the format of *Big Brother* invokes audience participation through the act of judgement. By building in a weekly eviction process decided by viewer voting, the programme demands that audiences continuously assess the participants, whether they actually cast a vote or not. This assessment is further promoted by the entire edifice of 'talk' about *Big Brother*, which includes watercooler discussions, magazine programmes (e.g. *Big Brother's Little Brother* (Channel 4/E4)), internet forums and press articles as 'a structural feature of the show's relational totality of involvements' (Scannell 2002: 277). Unlike game shows, however, the *Big Brother* format offers no objective criteria for such an assessment – no questions, challenges or points to accumulate – nor subjective criteria based on participants' talent, such as the voting process on *American Idol*. Audiences for *Big Brother* are thus left to draw, consciously or unconsciously, on their own social experience for making judgements of others, often applying moral standards to justify their (dis)like of or identification with one or another participant, just as they would in the social world. What complicates this process on *Big Brother*, however, is the viewers' awareness that the people they watch on screen are surrounded by cameras twenty-four hours a day: in other words, viewers know that the participants know they are being watched. This inevitably raises the spectre of performance and role-playing, which is especially problematic in an unscripted show that casts ordinary people to be themselves. Audiences are thus faced with deciding to what extent participants are 'acting up' for the cameras and to what extent are they being 'real'.

Audience research indicates that viewers tend to search for the 'real person' in the performances of participants and judge them accordingly (Hill 2002, 2004; Jones 2003). When American media scholar Mark Andrejevic, for instance, tracked internet discussions during the first series of the US *Big Brother*, he found that '[t]he repeated form of praise in the chat rooms, where the most common activity was to debate who should win and who the fans' favorite characters were, was that a cast member was being "real"' (2004: 125). By contrast, 'acting' was seen to be synonymous with deception and manipulation, so that the 'ultimate crime of a houseguest was, from the point of view of authenticity, to be caught being two-faced: presenting one façade to the houseguests and another to the producers (or the audience)' (Andrejevic 2004: 125). One such 'crime' occurred in the first season of the UK *Big Brother*, when 'Nasty Nick' Bateman – called this because of his attempt to manipulate fellow participants' votes through deception – was caught out by his housemates and evicted from the house. As Annette Hill notes, British audiences were suspicious of his subsequent break-down: 'Even though he appeared to break down and reveal his true self in a moment of personal conflict, according to these viewers [in a focus group discussion] . . . his tears could be perceived as part of a performance' (2004: 36). Because Nasty Nick had given audiences cause previously to be suspicious of his authenticity, they were now unwilling to believe that any subsequent display of his 'true self' would not also be as two-faced.

While performance and authenticity in these examples operate as opposing terms, audience research also suggests that viewers are aware they are watching a certain kind of performance *at the same time* as they judge participants on how 'real' they are. Participants often stress that they get used to the cameras, as explicitly noted by *Big Brother UK* season 2 participant Dean O'Loughlin in his *Big Brother* memoir (2004) and Holly Shand of *Road Rules* season 7 in an interview with Mark Andrejevic (2004: 107). For their part, viewers tend to oscillate between believing that no one can 'act naturally' in front of cameras and believing just as strongly that no one can 'hide' their true feelings for weeks on end (Hill 2004: 32-6). Contradictory viewing positions, then, are built into the programme, to the extent that viewers in the US accept the game premise of the show while also demanding that participants be themselves; they thus veer 'between describing the goal as an experiment in who could be the most "real" and as a competition in which houseguests [have] to "play the game" in order to win the grand prize' (Andrejevic 2004: 125). Rather than making the programme unwatchable, as one might expect, these paradoxical positions make the show more compelling by opening up the possibility that performance may be a channel for the production of the self.

More than any other programme before it, then, *Big Brother* bridges the conceptual divide between performance and authenticity, turning television cameras into channels for the discovery, through performance, of a 'true' self. In one exemplary instance, Josh Souza, the runner-up of the first US *Big Brother*, told fellow participant Brittany, who had accused him of flirtatiousness, that 'everyone should have an audience' because it helps them learn about themselves (Andrejevic 2004: 110). As Mark Andrejevic then concludes, surveillance on this show serves as a 'guarantee of the authenticity of one's uniqueness' (ibid.) rather than as a condition for dissemblance. Nonetheless, from the perspective of audiences, some people on the show come across as more 'real' than others, despite the fact that all of them are under the same conditions of surveillance. This suggests that authenticity operates on a sliding scale *within*, rather than opposed to, the framework of performance. Instead of using the term perform*ance*, normally understood as acting up, we might thus more accurately ascribe *Big Brother* participants' behaviour to perform*ativity*, or bringing oneself into being through acting out. John Corner has referred to this process in *Big Brother* as 'selving', or the apparent emergence of the self from the conditions of performance set up by the programme: 'One might use the term "selving" to describe the central process whereby "true selves" are seen to emerge (and develop) from underneath and, indeed, through, the "performed selves" projected for us' (2002: 261).

Three points are of particular interest about this process of 'selving' through reality TV. First, the media apparatus is not incidental or even opposed to the process; rather, it is *constitutive* of the production of this authentic self. The elements of surveillance, competition and intimacy under conditions of isolation all contribute to the evocation and expression of the participants' 'real' identity as mediated (in the sense of 'channelled') by performance. Second, Corner emphasises that the performance of the 'true self' 'requires a certain amount of the humdrum and the routine' to be plausible (2002: 262). Audiences, in other words, are primed to judge participants' performances as authentic by the domestic setting in which participants repeat everyday tasks and social interactions. Finally, the emergence of a true self 'from underneath' performed selves must happen unwittingly, free of any conscious or strategic performance aimed at the camera. The camera, in other words, must capture rather than spur the performance of the self. These three elements explain why *Big Brother* is such a watershed: with twenty-eight (or more) cameras and twelve ordinary people with nothing better to do than enact the routines of everyday life, albeit within a highly contrived and controlled environment, the *Big Brother* house becomes the setting for more or less convincing degrees of self-performance. Through watching the process of selving, audiences come to feel as if they know the participants (Hill 2004: 35), in an intimate relation that recreates the conditions of the social world in another medium.

This alone would not necessarily explain the 'reality' appeal of the show. Rather, the more radical insight is that, in creating the conditions for mediated self-performance, the show simulates the 'selving' that we regularly enact in our social lives. According to the sociologist Erving Goffman, whose work from the 1950s/1960s has gained a new prominence in the age of reality television, we are always engaged in some degree of performance for others. Goffman argues that we perform different selves in different contexts, undertaking 'legitimate performances of everyday life' (1959: 73) to produce a 'frontstage' self that matches the environment in which it is performed. In Corner's terms, this would be the 'performed self', behind which lies what Goffman refers to as our 'backstage' self, the core identity that is not performed for someone's scrutiny (Goffman 1959: 22). As Hill notes, *Big Brother* participants always perform for two audiences, those inside the house, who see a frontstage self, and those watching on television, who see both the frontstage and backstage selves (2004: 36). It is precisely this notion of two selves and two audiences that is exploited by second-generation reality TV: in a constructed media environment that offers a 'behind-the-scenes' view, the frontstage and backstage selves, which are normally perceived as unified in social life, can be separated out. The participants' frontstage self is performed for the other house-/island-mates, while the camera also captures a backstage self, which grounds the audience's judgement of participants' authenticity. Out of this flickering relation between selves, a 'true self' is seen to emerge from the performed self. Because this emergence is manifested through the camera, however, it suggests at the same time that *even our backstage selve*s involve a performance – to ourselves, to the camera, to the diffused social gaze as represented by unseen viewers. If authenticity can coincide with performance, because reality TV simulates the lived landscapes of sociality, then performance can mobilise authenticity. As Goffman notes, 'we all act better than we know how' (1959: 74).

Acting better than one knows how becomes a particular concern on the progenitor of the reality game, *Survivor*, where one's competitive performance becomes just as important as the performance of oneself to others. The following section will take seriously *Survivor*'s claim to be 'just a game' by applying the theory of play, or ludic theory, to see how competition on reality TV compares to more traditional notions of game play. Although the competitive aspect of *Survivor* has been much criticised, leading to a popular conception that the show promotes anti-social and unethical behaviour, it has yet to be studied in a context where competition is a necessary part of game structure. Sociological theories of what people do when they play games can offer insights into the success of *Survivor* beyond the claim that it introduced on-camera backstabbing.

## *Survivor*: Competition and the *homo ludens*

Competition is writ large in *Survivor*. Literally, it is inscribed onto the logo in three words that herald the competitive purpose of the show: 'Outwit, Outplay, Outlast'. The emphasis on strategy (out-wit), gamesmanship (out-play) and endurance (out-last) reframes the classical shipwreck narrative of the lone castaway stranded on a deserted island, as engrained by Daniel Defoe's *Robinson Crusoe*. After all, there is nothing necessarily competitive about a deserted island setting, as demonstrated by the BBC's millennial project *Castaway* (BBC One, 2000–1), which placed thirty-six people with diary-cams on a remote Scottish island in the Outer Hebrides for a year. In fact, the original idea behind *Survivor*, credited to UK producer Charlie Parsons, was to place 'ordinary' people in the real, if contrived, situation of being 'forced to cope with an absence of modern comforts' (Brenton and Cohen 2003: 45–6). The competitive element was added later, when Parsons and his team realized that having participants vote each other off the island would provide the format with narrative coherence as well as dramatic momentum (Brenton and Cohen 2003: 47). To the 'man vs. nature' dramaturgy of the deserted island format, *Survivor* thus added the element of 'man vs. man' familiar from sports, game shows and combat/adventure series.

Although Charlie Parsons conceived of the show in the early 1990s, he and his production company, Planet 24, had difficulty convincing broadcasters in the UK and the US at the time to take a risk on this 'new kind of television' which placed people in contrived situations rather than observing them in natural spaces (Parsons, cited in Brenton and Cohen 2003: 44–5). It was not until 1996 that a Swedish company purchased an option on the format and began producing it for Swedish television as *Expedition Robinson*. Although its initial season was marred by controversy when the first contestant voted off the show, Sinisa Savija, committed suicide shortly afterward,[9] *Expedition Robinson* found solid ratings for years in various European incarnations (especially in Sweden, Norway, Denmark and Belgium, where it has gone to ten seasons or more). Compared to the runaway success of the US version, however, *Expedition Robinson* is a minor footnote to the history of *Survivor*. In fact, in no country where it has aired as either *Survivor* or *Expedition Robinson* has the local version achieved the longevity and massive popularity of the US version (certainly not in the UK (ITV, 2001–2), where *Big Brother* proved to be much more to the viewing public's taste (Ellis 2001)). The difference between the US and other nations' versions can be attributed to Mark Burnett, a relatively unknown producer of adventure series who met Parsons in 1996, licensed the format and then successfully pitched it, against the odds, to CBS in a deal that marked a shift in traditional industry and advertising practices.

According to Burnett, the deal with CBS involved an unconventional profit-sharing arrangement struck on the basis of an innovative advertising model. Burnett claims to have offered to lower the network's risk by securing advertisers himself in exchange for 50 per cent of the after-profit advertising revenue (Carter 2001; Lotz 2007: 223). Leslie Moonves, President and CEO of CBS, has denied Burnett's version of the deal, saying that Burnett received only 50 per cent of additional ad revenues earned from the first *Survivor* finale (Carter 2001). It is no doubt in the interest of CBS to deny the existence of such a deal, since allowing a television producer to receive half of a show's revenue could establish a precedent that would, according to Amanda Lotz, be 'an unfathomable reallocation of [the] economic norms' of the TV industry (2007: 223). Nonetheless, in a *New York Times Magazine* article about Burnett published in January 2001, Bill Carter reports that Burnett also negotiated a 50 per cent ad-revenue deal with NBC for the ill-fated *Destination Mir* and another such deal with the USA channel for two *Eco-Challenge* shows (Carter 2001). Importantly, whatever the actual details of Burnett's deal with CBS, it offered a different advertising model precisely at a time when net-works were concerned about falling ad revenues. In what Burnett has called 'associative marketing', major sponsors received product place-ment in addition to commercial time and sponsorship tags, making *Survivor* a very 'commodity-friendly' format (McAllister 2006). The fact that the format incorporates a 'reward challenge' in nearly every episode makes it easy to integrate commercial products, despite *Survivor*'s pre-capitalist setting. Sponsorship products such as corn chips (e.g. Doritos), shower gel (e.g. Olay) and cars (e.g. GM) have routinely been offered – with the requisite brand-name close-ups – as rewards for team or individual challenges, and sponsors have received the added benefit of having their products discussed by participants in glowing terms. Sometimes, such as in the lacrosse game played on mudflats in *Survivor: Fiji* (episode 11), the reward challenges are created specifically with the sponsored product in mind – get dirty playing in the mud, get clean with Olay shower gel.

Burnett, whose previous producer credit had been for the adventure race *Eco-Challenge* (MTV, 1995; ESPN, 1995; Discovery Channel, 1996), made two further developments to Parsons's concept. First, he broke with the conventional low-gauge, low-expense documentary aesthetic of reality television, instead using a large production team (approx. sixty-five–eighty people) to make a show boasting 'cinematic' production values and carefully edited narrative arcs. Burnett has called the result 'dramality', thereby placing the emphasis on drama and avoiding the debates that have plagued docusoap-makers about how 'real' their product is. Second, Burnett drew on his background as a British paramilitary trooper and later producer of *Eco-Challenge* to turn Parsons's 'social experiment' (Brenton and Cohen 2003: 61) into a multi-layered nexus of games that narrows sixteen participants down over thirty-nine days to a single winner of a million dollars. The format, combining numerical simplicity with sociological complexity, was a huge ratings success for CBS in the summer of 2000. Regularly drawing nearly 25 million viewers per episode, the first season of *Survivor* attracted an astronomical 51.7 million viewers to its two-hour finale and Burnett was credited with 'single-handedly rejuvenat[ing] CBS' (Carter 2001).

Since then, the competitive structure has become key to the discourse of *Survivor*, with terms like 'voting off', 'alliances' and 'back-stabbing' – not to mention the ritualised rhetoric of challenges and Tribal Councils – becoming well established in the reality television lexicon. Of all of the competitive reality formats to follow the second-generation blitz in 2000, *Survivor* remains the most self-reflexive about its status as a 'game'. In its twenty-first season at the time of writing, *Survivor* has produced its own pedagogy of gamesmanship, as fans of the show have become participants, would-be participants have studied back series, and popular contenders have been brought back for second and even third seasons to put their winning strategies to the test (i.e. *Survivor All-Stars, Fans vs Favourites, Heroes vs Villains*). The result is that the game, rather than the show, has taken on mythical status. It operates discursively as both 'just a game' and '*the* game', that is, as a construct removed from social reality that nonetheless grants the ultimate measure of financial and social success with a $1 million prize and 'title of sole Survivor'. Although the show works as a generic hybrid of drama, adventure and game-play (Haralovich and Trosset 2004), its primary appeal lies in its distillation of game logic, which telescopes the chaotic scripts of quotidian social behaviours into tightly regulated performances. Numerous commentators have noted how readily *Survivor* functions as a metaphor for larger socio-cultural practices as diverse as office politics (Thackaberry 2003), capitalism (Andrejevic 2004), cultural imperialism (Delisle 2003) and the repressive mechanisms of the political unconscious (Wright 2006). Such an interpretive elasticity is a measure of the game's relevance to social reality, but it also suggests the relevance of play to social life.

The experimental back-to-basics isolation of *Big Brother* becomes a play on primitivism in Burnett's *Survivor*. The term 'play' here deserves emphasis, for it lies at the heart of the show's game discourse and ratings success. The element of play – often referred to as the 'ludic' element (from the Latin *ludus*, meaning play) – was first extensively studied in relation to culture by Johann Huizinga in his seminal book *Homo Ludens: A Study of the Play-Element in Culture* (originally published 1938). Huizinga's core premise is that 'we find play present everywhere as a well-defined quality of action which is different from "ordinary" life' (2000 [1938]: 4). Because play is 'not serious', Huizinga posits that 'it is free, is in fact freedom' (2000 [1938]: 8). At the same time, a player will become 'intensely and utterly' absorbed in a game because games are '"played out" within certain limits of time and place' (2000 [1938]: 9) which are controlled by rules that 'are absolutely binding and allow no doubt' (2000 [1938]: 11). Roger Caillois, a French sociologist who extended Huizinga's insights in the late 1950s, zeroes in on this contradictory aspect of play: it is both free *and* rule-bound. Indeed, the pleasure of play lies in the player being *'free within the limits set by the rules'* (Caillois 2001: 8; original emphasis), which allows the player to make 'constant and unpredictable' adjustments within the game-world.

Attempting to define the rubric of play, Caillois narrows it down to six characteristics. Play is

1. free: that is, not obligatory,
2. separate: circumscribed by limits of space and time,
3. uncertain: dependent on an outcome that cannot be determined in advance,
4. unproductive: 'creating neither goods nor wealth',
5. governed by rules, and
6. make-believe: 'accompanied by a special awareness of a second reality or of a free unreality, as against real life' (2001: 9–10).

Four of these defining characteristics – that play is free, separate, uncertain and rule-governed – fit *Survivor* easily, revealing its ludic underpinnings. The claims that play is 'unproductive' and 'make-believe', however, need to be updated for television, which is both a commercial enterprise and a technology of mediation. Television as commercial enterprise means that any game played out on the screen must create wealth, whether this refers to the massive revenues generated by televised sports or the relatively minimal revenues generated by daytime game shows. Television as a technology of mediation complicates the sixth claim that play is make-believe: television scholars, after all, have long noted that the domestic setting of television makes characters seem familiar from 'real life'. We will return to this point, but in the meantime it is worth noting that Caillois leaves out one characteristic on which his predecessor Huizinga had presciently insisted, namely, that play 'promotes the formation of social groupings' (2000 [1938]: 13). For Huizinga, who was thinking of playgrounds, clubs and secret societies, such social groupings 'tend to surround themselves in secrecy' (ibid.). On *Survivor*, of course, play is inextricably linked with social grouping and regrouping, much of which is pointedly kept secret from those who are excluded from alliances.

The game rhetoric that has emerged from *Survivor* thus makes manifest the core ludic elements of the format. All participants are 'free', in the double sense of having volunteered to be on the island (through a competitive process of application and interviews) and of having what Caillois calls the 'latitude' to respond to constantly changing conditions as they see fit. Here the unscripted aspect of 'dramality' is particularly important; although we know that producer control is exerted in the pre- and post-production stages, when participants are 'inside' the game they react freely to events and situations. At the same time, the entire island complex is a 'second reality', a contrivance built and controlled by the producers. The division into teams, the tribal challenges followed by individual challenges, the Tribal Councils and voting rituals, the system of rewards and punishments – all of these aspects, which are commonly cited as the 'unreality' of *Survivor*, manifest the ludic requirement that games be limited to a particular time and place, and that they be governed by rules which are 'absolutely binding' (Huizinga). The configurations within these limitations may be changed by the producers – such as the sudden reshuffling of tribes, as occurred in *Survivor: Africa* and *Survivor: Fiji* – but even then the basic rules established by the competitive framework of tribes, individuals and challenges have to be followed. It would make no sense, for instance, if the producers were suddenly to announce that all of the survivors were to be transferred to an island resort and share the million-dollar jackpot equally among them. This impossible eventuality reflects a point made by both Huizinga and Caillois that the apathetic player, or the heretic, is more destructive to a game than the resistant player, since the game disappears if someone refuses to acknowledge the rules, while the resistant player attempts to buck the system within the system's own rules. Any producer who would suddenly split the prize among all of the participants would thus be a heretic, and a game-destroyer.

From the ludic perspective, too, the primitivist setting of *Survivor* makes perfect sense. Several critics have argued that the 'tribalism' of *Survivor* is an orientalist fantasy, constructed entirely of post-colonial Western notions about an exotic, pre-colonial 'other' (e.g. Delisle 2003). While this is an insightful critique, it misses the ludic appeal of the setting. Viewers are not drawn to the programme as they might be to a travel show, where the wildlife of Gabon, traditional feasts of

Samoan villagers or breakfasts of Nicaraguan farmers (all highlighted in respective *Survivor* seasons) hold an ethnographic appeal. Within the ludic structure, the primitivist setting of *Survivor* functions not as an interface between civilisation and pre-civilisation, self and other, but rather as a fantasy of the place that is *most separate* from daily life in the West, which is imagined as a world of work, ownership, technology, noise, etc. Seeking 'freedom' from such trappings of daily life, *Survivor* viewers as well as participants rush to inhabit a ludic world.

There is more to the 'game' of *Survivor*, however, for in competitive games ludic freedom operates in a dialectical relation with power. For Caillois, the competitive game is one of four kinds of play, each of which corresponds to a 'powerful instinct': competition, chance, simulation and vertigo (2001: 12). While there are grounds for finding all of these forms at play in reality television, *Survivor* is above all an exemplar of the first category, competition, which turns on strategic attempts to gain power. This is why *Survivor* functions so well as a metaphor for politics, whether office, class, race or gender politics, since every participant is involved in 'the struggle for, and exercise of, power' (Wright 2006: 13). Power-play on *Survivor* means vying for control – of challenges, of voting decisions, of one's team-mates. Power, moreover, is strategically exercised, and much of the discursive content of *Survivor* has to do with discussions among participants about appropriate strategies. Some participants claim control outright, on the basis of their leadership qualities; others seek the residual control afforded by siding with powerful players; and the most memorable – and most controversial – participants are the 'manipulative' players who present different faces depending on the needs of the moment. As with *Big Brother*, duplicitous performance, even for the sake of strategy, tends not to be rewarded, drawing castigating comments from the jury of fellow participants and few to no prize-winning votes for the 'snake' (a term introduced in the first season's final Tribal Council by juror Susan Hawk, who famously castigated finalist Richard Hatch for being 'a rat and a snake').

*Survivor* as game-space further brings politics into conjunction with ethics. It is, after all, the baldness of the battle for power among *Survivor* participants that has led to the show being decried as an unethical programme that encourages backstabbing, manipulation and anti-social behaviour. And, indeed, although the logic of *Survivor* encourages social groupings – as is abundantly clear from the rhetoric of tribes, merges, alliances and voting blocs – the rules of the format require regular anti-social exclusions, just as chess requires opponents to take each other's pieces. Few people would read chess in terms of ethics, for board games are far more limited in terms of time, space and real-world analogies. On *Survivor*, however, the participants *are* the playing pieces, physically, mentally and emotionally. There are no pawns and boards, balls and pitches to mark a material separation of the game world from the social world; rather, players of *Survivor* bring their entire set of (anti-)social skills and behaviours to bear in the battle for power. Caillois's sixth definition of play, that it is 'make-believe' in the sense of being a separate 'second reality', thus fails to apply to *Survivor* precisely at the point where game strategy becomes a struggle for power with real-world ethical implications. While power-play on *Survivor* occurs in a 'second reality' separate from participants' ordinary lives, this is nonetheless not a 'make-believe' space because the relationships played out among participants are affectively, socially and materially real. Broken promises, dented egos, disappointed investments, palpitating likes and dislikes – these effects of social power-play are produced by but cannot be contained within the ludic logic of *Survivor*. This, at base, is what makes the show both gripping and provocative.

At the same time, the possibly constraining effects of power are offset by unpredictability, a necessary element of play. This is not the unpredictability of 'live' reality TV, like *Big Brother*, with daily shows edited from whatever has occurred in the previous twenty-four hours, but rather the unpredictability of game-play itself. The relatively simple rule structure of any game works precisely because the outcome cannot be predicted in advance. As Caillois points out, this has to do with chance but also with the freedom of the player(s), which in *Survivor* directly corresponds to the unscripted nature of events and interactions. On *Survivor: Nicaragua*, for instance, there was nothing to prevent Naonka from getting angry with her teammates and stealing food supplies, nor anything to prevent Marty from launching into an invective-laced diatribe against Jane at Tribal Council but, when they did so, the other players incorporated these outbursts into their own play and the game proceeded differently than it would have had either Naonka or Marty suppressed their responses. Given the number of *Survivor* participants, the opportunities for interaction and the extended time of play (thirty-nine days), this creates a huge number of variables in any one season. Haralovich and Trosset, in their aptly entitled article 'Expect the Unexpected', argue that '*Survivor* is more like a horse race than fiction' because it 'foregrounds the role of uncertainty due to chance in a way that fiction cannot' (2004: 84). They illustrate the magnitude of variability in the game by calculating that, if we focus only on the order in which the sixteen participants might be voted out, the possible outcomes number 16! (pronounced 'sixteen factorial'), or approximately 21 trillion (ibid.).

Such variability leads viewers to engage with the programme by making predictions, joining fan spoiler groups (see Henry Jenkins 2006: 25–58) or, perhaps most commonly, producing what I would call counterfactual narratives, that is, retelling the story in retrospect so that everything that happened seems necessary rather than contingent. Counterfactual narrativisation is aided by the formulaic ending of each episode, in which viewers see how each player voted and hear an edited version of the post-eviction interview with the ousted player. Based on this information, the narrative of the episode, or indeed of the game-so-far, can be woven together backwards as though every piece of the puzzle necessarily had to fall like that. Of course, this is possible only in retrospect, and it closes down the conditional possibility of every-thing else that could have happened had it not gone the way it had. It is in this counterfactual narrativisation, as in the engagement made pos-sible by predictions and spoilers, that viewers experience the pleasure of seeming to co-write the script.

The unpredictability of ludic structure is also important for the pro-ducers. Even though, as we know, producers manifest various kinds of control at different stages of the production process, they nonetheless do not have the same surety as scriptwriters of the outcome. Indeed, it is notable that over the course of ten years and more than twenty seasons, there is no decipherable pattern among *Survivor* winners and no specific set of identity attributes that repeatedly characterise a winner. The characteristics one finds paraded elsewhere in the media as social markers of privilege – being male, white, middle-class, het-erosexual, urban, physically fit, youthful – provide no guarantee, either individually or cumulatively, that their bearer will win *Survivor*. Past winners have included a middle-aged white woman (Tina Wesson from *Survivor: The Australian Outback*), a white man in his late fifties (Robert Crowley from *Survivor: Gabon*), two openly gay men (the first series winner, Richard Hatch, and Todd Herzog of *Survivor: China*), two African Americans (Vecepia Towery of *Survivor: Marquesas* and Earl Cole of *Survivor: Fiji*), an Asian American (Yul Kwon of *Survivor: Cook Islands*) and a Latina woman, who is also the first person to win *Survivor* twice (Sandra Diaz-Twine of *Panama* and *Heroes vs. Villains*). In contrast to *Big Brother*, which is often criticised for being nothing but a personality contest, not even likeability is a guaranteed posi-tive attribute on *Survivor*; as Marty of *Survivor: Nicaragua* has noted, 'anybody that's on the chopping block [for being unlikeable] can be useful to someone else'.

Despite this level of unpredictability about the outcome, many commentators of *Survivor* have argued that the producers' casting choices as well as editing tactics have resulted in character stereotyping, especially when it comes to race. Christopher Wright, for instance, claims that *Survivor* has added to the negative portrayal of African Americans on television by stereotyping African American participants as clownish, aggressive or sassy (2006: 109–33). Nonetheless, *Survivor: Cook Islands* (2006), which was highly controversial for dividing tribes into four ethnic groups (African American, Asian American, Hispanic American and white American), successfully increased not only the number but also the diversity of minority representation on the show, while the season that followed, *Survivor: Fiji*, ended up with three African Americans in the final voting round (Earl Cole, Cassandra Franklin and Andria 'Dreamz' Herd). As with the issue of power, the question of whether and to what extent the show deals in stereotypes matters because *Survivor* is both a 'second reality' and an open-ended game with a highly porous relationship to social reality. Yet I would argue that the same elements of play which make the outcome of any *Survivor* season uncertain also loosen the strictures of stereotypical representations on the show.

Even more so than on *Big Brother*, *Survivor* participants are utterly caught up in their performance as game-players while simultaneously being invested in producing an authentic performance of their selfhood. The ludic structure allows participants to try on roles and identities within the confines of game-play, at the same time as these roles are coterminous with their social performances of selfhood outside the game (see Goffman 1959). As part of *Survivor* strategy, players thus perform themselves as authentic – even if that authenticity involves manipulation or deceit as one of their social skills. The ludic structure helps to coalesce these two seemingly contradictory conditions, performance and authenticity, in the same way that it brings together freedom and rules. It is in this combination of apparent opposites that we find the importance of the game to reality TV, especially to competition shows which require strategic yet authentic role-playing. But the porous interface between the ludic and the social suggests that this is about more than simply television. Cultural theorist Vilém Flusser, reflecting on Huizinga, has claimed that the *homo ludens* involves nothing less than a redefinition of the human:

The new human being is not a man of action anymore but a player: *homo ludens* as opposed to *homo faber*. Life is no longer a drama for him but a performance. It is no longer a question of action but of sensation. The new human being does not wish to do or to have but to experience. He wishes to experience, to know and, above all, to enjoy. As he is no longer concerned with things, he has no problems. Instead, he has programs. (1999: 89)

Flusser, writing in the 1980s, was referring to technological programmes. For our purposes, however, we might offer a slight amendment. The new *homo ludens* wishes to experience, to know and, above all, to enjoy. For this, s/he has reality TV programmes.

## Conclusion

This chapter has focused on three programmes that have variously been credited with representing the 'start' of reality TV: *The Real World*, *Big Brother* and *Survivor*. I have argued that none of these shows should be taken as the sole origin of reality television, since this goes against the genealogical enterprise; rather, they should be considered as trend-setting programmes for a new generation of reality TV that is framed by competition under conditions of comprehensive surveillance. Although *The Real World* does not incorporate competition into the format, it is an important precursor of the second generation because it introduces the concept of 'intimate strangers', creating a show out of the unscripted interactions of strangers selected to live together in close quarters over a set period of time. The fact that this is a contrived environment for which participants must be selected also introduces the importance of casting, which along with editing are the two main areas of second-generation unscripted programming over which producers have control. Cast selection and editing, moreover, are also the points where generic hybridity is introduced to these shows by incorporating story-telling tactics from fictional programming.

As we have seen, *Big Brother* has much stronger links than *The Real World* to the tradition of observational documentary and to reality TV's earlier concerns with authenticity and ordinariness. The major difference between *Big Brother* and first-generation formats lies in the purpose-built, enclosed environment of the *Big Brother* house, which is outfitted with a 24/7 surveillance system that captures housemates' every move and interaction. As a groundbreaking social and televisual experiment in monitored isolation and lack of privacy, *Big Brother* caused controversy in nearly every country in which it was screened (but for the US and the UK), provoking public outcry against the inhumane treatment of participants and scholarly comparison with discipline societies based on panoptic surveillance. As an international new media object, however, *Big Brother* changed the production, distribution and consumption patterns of television, turning the format into a global commodity and pioneering the convergence of television with other media platforms to increase audience interactivity and programme revenues. *Big Brother* is also credited with reconfiguring the relation between television and everyday life, as viewers watch ordinary people like themselves carrying out humdrum tasks familiar from their own lives. Called to assess these performances of everyday life by regular eviction votes, audiences search for evidence of the participants' 'real' selves while also acknowledging that the cameras turn the entire house into a performance space. Performance, however, is no longer necessarily opposed to authenticity, and many participants treat the camera as a means of self-expression. As this chapter has aimed to demonstrate, with *Big Brother* televisual surveillance becomes an expressive accessory to everyday life.

Although the *Big Brother* format has a competitive structure that features eliminations and a final winner, the discourse of competition is much more in evidence on *Survivor*, which places participants in a remote environment and challenges them to survive the conditions as well as each other. As we have seen, the self-conscious game rhetoric of the programme and participants can be analysed according to the influential sociology of the *homo ludens* (or 'playing man') introduced by Johann Huizinga and developed by Roger Caillois. While many features of this game theory, such as the emphasis on rules, freedom and unpredictability, apply neatly to *Survivor*, I have argued that we need to update the notion of play in relation to (reality) television as both a commercial enterprise and a mediating technology. Further, in this chapter I have argued that the 'second reality' of games, which according to Caillois is a space of make-believe, actually has a porous relation with social life when those games play out on reality TV. Because reality television seeks to collapse the perceived boundaries between reality and fiction, authenticity and performance, private and public life, reality games have real-world implications. This means in turn that the second-generation reality TV shows that follow *Big Brother* and *Survivor* are much more likely to embrace an interventionist role. In the next chapter, we will look closely at the programming trends arising in the immediate wake of *Big Brother* and *Survivor*. As we shall see, surveillance becomes personalised, competition is refigured as challenge, and reality TV mechanisms intervene openly into people's lives as an aid to their self-transformation.

## Notes

1. *Who Wants to Be a Millionaire* distinguished itself from decades of quiz show predecessors through its 'focus on the individual' (Holmes 2008a: 69). Individual players were highlighted as ordinary through techniques such as having the presenter ask about the player's home life and offering players the option of 'calling a friend' if they did not know the answer to a question.
2. A similar idea spawned the 1993 British programme *The Living Soap* (BBC), which placed six students into a shared house in Manchester and filmed their everyday lives. Although *The Living Soap* was meant to continue for a year, it was taken off air after five months.
3. The following continental European countries began screening series of *Big Brother* in 2000: Belgium (Kanaal Twee), Germany (RTL2), Italy (as *Grande Fratello*, Canale 5), Portugal (TV1), Spain (as *Gran Hermano*, Telecinco), Sweden (Kanal5) and Switzerland (TV3).
4. There were of course some exceptions to the minor broadcaster rule, such as Argentina, where *Big Brother* aired on the number-one rated private channel (Telefe); Australia, where it was bought by a major commercial network (Network 10); and the US, where it appeared on the major network CBS in a (not very successful) bid to revive flagging summer ratings.
5. The original working title of the programme was 'The Golden Cage' (*De Gouden Kooi* in Dutch), which highlights the aspect of confinement rather than the omniscient gaze implied by the title 'Big Brother'. Notably, in 2006 Jon de Mol resuscitated 'The Golden Cage' (Tien, 2006–7; RTL5, 2007–8), using it as the title for an open-ended version of *Big Brother*: in this format ten strangers are confined in a luxury mansion, competing with one another for visiting time with family and friends, and able to leave only if they are unanimously voted out by all housemates or choose to leave of their own accord. The lack of regular eliminations meant that the one – and only – Dutch season of *The Golden Cage* ran from September 2006 to May 2008 before a housemate was named the winner.
6. Wolfgang Thaenert, director of the media regulatory commission in Hessen, quoted in *Spiegel Online*, 2 March 2000, <http://www. spiegel.de/kultur/gesellschaft/0,1518,67477,00.html> (retrieved 9 May 2010; my translation).
7. See 'Loft Story under Siege', *BBC News World Edition*, 20 May

2001,    <http://news.bbc.co.uk/2/hi/entertainment/1341239.stm>
(retrieved 10 May 2010).

8. Few scholars have discussed the lack of controversy surrounding
the first series of *Big Brother* in the UK, but it might well have to do
with the fact that the docusoap had already been at the centre of a
'fakery' scandal in the late 1990s (see Chapter 2), so the viewing
public were less prone to be perturbed by the *Big Brother* mix of
actuality and artifice.

9. Savija's suicide caused an outcry in Sweden, where many critics
(including his fiancée) drew a link between the humiliation he suffered on eviction from the show and his later death. Not surprisingly, television producers, including Burnett himself, attributed
Savija's suicide to his depressed and unsettled condition as a
Bosnian refugee in Sweden <http://articles.cnn.com/1999-10-
21/entertainment/9910_21_survivor_1_expedition-robinson-game-
show-bosnian-refugee?_s=PM:SHOWBIZ> (accessed 30 March
2011). The debate resulted in more stringent screening procedures
for reality TV participants.

# 4 The Second Generation Comes of Age (2001–5): Challenge and Transformation

In the first half of the 2000s, the number of reality TV programmes exploded across primetime schedules, causing commentators to ask whether this was just a trend or the evolution of a new programming staple. Whereas in the 1990s an upsurge of reality TV programming had meant a spike in the number of 'copycat' or franchise programmes, (e.g. real-crime shows following the *Cops* model, docusoaps following the *Airport* model, the international spread of *Big Brother*), from 2001 it meant a dizzying increase in the array of reality subgenres being produced, each with its own clutch of similar-but-different shows. What allowed these programmes to be lumped under the 'reality' label – and to be recognisable as a genre – was a combination of four elements: *ordinary* people in a *contrived* situation facing some kind of *challenge* surrounded by *cameras*. This was in effect the Endemol model introduced by *Big Brother* and developed separately by *Survivor*. Non-competitive incarnations of reality television continued to exist: groundbreaking shows like *Cops* and *The Real World* remained on air while *The Osbournes* (MTV, 2002–5) resuscitated the family docusoap with a successful celebrity twist (see Chapter 5). Celebrity versions of competitive formats were also developed (e.g. *Celebrity Big Brother UK* (Channel 4, 2001–10)), but such shows were successful precisely because they treated celebrities as ordinary people (see Chapter 5). Overall, however, in this period the documentary underpinnings of reality television were increasingly diluted by the importation of competitive elements from the game show, personal confession from the talkshow and narrative arcs from television drama. Television now celebrated its capacity to intervene in people's lives rather than just represent them, and reality programmes justified such contrivances by offering participants the opportunity of self-fulfilment through challenge.

Competition not only transformed reality TV formats but also gave reality TV a competitive edge in the industry, turning format development and sales into big business. After the record-smashing twelve months between the launch of Dutch *Big Brother* in September 1999 and the end of US *Survivor: Borneo* in August 2000, elimination-based reality television formats spread rapidly across TV schedules around the globe. This short period brought radical changes in ratings expectations, sales platforms and business models in the television industry. No longer the poor cousin among television genres, reality television shows became highly saleable global commodities. As Ted Magder argues, reality TV represented three changes in television production: 'the increasing use of formats as the basis for program production; the increasing tendency to use TV programs as the basis for a multimedia exploitation of creative property; and the increasing strength of European program suppliers in the U.S. market' (2004: 145).

Although the establishment of a global trade in television programme formats preceded second-generation reality TV (see Moran 1998), the competitive reality model proved to be particularly adaptable to international format sale because of its cross-cultural portability. In format sales, a programme is stripped down to its production and marketing template and sold to a foreign production company, which injects cultural specificity to give it local flavour (Moran 1998). In the costly world of programme development, this practice decreases the trial-and-error risk that comes with new television programmes (which have a notoriously high rate of failure) while providing evidence of previous ratings success to advertisers and a platform for attracting audiences. The reality game model, because it is so strongly rule based and allows for marketing tie-ins (see Chapter 3), has been at the forefront of these changes in television production and distribution, with Endemol leading the way. As Magder reported in 2004, '[a]t any one time, [Endemol] has as many as three hundred formats in production around the world' (2004: 146), consisting mostly of game shows and reality TV formats. As a commodity potentially worth millions, the competitive reality format also became the site of legal disputes about intellectual property, as networks and production companies attempted to prevent copycat formats from cutting into their profits.

This is not to say, however, that reality TV programmes in the flush of the second generation were all game based. Rather, second-generation reality TV quickly fractured into a range of subgenres that reframed the 'second reality' of classic games (see Caillois 2001) in terms of obstacles that people encounter in the primary reality of social life. Dating, marriage, childrearing and self-presentation all became viable topics for reality TV. New shows retained the focus on relationships played out within a confined setting, as found on *Big Brother* and *Survivor*, but these relationships were now transferred to the context of domesticity and personal care. The driving force of reality TV shows was thus broadened from competition to *challenge*, a term which can equally mean an oppositional encounter, a test of one's abilities, or a stimulating task with a set goal. All three of these aspects are folded into second-generation reality TV shows, with US formats tending more heavily to goal-orientation as the basis for personal growth and UK formats tending more to the test as the basis of socio-logical experimentation. In either case, the challenge as a stimulating task – whether this involves scaling a wall or solving one's personal problems – underwrites the bulk of these formats. Rules remain, hence the adaptability and saleability of formats, but within the framework of the challenge they operate not as constraints but rather as the productive means for overcoming obstacles found in one's own life. The distinction between televisual reality and social reality in the challenge programmes is more porous than on *Big Brother*, since the lessons gained in one reality can be applied to make sense of problems encountered in the other reality and vice versa. Television, through its ludic interventions, becomes a route to fantasy as well as a tool for pedagogy, teaching viewers how to behave while entertaining them with and through play.

This is serious play, however – people go on TV to prove themselves and to achieve self-improvement through transformation. There is both a value and an ideology to such transformations. Participants are rarely just after a cash prize; even when money is the main motivation, the monetary value of the prize tends to reflect a set of social values that are ideologically determined. The ideological determinants are most strongly articulated in the transformation formats, which seek to mould participants' lives and appearances in a particular direction, but they are evident in all challenge formats which are based on socially accepted standards of success (or failure).

The common criticism that reality television has no socially redeem-ing value comes up for reappraisal in the second-generation formats, since many of them enact redemption narratives for the sake of par-ticipants' personal benefit as well as the public good. It is thus no longer adequate to write reality television off as light entertainment for a dumbed-down audience. Rather, the more reality TV formats embrace contrivance and intervention, the more the genre can lay claim to having social effects. In this chapter I shall therefore examine the discourses of social value and ideology that are mobilised by these programmes to justify narratives of redemption and transformation.

Further, if second-generation formats exhibit an increasing porous-ness between televisual reality and social reality, then we must consider how the 'reality' of second-generation reality TV takes on different discursive meanings from first-generation programmes. The criti-cal tradition of understanding reality television as a form of 'factual programming' (Hill 2005) has aligned it with documentary, especially in British television studies, but the programmes of the early to mid-2000s suggest the demise of the relevance of documentary strategies and comparisons. The pressing question of the 1990s, 'how real is reality TV?' – which was inevitably answered 'not!' by its critics – becomes less appropriate in the later second-generation formats than the question, 'what does reality TV *do*?' Whereas in the documentary tradition reality is what lies before the camera, supposedly untouched by the documentary-maker, in second-generation reality TV reality is framed as something that lies 'before' the participant, that is, in the participant's future as a result of the interventions of the reality TV apparatus. In this era, the 'reality' of reality TV is thus less about its claims to a privileged relation with reality (Jermyn 2004) than about its capacity to intervene in a range of social discourses about the self, the family and the community.

This chapter will address the intersection between reality TV and social discourses by tracing the notion of 'challenge' across the development of second-generation formats in the first half of the 2000s. Beginning with the competitive challenge of the game shows that sprang up after the success of *Survivor*, we will then consider the romantic challenge of finding love in real-love shows like *The Bachelor*, the self-improvement challenge of transforming property and per-sonal appearance in makeover formats, and the citizenship challenge of transforming one's family, community and nation through better governance. As a bridge to social discourse, this chapter will also high-light the ideologies associated with each of the subgenres under con-sideration: the key ideology of winning in the post-*Survivor* formats, the heteronormative ideology of coupling in real-love formats, the conflicting ideologies of self-realisation in makeover formats, and the neoliberal ideology of 'biopower' in life-transformation formats. Although each of these programming strands has been addressed separately by various scholars (e.g. Kavka 2006, 2008; Weber 2009; Ouellette and Hay 2008), it is worth considering them together in order to understand how reality television becomes a social force that seeks to regulate, rather than simply document, ordinary people's lives and interactions.

## Post-*Survivor* Challenge Formats

As we saw in the previous chapter, the reality game format is attribut-able to British producer Charlie Parsons, whose idea for a show to be called *Survive!* combined a desert-island setting with challenge-based eliminations that pared a group of contestants down to one eventual winner (Brenton and Cohen 2003). This relatively simple idea of asking participants to give up their 'normal' lives in order to enter a ludic world created by television represents a key premise of second-generation reality TV. Although *Survivor* has become the touchstone of game discourse on reality TV, there have been numerous other attempts internationally to capitalise on its success or that of its European predecessor, *Expedition Robinson* (SVT, 1997–; see Chapter 3). Shows like *Treasure Island* (TVNZ, 1997–), a South Pacific version of *Expedition Robinson* produced for New Zealand television, and the Belgian production *The Mole* (VRT, 1999–2003) are early examples of elimination formats that put participants through a series of physical and mental challenges as part of an overt game. *The Mole* proved so suc-cessful that, like *Big Brother*, the format was licensed in forty countries, with the longest-running version still screening in the Netherlands (ARVO, 1999–). For the US networks, the next 'big thing' in reality television after the success of *Survivor* were competitive challenge shows, with *Fear Factor* (NBC, 2001–8), *Boot Camp* (FOX, 2001) and *The Amazing Race* (CBS, 2001–) all appearing in 2001, along with two seasons of the US version of *The Mole*. The executive producer of *Survivor*, Mark Burnett, capitalised on his own success by applying the competitive premise to other settings, most notably the boxing ring with *The Contender* (NBC, ESPN, Versus, 2005–) and the corporate boardroom with *The Apprentice* (NBC, 2004–; BBC, 2005–). In Britain, where the UK *Survivor* (ITV, 2001–2) did not do well in the ratings and *Big Brother* continued to rule the roost (Ellis 2001), there appeared to be little interest in competitive challenge programmes except for the surprising success of the celebrity format *I'm a Celebrity . . . Get Me Out of Here!* (ITV, 2002–; see Chapter 5). As this section will argue, however, it is less helpful to think of these competitive challenge pro-grammes as a specific subgenre than as a spectrum which runs from the enclosed game world to formats which offer greater porousness between the second reality of the game format and the primary reality of the social world.

The underlying stimulus, and source of value attribution, for all of these reality game formats is the ideology of winning. No matter whether the show represents an enclosed game world with a complex

set of rules, as on *The Mole*, or a more open competitive environment where participants bring their social and work experience to
bear, as on *The Apprentice*, the incentive of such programmes lies in
the payout that goes to the winner at the end (e.g. 1 million dollars
for *The Amazing Race*, a one-year paid position as Donald Trump's
apprentice in *The Apprentice*). I call this emphasis on winning an
ideology rather than a defining game characteristic because it seems
natural and incontrovertible that the goal of any participant on these
shows must be to win. As Roland Barthes argued in his classic book
*Mythologies* (1993; orig. 1957), ideology regulates social meanings
and behaviours precisely because it disappears from view, becoming
'naturalised' as common sense. In these programmes, the ideology of
winning operates as common sense; it is enforced by the structure of
the game and repeatedly expressed by participants when they frame
other contenders as rivals, although it also serves as grounds for reflec-
tion on what lengths one (or one's rival) is willing to go to in order to
win. Most importantly, the ideology of winning is linked discursively
to the 'challenge' of self-improvement understood as having moral
value. Over and over again, participants in these formats assure each
other and the camera that it is a good thing to undertake a challenge,
whether in the form of individual tests, team games or participation
in the programme itself. The moral value lies in the achievement:
completing the task, functioning as a member of the team, coping with
difficult conditions or overcoming particular fears are all reasons given
by participants for expressing pride in their accomplishment. As many
of the eliminated participants claim in the final interview, the sense of
achievement 'means more' than the cash prize. This attitude, whereby
a challenge is framed as a moral test in the interests of self-improvement, is particularly – though not uniquely – American. It has been
exported through sales and spin-offs of US-produced game formats
(e.g. *The Amazing Race*), and injected into the Americanised version
of formats imported from elsewhere. For instance, the first season of
*Big Brother* in the US, which followed the Dutch format 'bible', drew
only average ratings as well as criticism from audiences who found it
too boring (Pamela Wilson 2004). In the second season, the US *Big
Brother* received a *Survivor*-like makeover which foregrounded the
importance of challenges, ritualised the process of nominating housemates for eviction, and created status divisions within the house to
encourage competition.

*Survivor* not only introduced a game format structured around
physical and mental challenges but also highlighted the importance
of setting. Because producers never permit the contestants to actually

starve or come into contact with life-threatening elements, *Survivor* participants in some sense *play at* surviving. In the terms laid out by Roger Caillois, they engage in mimicry, just as children might play at being pirates (Caillois 2001: 12). A clutch of other shows followed this lead by creating settings in which participants would play-act as well as play a competitive game. *The Mole*, winner of light entertainment award the Golden Rose in 2000, borrows the secret intelligence context familiar from popular novels and films to create a multi-layered game in which participants play at being secret agents in foreign countries. The team challenges often involve search and scavenge missions, with the twist being that one member of the group is secretly a 'mole', or counter-spy, whose job it is to sabotage the missions' success. Unlike the isolated environments of *Expedition Robinson*, *Survivor* or *Big Brother*, *The Mole* sends participants outward, into foreign settings where they interact with inhabitants, while at the same time keeping them firmly within the world of the game. The cash prize is not set at the beginning but becomes part of the game stakes: participants team up in regular challenges to earn money for the collective jackpot, with the 'mole' attempting to sabotage the challenge without drawing attention to him/herself. Uncovering the mole is the main task for participants as well as viewers: the elimination of participants is based on end-of-episode quizzes which test their suspicions about the identity of the mole, with the lowest scorer being sent home, while viewers are treated to opaque clues in each episode to supplement their hypotheses about whether so-and-so is the saboteur or just a poor performer in a particular challenge. The layering of challenges, quizzes, clues and cash prize thus creates a game world within a real world. Participants play at being secret agents and saboteurs, engaging in the pleasure of mimicry as well as the personal value of having challenged oneself.

In the US-produced *Boot Camp*, by comparison, participants play at being military recruits but in the real setting of a military base. They are trained by drill sergeants to undertake basic group exercises involving strength and endurance. As part of the mental challenge, participants are treated like recruits, called only by their surnames, yelled at by the drill sergeants and permitted little rest. Training drills prepare participants for regular 'missions', which in turn lead to a ceremony on 'elimination hill' where two participants are 'discharged' per week (and have to hand over their dog tags). The final reward, $500,000 for the winner, follows a showdown between the last two participants pitted against one another in a series of seven challenges. The interest of *Boot Camp* is twofold. First, like *The Mole* it is an enclosed reality game which mimics a socially institutionalised space of challenge. Both secret intelligence services and the military are real-world social institutions whose members must undergo physically and mentally challenging training regimens to prepare them for engagement with an enemy or foil. As such, they are particularly adaptable to play understood as mimicry, as age-old children's games of 'playing soldier' indicate. At the same time, the reflexive relationship between game world and real world lends social weight as well as moral value to these programmes, as is neatly exemplified by the fact that ABC executives decided to place *The Mole* on hiatus after the 9/11 attacks because the show seemed inappropriate in a world where American intelligence and military forces were 'really' fighting Al Quaeda.[1] The second point of interest has to do with the comparative commodity value of these programmes. Since its inception, Belgian-produced *The Mole* has been licensed to forty countries, making it one of the more successful commodities in reality TV format sales. *Boot Camp*, however, found itself at the centre of a legal controversy over copyright. In April 2001, Mark Burnett and CBS filed a lawsuit against FOX claiming that *Boot Camp* breached the intellectual copyright of *Survivor*, 'including its highly ritualised elimination ceremony, its provision for immunities from elimination, its technique of interspersing interviews with contestants as to their voting and playing strategy and their personal views concerning the other contestants, and its look and feel' (cited in Huff 2001). In filing this suit, Burnett and CBS effectively staked ownership of the concept as a commodity, arguing that intellectual property infringement by other networks would result in financial loss to the originators. The details of the settlement were never released (Huff 2006: 97), but the lack of a clear 'winner' in this case gave an early indication of how difficult it would be to claim copyright of format concepts.

Interestingly, CBS and FOX had come to legal blows a year earlier, when FOX sought a court injunction against CBS to stop work on a show to be called *Global Adventures* in which teams travel around the world while competing with each other. FOX had deemed *Global Adventure*, produced by Jerry Bruckheimer, to be too similar to its own planned programme *Race Around the World*. In the heady days of competitive challenge programming, it is perhaps no surprise that different networks would independently come up with the idea of combining a race with travel to exotic locations, which recalls Jules Verne's classic adventure novel, *Around the World in 80 Days*.[2] In this instance, FOX was refused the court injunction (Dehnart 2000) and presumably put *Race Around the World* on permanent hiatus, while CBS renamed *Global*

*Adventures* and began screening it as *The Amazing Race* in September 2001. Although the first season did not rate particularly well, as it was launched a week before 9/11 and suffered from the American public's ensuing isolationism, *The Amazing Race* went on to earn seven Emmy Awards for Outstanding Reality-Competition Programme (a category created in 2003) and continues to be in production.

In contrast to other competitive challenge shows, which vacillate between team and individual challenges, the success of *The Amazing Race* format lies in its casting of pre-existing couples (or, in one season, families) as participants in 'the most daring competition ever attempted' (as claimed in the opening credits). These couples do not necessarily have to be in romantic or conjugal relationships: they may be relatives, friends, colleagues or, in a twist that reflects the complexities of contemporary relationships, ex-domestic partners. The variability of couple configurations lends openness to the dramatic arcs, since mother/daughter relations, for instance, are articulated differently from husband/wife or best friend relations. The openness is further underscored by the demographic breadth of the casting selections: the first season, for example, included a retired couple, two African-American couples (one of whom was billed as 'separated parents') and a middle-aged gay couple (billed as 'life partners'). This clearly takes a page from the *Survivor* book of casting but introduces greater complexity because the participants come pre-paired, so that the challenge of foreign travel is simultaneously figured as a challenge to the relationship. Despite the competitive race structure, which provides the narrative impetus and suspense as teams compete in a series of challenges at each stage of the journey, the interest of the programme arises from its focus on relationships. As Lynne Spillman, casting director for *Survivor* and *The Amazing Race*, has admitted, 'For me in casting, and production will probably hate that I say this, [*The Amazing Race*] is a relationship show, period' (Dehnart 2008). The show thus has a competitive structure but a relationship focus, which, combined with the real-world settings, means that the line between game world and social world is highly porous. The ideology of winning (a million dollars, no less) is to a large extent overridden by the moral value of undertaking the challenge – not simply for sake of self-fulfilment but in the interests of strengthening and improving relationships. As host Phil Keoghan's exit interviews with eliminated couples show, the moral of this tale of exotic journeys lies in the internal 'journey' that inevitably causes each partner to gain 'new respect' for his/her race-mate.

The most porous division between the secondary reality of the competitive game world and the primary reality of the social world is to be found in those programmes which demand that contestants draw on their pre-existing social and professional experience in order to 'win the game'. These challenges mimic the tests that participants would be, and often have been, set in the social world. Programmes like *The Contender* and *The Apprentice*, both produced by Mark Burnett, take the format of *Survivor* and replant it in the professional spaces of the real world. On *The Contender*, amateur boxers, some with fledgling professional careers, train and live together in an enclosed space, but elimination challenges are decided by 'real' bouts in the boxing ring decided by professional judges. On *The Apprentice*, participants with professional experience in the world of business, law and/or commerce are given team challenges that involve sales, advertising and events organisation, with each group led by a 'project manager'. The tasks are developed in tandem with the services of actual companies (who receive brand publicity in return), and the discourse of the participants is unremittingly entrepreneurial. Elimination is decided by bringing whichever team makes the least money on a task into 'the boardroom', notoriously overseen by Donald Trump in the US version and Lord Alan Sugar in the UK version, where participants are encouraged to defend themselves by attacking the performance of others in the name of 'business'. This is both a contrived game world – it is hard to imagine such desperate sniping going on in actual boardrooms – and a setting that spills over into the real world. Challenge winners often produce advertising materials used by actual sponsors, and participants are repeatedly told that they are undergoing 'a 16-week job interview' for a one-year position in Trump's or Lord Sugar's organisation. If *Survivor* promotes the value of 'challenging oneself' in a stripped-back, primitivist environment, then *The Apprentice* relocates this value within the ideology of entrepreneurship. In a sense, *The Apprentice* is simply the flip side of *Survivor*, suggesting that in contemporary life the deserted island is never anything more than a stage set for corporate team-building exercises and office politics (see Thackaberry 2003). The competitive aspect of the game, in other words, has long since invaded real life, which is why reality TV can borrow so heavily from game discourse. As the motto for *The Apprentice* maintains, 'it's not personal, it's just business'.

## Love Relations: Before and After *The Bachelor*

Following hard on the heels of competitive challenge programmes came the reality TV resuscitation of a generic staple, the dating show.

Just as the competitive challenge format is a hybrid of game show, drama and adventure (Haralovich and Trosset 2004), so reality love programmes combine the rule-bound play of the dating show with the narrative arc of romantic drama and wrought emotions of talkshow confessions. In its earliest configuration, developed by US television producer Chuck Berry in 1965 as *The Dating Game*, the dating pro-gramme was a studio-based show presenting a bachelor/ette's blind selection of a romantic partner based on answers to a series of usually whimsical questions. This format proved so popular that *The Dating Game* remained in syndication off and on for over three decades, until 1999, and served as the inspiration for *Blind Date* (ITV, 1985–2003) in the UK and *Perfect Match* (Network Ten, 1984–9, 2002) in Australia. There followed numerous twists on the programme, such as the long-running *Love Connection* (synd., 1983–94, 1998/9), which integrated studio audience voting with post-date reporting. All of these earlier shows, however, were limited in their setting and reach: television played matchmaker, but the studio was the place in which couples met and the single date was the extent of their programmed commitment to one another. Once absorbed into reality TV, the dating show was reconfigured as both contrivance and reality, both a competitive game *and* real life. The stakes were now raised: television played match-maker not for a single date but for marriage. The element of challenge that defines second-generation reality TV remains, but here challenge becomes the basis for a lifetime opportunity.

The first programme to raise the stakes, the heavily criticised *Who Wants to Marry a Multimillionaire?* (FOX, 15 February 2000), mod-elled itself openly on the game show in an effort to ride the wave of success of ABC's *Who Wants to Be a Millionaire?* Realising that ABC's game show functioned as 'wish fulfilment', FOX Television's Mike Darnell came up with a format that would offer romantic wish ful-filment by mixing beauty pageant and game show in a matrimonial contest (Smith 2000). On *Who Wants to Marry a Multimillionaire?* fifty women competed to be the bride of an unseen 'multimillionaire', Rick Rockwell, in a two-hour programme which culminated in an on-stage engagement and legally binding marriage for 'winner' Darva Conger. The programme was met by immediate backlash: Conger publicly claimed not to have consummated the marriage and had it quickly annulled; journalistic probing revealed that Rockwell had been subject to a restraining order for domestic violence and was possibly not so rich after all; disapproval from left-wing organisations like the National Organization for Women joined the outcry of right-wing organisations like the Media Research Center, proving the show to be 'an equal-opportunity offender' (Smith 2000). In response, FOX cancelled a scheduled rebroadcast of the programme, but continued to produce reality romance shows which many critics saw as salacious and harmful intrusions into people's lives (e.g. Alexander 2004). The notorious *Temptation Island* (2001–3), for instance, placed four 'committed' couples on an island resort to test the strength of their relationship with romantic temptations from a bevy of shapely singles (see Andrejevic 2004: 173–94), while *Married by America* (2003) combined studio-based panel selection of a fiancé(e) for four singles with a subsequent 'engagement' period of on-camera cohabitation to test the new couples' fitness for marriage.[3] These programmes, especially *Temptation Island*, have been widely criticised for profaning the institution of marriage and turning audiences into voyeurs of bodies as well as emotions. It would seem, on this basis, that marriage would be the limit point for televisual intervention and intrusion. And yet, the lesson to be learned from FOX's foray into the reality romance subgenre turned out to be about the approach rather than the content. In terms of ratings and acceptability, the problem with FOX's offerings lay not with the voyeuristic intrusion of television into conjugal life but rather with the lack of alignment between its programmes and the heteronormative ideologies of marriage.

The person who best learned the lesson of alignment, perhaps, was Mike Fleiss, the creator of the highly successful *Bachelor* franchise for ABC and the producer, two years previously, of the disastrous *Who Wants to Marry a Multimillionaire?* for FOX. *The Bachelor*, currently in its fifteenth season, first screened in early 2002 with spin-offs *The Bachelorette* following in 2003 (ABC, currently producing its seventh season) and *Bachelor Pad* in 2010. In the basic format of the show, a central bachelor/ette winnows down a field of twenty-five suitors over several weeks and several stages of dating (group dates, one-on-one dates, hometown visits and overnight dates), with each stage ending in a highly organised 'rose ceremony' that uses the rose as a symbol of a potential love relation. At the last rose ceremony, one of the two finalists is rejected and the other, so producers hope, receives a ring as the seal of an engagement. In 2002 *The Bachelor* overturned the perception that reality romance shows were voyeuristic publicity stunts by fully espousing the ideology of marriage and the heteronormative trajectory it represents. As with competitive challenge shows, there is a firm ideological basis to *The Bachelor/ette*: there is no question in this series that self-fulfilment can and should be achieved through a monogamous relationship with a member of the opposite sex. This goal is taken for granted, and the programme presents itself as a serious opportunity for its fulfilment at the same time as it functions as romantic fantasy.

The ideological infrastructure is manifested as a story of 'finding true love', which involves a heteronormative trajectory that comes pre-scripted from social life. Heteronormativity, understood as the standardised institutions and practices that make heterosexuality seem normal, coherent and privileged (Berlant and Warner 1998), is dependent on a particular romantic myth: it begins with a 'connection' between two people of the opposite sex, then develops into a proposal, an engagement, a wedding and children – in that order. The insight behind *The Bachelor/ette* is to recognise that this well-known trajectory can double as a prescriptive narrative arc for an unscripted television series, telescoping the heteronormative trajectory of real, if romanticised, life into a six-week timeline. Participants on *The Bachelor/ette* unselfconsciously reproduce the rhetorical terms of the social script, eliding any need for cue cards or a screenplay precisely because they are *already* well practised at their role in the ideological narrative of monogamy. Over and over again, participants assure the camera and each other that they are there 'for the right reason', not for sex or for fame but to find their husband/wife; as Jake Pavelka, the bachelor of season 14, intones, 'I'm not looking for the most beautiful girl, but the girl with the most beautiful heart'. Of course, the patent difficulty for the show is that, by compressing the common heteronormative trajectory from years into weeks, the search for monogamy is carried out through a painfully polygamous process, starting with group dates and ending with 'overnight dates' in which the bachelor/ette literally seems to jump from one bed to another. In the discourse of the show, however, the 'enormity of the decision' facing the bachelor/ette (Chris Harrison's EW blog, 6 July 2010) requires such drastic tactics, and the moral message of having made the 'right decision' overrides the muddy methods when the bachelor/ette chooses Mr/Ms Right. The boundary between monogamy and polygamy, moreover, is firmly policed, with polygamy permitted only in the long-term interests of monogamy. The 'scandal' of season 14, for instance, proved how quickly any other kind of polygamy is to be closed down: when contestant Rozlyn Papa was suspected of having an affair with a staff member during the filming, she was immediately and publicly thrown off the show. The phrase 'inappropriate relationship' became the byword of the Papa scandal, repeated by host Chris Harrison and bachelor Jake Pavelka in interviews, blogs and talkshows as the explanation for why Papa had to be summarily dismissed. The choice of the word 'inappropriate' reveals the moral and social regulation at work; certain relationships are accepted within the framework of *The Bachelor* and others are not.

Of course, the 'appropriate' relationships confirmed on *The Bachelor* have a high rate of failure after the show's end. Only two relationships of the twenty completed *Bachelor* and *Bachelorette* series to date have led to marriage,[4] while numerous newly minted couples have broken up within a few months of the show's screening, including the highly acrimonious and very public split of Jake Pavelka and Vienna Girardi (see Chris Harrison's blog, EW.com, 6 July 2010). This has led many critics to argue that reality romance shows operate purely as spectacle, peddling a romantic fantasy that is staged for the camera in the same way as scripted, fictional television. It is certainly the case that *The Bachelor* franchise provides a luxurious, no-expense-spared stage set for love, replete with mansions, limousines, lavish evening wear and romantic getaway destinations. Clutching symbolic roses, participants are surrounded at every turn by the props familiar to viewers from the genre of popular romance, beginning with fairy tales (see Bratich 2007). As I have argued elsewhere (Kavka 2008), however, these props are also supports for the participants' *performative* acts of love. In order to engage with the ideology of marriage as seriously as the programme does, in order to be there 'for the right reasons', participants must enact their roles in the love plot as though they were *already* the subjects, or objects, of love. That is to say, contestants come to the programme expecting to find love; they thus behave as potential lovers; and as a result they feel love – at least as far as their time within that setting goes. This does not mean that they perform 'false' love but rather that the setting is part of the performative enactment of love, just as a promise is real in the moment it is made, even if it remains unfulfilled.[5] This explains both the appeal and the discomfort of the programme for viewers. On the one hand, *The Bachelor/ette* offers viewers the chance to participate in a romantic fantasy whose climax is the formation of the happily-ever-after, monogamous couple – with none of the dull quotidian aftermath. On the other hand, the programme opens up the uncomfortable possibility that the emotional highs and distressed lows in this love myth are real and that as viewers we are seeing too much: we are positioned as psychological voyeurs of private intimacies by the scopic technologies of reality TV.

The success of *The Bachelor* opened the door to copycat programmes which took a more ironic, even playful stance on the heteronormative ideology of romance. In an ironic reversal of the opulent props of the format, for instance, *Outback Jack* producers (TBS/ABC Australia, 2004) took American 'beauty queens' and sent them to meet an antipodean bachelor in the Australian outback, going so far as to para-chute the unsuspecting women into the outback wearing full-length evening dresses underneath their skydiving suits. The Australian 'Jack', who was introduced in the first episode using the slow-motion, long-shot film techniques reminiscent of the spaghetti western, was in fact a generic construct of virile masculinity created around New Zealand underwear model Vadim Dale (although, in a further irony, this turned out to be one of the few reality romance programmes to result in a marriage).

Other shows combined sociological experimentation with a similar degree of self-reflexivity about the constructed nature of the reality romance genre. The most popular of the post-*Bachelor* shows, *Joe Millionaire* (FOX, 2003), purported to test women's attraction to money – and men's ability to differentiate between gold diggers and 'real' love – by casting a working-class bachelor (construction worker Evan Marriott in the first season) but informing the twenty potential brides that he had just come into a huge inheritance, which included the French chateau where the programme was set. The 'trick' of the programme, having a manual labourer masquerade as a millionaire, created the conditions for an implicitly conservative moral message about money and romance, but it also produced a double mode of address – a limited story for the female participants and a more full one for the viewers – which lent the programme an ironic tone. *Average Joe* (NBC, 2003–5) equally played on expectations of the romance genre, but this time at the expense of the beauty queen bachelorette, who found herself in the first episode not with handsome, buff men alight-ing from individual limousines but rather a busload of sixteen 'average' guys. The show's moral message that beauty is more than skin deep was undercut, however, with the later introduction of four typically handsome men, one of whom was the bachelorette's chosen winner in each season.[6] If anything, this test of romantic attractions served as a twofold reminder. First, it highlighted the fact that heteronormative ideology regulates not only the sexual but also the social suitability of desire. Indeed, reality TV has repeatedly returned to the issue of heteronormative suitability as the basis for social experimentation, as for instance in the internationally successful *Beauty and the Geek* (WB, 2005–6; CW, 2007–8), which pairs physically attractive young women with 'nerdy' young men to share a bedroom and compete in challenges for a stake in the final prize. Second, *Average Joe*'s insistence on casting male suitors of non-ideal proportions (e.g. short, stick-thin, buck-toothed or obese) draws attention to the fact that the bodies of par-ticipants are part of the *props* of the televised romantic fantasy. In this light, it is worth noting that *The Bachelor* franchise attempts to secure its longevity by turning the participants themselves into the commodities of future *Bachelor/ette* series: all bachelorettes and a number of the bachelors have been drawn from the pool of rejected participants of previous series, as has the entire cast of *Bachelor Pad*.

Part of the post-*Bachelor* experimentation with heteronormative ideology has also involved taking issue with the heterosexual romance at the centre. Although there have been relatively few of these shows, the single-season programme *Boy Meets Boy* (Bravo, 2003) used the *Bachelor* format as the basis for a gay reality romance and coincided, in terms of scheduling, with the makeover programme *Queer Eye for the Straight Guy*, also on cable channel Bravo. The game twist in *Boy Meets Boy* depended on the revelation that only some of the suitors were actually gay, so that the bachelor had to use his skills to figure out whom to desire. A similar tactic was applied in *Playing It Straight* (FOX, 2004) but in reverse, with a heterosexual bachelorette having to figure out which of her male suitors is straight and which gay. It is arguable, however, that both of these programmes maintain the heteronormative trajectory, with *Playing It Straight* peddling in sexual stereotypes and *Boy Meets Boy* centring the narrative on a hetero-social pair, the gay man and his female best friend, not unlike *Will and Grace* (see Kavka 2008). The more recent reality soap *The Real L Word* (Showtime, 2010–) to some extent breaks the grip of heteronormativity by chronicling women in pre-existing rather than contrived romantic relationships, but it is worth noting that *The Real L Word* is a docusoap rather than a competitive format. As such, it lacks the element of challenge, which, in the context of the heteronormative real-love show, is recoded as an opportunity for love.

As we have seen, participants on programmes like *The Bachelor* repeat the mantra of being on the show to 'find love', that is, of taking the opportunity created by television to complete their own romantic narrative of self-fulfilment. To some extent, programmes in this sub-genre are able to reflect on this romantic narrative, but it is interesting to note that the most successful and long-running of these shows, *The Bachelor/ette*, is at once the programme with the least degree of self-reflexivity and the one that takes its television-derived rituals most seriously. As I have argued, the performative 'as if' attitude is crucial to the operation of the real-love show: participants must act 'as if' they are already the subject/object of love, and viewers must act 'as if' the epigraph to the final episode will indeed be marriage happily ever after. The interest of this strand of reality TV lies in the fact that it can make the 'as if' seem real, in no small part because of its ability to transfer the props of romantic fantasy into an actual stage set for falling in love. Television in this subgenre functions as interventionist matchmaker, provider of opportunity and fulfiller of fantasy – if only one is willing to take up the challenge on offer.

## Makeover Shows: Properties of Self-Transformation

In a sense, the reality romance programme represents a category of the makeover show, with its heavy emphasis on the fantasy of transforming one's life by 'finding true love'. Both reality romance and makeover shows reconfigure challenge as opportunity, providing participants with a chance at self-improvement through the auspices of televisual intervention. Both kinds of shows, moreover, rely on commodity consumption, with the *Bachelor* subgenre linking the enactment of love to luxury settings and toned bodies, and the makeover show connecting self-improvement to the guided consumption of housewares, personal consumer goods and even cosmetic surgery procedures. Moreover, both subgenres invite viewers to participate in the fantasy of transformation as something which can 'really' happen, as proven by the emotional and material investments of on-screen participants. Of the two, however, the makeover provides the larger, more elastic framework that encapsulates the transformative effects of reality television as a whole. According to Dana Heller, writing in the introduction to the volume *Makeover Television: Realities Remodelled*, 'contemporary makeover programming provides the paradigmatic example of reality television's prominence and far-reaching mass appeal' (Heller 2006: 3). In her list of programmes that constitute the makeover subgenre, Heller includes transformations of the home as well as the body, reconfigurations of heterosexual courtship (including *The Bachelor*) and family life, the remaking of ordinary people into celebrities and celebrities into ordinary people, and the overhaul of consumer lifestyles as well as social identities. For Heller, all of these transformations and renovations are driven by reality television's power to make things over. Jack Bratich makes the claim more boldly: '"making over" and transformation define the very essence of reality TV itself' (Bratich 2007: 6).

In this section, I will look at the makeover programme in narrower terms, considering makeovers of the home and body as the key material for transformations of lifestyle and the self. If transformation is central to the makeover show, then its main trope is the 'before-and-after' structure (Moseley 2000), whether condensed into two juxtaposed pictures or extended into a narrative of progression from the bad 'before' to the good 'after'. In between the before and after, of course, is not only the labour of making over, which is often edited out, but also the guidance of the *expert*, whose knowledge and taste are highlighted in the process of transforming bad into good. Ideologically, what all makeover programmes have in common is a core belief that transformations of the self's properties – whether real estate or personal attributes – will result in *self-realisation*.

It is worth noting that the makeover format has genealogical forebears which stretch well past second-generation reality TV. As many critics have noted, the makeover show has strong resonances with the traditional fairy tale, which in its most optimistic form presents obstacles being overcome through supernatural wish fulfilment. As Bratich points out, '[t]he fairy tale was, in its essence, about powers of transformation', both in the enchanted world itself, where creatures as well as things were subject to metamorphosis, and in the tale's effects on recipients, who were taught to hope for change by such stories of wish-granting and magical powers (Bratich 2007: 17–18). For Bratich, the phrase 'powers of transformation' equally describes the instructional, wish-fulfilling functions of reality TV, especially as performed by experts on makeover shows who proffer solutions and services as effortlessly as fairies might wave a magic wand. The fact that by the nineteenth century fairy tales had come to have a specific educational and moral function (Bratich 2007: 17) suggests a cultural overlap with another genealogical predecessor of the makeover programme, namely, the etiquette books and domestic advice manuals which can be traced to the same era (see Lewis 2008). Both advice manuals and makeover shows, according to Tania Lewis, 'have sought to provide social, moral and personal guidelines for everyday living' (Lewis 2009: 2), thereby shifting the fairy tale scene of transformation from an enchanted castle to one's own living space.

In terms of contemporary television history, Charlotte Brunsdon has argued that the popular makeover show has its roots on British television in the tradition of DIY hobbyist programming. Such programmes taught handy skills through display, showing viewers 'how to do or make things' often associated with the home or garden (Brunsdon 2004: 80). The emphasis on skill acquisition in the hobbyist programmes gave way in the 1990s to what Brunsdon calls a 'lifestyling' of the primetime 8–9 slot. In a profusion of shows 'about cookery, home decorating, clothes and gardening' (Brunsdon 2004: 76), the didactic element remained but was 'subordinated to an instantaneous display of transformation' (2004: 80). The most popular and most innovative of these shows was undoubtedly *Changing Rooms* (BBC,

1996–2004), which combined challenge with the spectacle of transformation: two sets of neighbours were each given a limited budget
(£500) and limited time (forty-eight hours) to remodel one room in
each other's houses, leading to a mutual 'reveal' at the end of each
episode. As the first programme to combine a challenge structure with
the 'before-and-after' narrative of the makeover (Kavka 2006: 215),
*Changing Rooms* paved the way for numerous competitive renovation
shows (e.g. *The Block* (Australia, Nine Network, 2003–)). The viewing
pleasure of display in *Changing Rooms*, moreover, lay not only in the
revelation of transformed rooms but also in the emotional spectacle
of subjects' responses to these transformations: later makeover shows,
whether of properties or selves, would make much of the double
reveal, amplifying the display of the transformed object with the
spectacle of the subjects' wide-eyed response. By the early 2000s, the
combined didacticism and display of property renovation had become
a televisual obsession in Britain (e.g. *How to Rescue a House* (BBC2),
*House Doctor* (Channel Five), *Property Ladder* (Channel 4)). By contrast,
US television had only a limited tradition of property makeover programming (most notably *This Old House* (PBS, 1979–)). The *personal*
makeover, however, had long been familiar to US audiences from
cosmetic counters, women's magazines and daytime television shows
like *Glamour Girl* (NBC, 1953–4; see Cassidy 2006).

If the UK makeover boom can be tied to the transformative 'lifestyling' of the primetime schedule, then the US makeover show in
primetime is linked mainly to transformations of the self, with lifestyle reserved for niche cable channels (Kavka 2006). Although UK
makeover shows expand into the area of personal transformation
throughout the 2000s, the emphasis on beauty and the body origi-
nates in US versions of the makeover. The *Oxford English Dictionary*'s
definition of 'makeover', for instance, states that the word is of US
origin, meaning 'a complete transformation or remodeling, esp. a
thorough refashioning of a person's appearance by beauty treatment'.
The emphasis on *appearance* suggests that in the US the makeover
is about the perfectibility of image rather than the improvement of
lifestyle. Indeed, at the turn of the millennium in the US, the pressure
of rampant image culture met with the increased medicalisation of
everyday life to produce a new understanding of 'beauty treatment':
rather than cosmetics, 'treatment' came to mean cosmetic surgery in
what Naomi Wolf heralded as the 'Modern Surgical Age' in *The Beauty
Myth* (1991). By the mid-2000s, the accepted phrase was 'cosmetic
procedures', which encompassed medical intervention on all areas of
the body deemed to have 'failed' by the standards of image culture:

sagging skin, undersized breasts, misshapen noses, excess fat, balding pates, discoloured teeth, etc.

When the ABC network began screening its 'reality surgery' show *Extreme Makeover* in late 2002 (ending in 2007), it brought the makeover show in line with the 'Modern Surgical Age' while contributing to the culture of self-transformation. In its first series, the show sparked a great deal of controversy (and attendant publicity, averaging 11 million viewers per episode) between those who considered it sadistic to promote surgery on medically healthy bodies and those who believed it to represent a normalised modern practice (Woods 2004). In each episode of the programme two participants, selected because they were unhappy with their appearance and lives, were subjected to a raft of surgical procedures, physical training, life coaching and restyling before presenting their magical transformation to friends and family in a 'big reveal'. With *Extreme Makeover*, a new iconic image entered the canon of the makeover programme: from now on, viewers would recognise dotted lines stencilled directly onto bodies as doctors' notes for future scalpel cuts. What further differentiated the format from earlier makeovers was the inclusion of on-camera surgery, so that the 'extreme' of the title referred not only to the scale of the makeover but also to the degree of intrusive spectacularisation. As Gaby Woods notes, 'the reality shows have not just made a spectacle out of plastic surgery; they have turned it into something ordinary people feel comfortable having in their living rooms' (2004). Indeed, the normalisation of cosmetic surgery through programmes like *Extreme Makeover* – followed by post-op beauty pageant *The Swan* (FOX, 2004), celebrity-worshipping *I Want a Famous Face* (MTV, 2004) and surgeon-focused *Dr. 90210* (E!, 2004–8) – led to a marked increase in the number of plastic surgery procedures performed in the US. In 2004 Rod Rohrich, president of the American Society of Plastic Surgeons, noted that 'the growth of plastic surgery has been nothing short of phenomenal. With all these reality shows, the interest has sky-rocketed', making plastic surgery seem accessible 'for everybody, for anybody that wants it if they want to save for it' (cited in Woods 2004). By the time *10 Years Younger* appeared on UK television in the mid-2000s (Channel 4, 2004–), it seemed natural that any age-defying makeover would involve bodily modification as well as style advice, but it also prepared the way for a backlash in the form of transformation shows that refuse to recommend cosmetic surgery (e.g. *How to Look Good Naked* (Channel 4, 2006–; Lifetime Real Women, 2008–)).

Ultimately, the bodily modification makeover not only inured audiences to the sight of blood (paving the way for *Cosmetic Surgery Live* (Channel Five, 2004–) on UK television) but also encouraged viewers to participate in the fantasy of self-realisation through radical transformation. The makeover's contradictory promise of a 'new you' who is at the same time the 'real you' is exacerbated by surgical makeover shows, in which post-transformation participants repeatedly wonder 'is that really me?' while simultaneously assuring themselves and the camera that the 'real me' has finally come out. As Brenda Weber has noted, this is a key thematic contradiction of the makeover show, especially since the appearance of *Extreme Makeover*: participants and viewers are taught that 'to communicate an "authentic self" one must overwrite and replace the "false" signifiers enunciated by the natural body' (Weber 2009: 4). At the same time, the transformative narrative of these shows collapses distinctions between image, body and selfhood by suggesting that all failings of the self can be resolved by making 'corrections' to the body, resulting in an image with which the self can (finally) identify.

This relation of co-dependence between image, body and selfhood is not just a televisual construct; it is also sustained by the social gaze, a term which refers to the collective acts of looking at and judging one another which underpin social life. The televised makeover both represents *and* mobilises this gaze (Weber 2009: 85), sometimes literally: on *10 Years Younger*, for instance, participants stand in a plexiglass box in a public place while passers-by are asked to guess their age, and on *How to Look Good Naked* participants' headless bodies are plastered on billboards or buildings while passers-by are invited to gaze and comment. The premise on these shows is that subjects tend to misapprehend how others see them from the outside; they must thus have the gaze enacted so as to better understand the image projected by their bodies. At the same time, however, the social gaze is normative. It co-creates the image of the subject by making judgements according to social norms of attractiveness – which the subject has also internalised. The tension between authentic self-expression and having to negotiate the social gaze results in a contradictory message about self-empowerment on makeover programmes: in order to 'be yourself' you must be like everyone else (Weber 2009: 255); to take control of your life, you must submit to experts and/or the knife; to become empowered, you must 'surrender to transformation', as Nely Galán, executive producer and life coach of *The Swan*, succinctly put it (season 1, episode 1). Although detractors claim that makeover programmes are dangerous because they *prescribe* adherence to such norms (e.g. Marwick 2010), more sympathetic critics suggest that these shows usefully *describe* the contradictory pressures brought to bear, especially on women, by image culture.

Not all personal makeover programmes require surgical attainment of a normative ideal but they do recognise the existence of such an ideal and the damaging impact it can have on subjects' sense of self. The personal makeover show is thus presented as a form of *therapy*, offered by experts often through the lessons of tough love, or what Brenda Weber calls the 'affective domination' of love-power (2009: 96–9). Subjects are stripped back or even stripped bare on these shows; they are unmade by 'bullying' experts in order to be remade in a form that better suits current social norms. While surgical makeover shows take the body itself to be the transformable medium of the subject, style shows focus on the transformative potential of clothing, make-up and hairstyle in order to cure subjects of debilitating flaws in self-presentation and self-confidence. The most notable of these shows is the *What Not to Wear* franchise, which originated in the UK with the unapologetically upper-middle-class 'fashion gurus' Susannah Constantine and Trinny Woodall in 2001 (BBC, 2001–7; US version: TLC, 2003–). Although Trinny and Susannah have been heavily criticised for being snooty, bossy and rude, overriding participants' wishes in favour of their own 'rules' for dressing women's bodies, this misses a key point of the programme. On *What Not to Wear*, women's bodies are accepted whatever their age, condition or shape, even though the 'rules' for how they should dress are formulaic. Indeed, they are often enthusiastically squeezed and petted in displays of Trinny and Susannah's 'love-power' to convince the participants that they should not change their bodies to suit the demands of image culture but should rather make the most of their assets through clothing and hairstyle. As Frances Bonner points out, this attitude represents 'a different response to the televisual dominant where beauty and attractiveness is solely the preserve of the young and slim and those willing to ape those qualities surgically' (2009: 109). The social gaze remains, and the presenters insist that one dress to meet it, but the therapeutic message of the show – to participants and viewers alike – is about self-acceptance through the small-step transformations available in high-street shops.

There is, as Weber has noted, a strong current of shaming that runs through these programmes, especially in the initial stage that participants must pass through in order to accept themselves as beautiful. This stage of tearful humiliation is even found in the rampantly optimistic 'anti-makeover' show *How to Look Good Naked*, in which women participants are taught by the gay male stylist (Gok Wan in the

UK, Carson Kressley in the US) to love their bodies *without* clothes on. In both *What Not to Wear* and *How to Look Good Naked*, participants undergo the ritual of having to undress in a 360-degree mirror box (*What Not to Wear*) or to face larger-than-life projections of their bodies on hoardings and billboards (*How to Look Good Naked*) while the camera captures the display of their bodies and their pained reactions. The point of this shaming surveillance, however, is to re-empower the subjects' own gaze over their bodies. Participants who feel out of sync with their bodies – from the mild form of dressing in outdated clothing to the more serious form of body dysmorphic disorder (BDD) – come to the programmes *already* feeling shame from their perceived inability to meet the social gaze. The makeover show then 'spins a story of shame and redemption' (Weber 2009: 87), with the presenters bossing and cajoling, touching and identifying to redeem the subject – in her own eyes. If media images have been the cause of the problem then the redemption narrative of the makeover show seems to claim that media can be the source of its reparation, too.

The crucial point so far left out of this discussion is that the transformative redemption of the makeover is inextricably connected with the consumption of material goods and services. Whether a show operates by highlighting brand names (*Extreme Makeover: Home Edition*), shop signs (*Queer Eye for the Straight Guy*) or the services of particular providers (e.g. dental surgery on *Extreme Makeover*), the makeover subject is seen to achieve self-realisation through the consumption of commercial products (Redden 2007: 152). The makeover show must thus be understood as a product and lynchpin of consumer culture, a 'shame and redemption' narrative updated for the commercial age. This relationship between consumption and redemption is perhaps most visible in the surprise US cable channel hit of 2003, *Queer Eye for the Straight Guy* (Bravo/NBC, 2003–7). Focusing solely on male subjects of transformation, the premise of *Queer Eye* is the same as other makeover shows: an inadequate, unrealised subject is made to come out of his shell, to reveal the 'real me', with the help of guidance from experts. The difference is that, first, the subjects are all (heterosexual) men; second, this is a holistic makeover, transforming everything from body to clothing to décor and lifestyle consumables; and third, it positions gay men as the arbiters of masculine taste and consumption. In a clever twist on the traditional format, the programme multiplies the opportunities for guided consumption by dividing self-transformation into five areas, each overseen by an expert: Ted Allen for food and wine, Kyan Douglas for grooming, Thom Felicia for interior design, Carson Kressley for fashion and Jai Rodriguez for 'culture' (although

Jai's job seems largely to involve teaching the straight men how to improve romantic intimacy with their wives or girlfriends).

In the successful formula established in the first season, the 'Fab Five' barge into the subject's house to engage in an exuberantly chaotic flurry of shaming the man and trashing his apartment before taking him on a shopping expedition while unseen crews clean and redecorate the house. After a reveal of the new décor and a tutorial on the proper use of the consumer items by each expert in turn, the participant then puts his new talents to use by preparing an event for friends or family while the Fab Five scrutinise the performance on big-screen CCTV in a loft far away. The initial unmaking of the man and his lair thus leads to his personal and material remaking through consumption and his final redemption through lifestyle education. As the fulcrum of this process, the shopping expedition gives the experts an opportunity to advertise the stores they have selected as the means of transformation. In season 1, episode 11, for example, Carson takes Alan Corey to H&M, informing him it has 'hip clothes, moderate prices, you gotta love it', while in the furniture store Innovation Thom tells Alan, 'the thing about Innovation is that their aesthetic is cool, kinda young and hip but it actually works' – all while the camera zooms in on the storefront signs. Along with Kyan's assurance that Chelsea Barbers (cue zoom-in) is 'really cool', the repetition of the words 'hip' and 'cool' indicate that the experts are *fashioning* a style for Alan, giving him a 'vision' that transforms his previously tight-fisted lack of taste into competencies that can be 'channell[ed] towards certain culturally valued ends' (Redden 2007: 151).

The ratio of five gay experts to one straight participant grounds both the 'Fab Five' branding and the metrosexual logic of the show. As Jai and Ted croon in an improvised ditty in Alan's trashed apartment, 'all it takes is one dirty straight guy – and five gay men'. The insistence in this programme that the style experts are queer has caused a great deal of debate among critics about whether this is a positive or negative representation of male homosexuality, whether in effect the show makes gay men visible on their own terms in mainstream culture or simply promotes stereotypes of gay men as wisecracking, materialistic style queens removed from heteronormative life (Straayer and Waugh 2005). Without attempting to resolve this debate, it is worth making two points about the show's self-location on the corner of 'Gay Street' and 'Straight Street' (opening credits, season one). First, as Toby Miller and others have noted, *Queer Eye for the Straight Guy* is more about metrosexuality than sexuality; it is thus concerned with the thrill of consumption and commodity fetishism rather than the thrill, or any particular object, of desire. As Miller argues, queerness in this programme is harnessed 'as a form of management consultancy for conventional masculinity' (2006: 116), since it is figured as lifestyle practices that can be taught and bought by straight and gay men equally. Second, the insistence on five gay experts and one straight participant draws attention to the identity coding of the heterosexual participant as much as the homosexual experts. The straight man – whether white or Asian-American (there seems to be a dearth of African-American participants), WASPish or Jewish, young or middle-aged, married or single, professional or working class, homeowner or renter – becomes differentiated as a set of identity attributes, which often struggle to be realised into coherent selfhood. This in turn means that *Queer Eye* highlights not only the role of consumerism in the makeover but also the connection between consumerism, processes of identity formation and the role of television as go-between.

If the makeover programme sells the personal challenge as a transformative opportunity for self-realisation then it does so fully in line with the premises and practices of capitalism. Seen from a broader perspective, the makeover show points to a shift in the role of (reality) television as apparatus and as business. By the mid-2000s, television is not just one industry among others that functions on a capitalist business model, nor is it any longer simply a mass advertiser of consumer goods. As we shall see in the next section, reality television in this period becomes refined as a pedagogical tool that teaches consumers how to be better citizens within the capitalist framework of neoliberal society. This counteracts earlier assumptions that reality TV is just light entertainment with no social value; on the contrary, in the programmes to be discussed, television itself is reconfigured as a facilitator of the public good through pedagogies of self-management.

### 'Life Interventions': Domestic Pedagogies and Citizenship

So far we have been discussing the televised makeover in terms of personal transformation, whether this is achieved through property renovation, bodily modification and/or changes in fashion and (life) style. There is, however, an important trend in transformation television that positions the self less as a marker of personhood than as a key constituent of larger formations like family, community and nation. In these programmes, participants are addressed in terms of their place in a web of social relations and are judged according to the impact of their behaviour on the group. Transformation implicitly occurs at the level of community as well as self when reality TV uses its resources to make 'life interventions' that change '"needy" individuals into functioning citizens' (Ouellette and Hay 2008: 6).

Many of these programmes follow a self-help model, with experts showing participants how to solve their own problems on a range of issues, such as nutrition and weight loss (e.g. *You Are What You Eat* (Channel 4, 2004–7), *The Biggest Loser* (NBC, 2004–)), parenting (e.g. *Supernanny* (Channel 4, 2004–; ABC, 2005–), *Little Angels* (BBC, 2004–6)), addiction (e.g. *Intervention* (A&E, 2005–)), juvenile and social delinquency (e.g. *Brat Camp* (Channel 4/ABC, 2005–7)), and even domestic cleanliness (e.g. *How Clean Is Your House?* (Channel 4, 2003–9)). In a further development of the life intervention format, shows like *Extreme Makeover: Home Edition* (ABC, 2003–), *Miracle Workers* (ABC, 2006) and *Secret Millionaire* (Channel 4/ABC, 2006–) mobilise the not inconsiderable resources – sometimes into six and even seven figures – of corporations and wealthy individuals to provide housing, healthcare, income/tuition assistance and disaster relief for those who cannot help themselves. By and large, the community-transformation ethos has its strongest roots in the US for reasons, as we shall see, that have to do with the spread of neoliberalism since the 1980s. Nonetheless, shows about universal topics of self- and family management, such as parenting, weight loss and cleanliness, have also had broad international appeal.

All of these programmes, whatever their provenance, figure self-hood as a condition of citizenship, understood in its broadest sense as productive membership of a group that comes with attendant rights and responsibilities. Reality-citizenship in turn is supported by the surveillance and interventionist technologies of reality TV. The social gaze that is mobilised to shame and redeem subjects in personal transformation programmes is reoriented in the 'life intervention' shows as a monitor and elixir of social welfare. Self-management or self-realisation continues to be the means, but the ideological goal is the greater good – to maximise the potential of one's family, one's neighbourhood or the entire population. Moreover, these shows are didactic, because by teaching participants self-management they also address viewers as citizens who can learn how to do things better for their family and community. These programmes thus present reality TV as domestic and social pedagogy. By offering stories, often backed up with public service information about nutrition, parenting, housekeeping and volunteerism, reality TV teaches participants and viewers alike valued techniques of self-governance in the interests of the group. In so doing, it meshes with larger governmental structures without having to budge from its commercial base.

As an example, let us consider *The Biggest Loser*, a highly successful show about weight reduction that straddles the personal makeover and the life intervention show by teaching people how to look better *and* be healthier. The format of *The Biggest Loser* borrows heavily from the US reality challenge programmes but focuses on obese participants who are struggling to lose weight. In rounds of weekly eliminations, they take part in gruelling challenges and suspenseful weigh-ins until the person who has lost the greatest percentage of weight ends up winning the cash prize. The original concept behind the show was trialled with much less success in 2001 in The Netherlands and Germany: produced by Endemol and called *Big Diet*, it attempted to capitalise on the success of *Big Brother* by placing participants in a *Big Brother*-style house and setting them weight-loss targets. Although the Dutch version finished its season, the German version (RTL2, 2001) was cancelled for poor ratings,[7] and in 2003/4 Endemol shifted to a text-messaging diet service for subscribers, thereby bypassing television altogether (Moran with Malbon 2006: 93). The point here is not that a *Survivor*-type challenge format works better for dieters than a *Big Brother* format – although that does seem true in the US – but rather that the success of weight-reduction reality TV depends on its ability to intersect with wider discourses about obesity and its impact on families and the nation. Such discourses, while less prevalent in northern Europe at the start of millennium, have expanded exponentially in recent years in the image- and health-conscious US. *The Biggest Loser* reflects and magnifies this trend by using participants and trainers as mouthpieces for public information messages about the impact of obesity on life expectancy, family stability and national healthcare costs. Rather than simply offering subjects an aesthetic makeover, then, the show takes on the greater purpose of life intervention conjoined with messages of good citizenship. While we watch individuals undergo a personal programme of self-revitalisation as they shed kilograms, the more important transformations implicitly occur across participants' social networks: children and spouses welcome home a happier, healthier family member; the economy has a more productive worker; and the nation comes one step closer to curing its problem with obesity. By watching, audiences are taught not only the routines of weight loss but are also challenged to set their own targets, so that they too can improve the health and security of their family and community through better self-management.

This kind of message readily translates into nutrition programmes such as *Honey, We're Killing the Kids* (BBC, 2005–), which locates the burden of family health on parents' food provision habits, and *Jamie's School Dinners* (Channel 4, 2005) as well as *Jamie Oliver's Food Revolution* (ABC, 2010–), in which celebrity chef Jamie Oliver targets British and American schools, respectively, as sites of food education for the sake of national health. A similar relation between the challenges of personal or domestic self-regulation and the gains of social improvement can be found in shows that aim to improve the delinquent behaviour of children, youth or the underclasses, such as *Supernanny*, *Brat Camp*, *From Ladette to Lady* (ITV, 2005–) or *Charm School* (VH1, 2007–9). Here, too, participants are trained to govern themselves and/ or those in their care along specific cultural and class-based guidelines, in order to improve their well-being and thus secure the larger social body. Despite the differences between controlling toddlers and teaching brash party girls the intricacies of upper-class etiquette, these shows are comparable because they are 'bound to a logic of citizenship that emphasize[s] personal responsibility' (Ouellette and Hay 2008: 21). They are thus part of the political sphere of governance, which has become dispersed across private institutions and individuals. Parents, for instance, are seen to govern the domestic sphere of home and children, but they do not always know how to do this correctly. They need the expert guidance of 'supernanny' Jo Frost, who introduces not only disciplinary techniques such as the 'naughty chair' but also a domestic routine in the form of a 'household constitution' that secures every member's productive place in the familial micro-society (Ouellette and Hay 2008: 170). Assigning personal responsibility for individual, domestic and social health is the goal of this broad range of pedagogical programmes. Whether treating overeaters (*Fat Camp* (MTV, 2006)), over-consumers (*Hoarders* (A&E, 2009–)), chaotic parents (*Supernanny*) or slutty women (*Charm School*), the shows never address participants' failings in terms of social inequality or the uneven distribution of economic and cultural capital (see McAlister 2010; McMurria 2008). Rather, the faults are taken to be personal and hence the cure requires learning techniques of self-governance played out on the bodies and in the households of private citizens.

To adopt Michel Foucault's terminology, these programmes belong to current discourses and practices of 'governmentality', a term which refers not only to political governments but also to the ways in which government has become 'more privatized and dispersed' (Ouellette and Hay 2008: 8). From a Foucauldian view, reality TV is one such mode of privatisation and dispersal: it does not act alone, confined to the category of entertainment, but fits into a larger political mechanism that contemporary critics, following Foucault, call 'biopolitics'.

In a 1976 lecture on power ('Society Must Be Defended'), Foucault briefly introduced the term 'biopower' to indicate a shift in the early modern era (sixteenth–seventeenth century) from an older political sovereignty to a new 'power of regularization': 'Sovereignty took life and let live. And now we have the emergence of a power that I would call the power of regularization, and it, in contrast, consists in making live and letting die' (2011: 127–8). While feudal sovereignty can be caricatured as the queen who screams 'off with his head!' because she has the right to kill whomever she wishes, what Foucault calls the 'technology of biopower' lies in governmental strategies that organise populations to live and prosper *in the interests of the state*. This technology, according to Rabinow and Rose, involves 'more or less rationalized attempts to intervene upon the vital characteristics of human existence' (2006: 196–7). In describing 'Biopower Today', Rabinow and Rose list a minimum of three elements that are involved: 'one or more "truth" discourses about the vital character of living human beings'; 'strategies of intervention upon collective existence in the name of life and health'; and 'modes of subjectification, through which individuals are brought to work on themselves, under certain forms of authority, in relation to truth discourses' (2006: 197). Although Rabinow and Rose are concerned with political theory rather than media studies, they provide a remarkably apt rubric for understanding how reality TV transformation programmes combine discourses about correct forms of *living* with strategies of *intervention* and modes of *subjectification* under authority. The faulty subjects of reality TV are 'made to live (better)' by experts who teach them how to become more vital, to thrive and prosper, through strategies for controlling, monitoring and regulating themselves and their households.

Strategies of self-governance are necessary not only because governmentality has been rationalised and dispersed but also because the liberal model of political governance is based on a notion of individual liberty, with government acting on individuals from a distance. Foucault's analysis of liberalism proves helpful here as well. The term liberalism, as Ouellette and Hay point out, 'does not refer to a political ideology (as in conservative versus liberal), but instead to a "governmental rationality", or approach to governing through freedom' (2008: 9). Liberal rulers govern with a light hand, seeking to facilitate the actions of markets and individuals, while at the same time 'expect[ing] individuals to govern themselves properly – to choose order over chaos and good behavior over deviance' (Ouellette and Hay 2008: 10). This is the basic contradiction of liberalism: government must stay off the backs of the citizens, yet the system only works if its citizens govern themselves. This contradiction remains inherent in the post-1980s 'reinvention of government' which is referred to as neoliberalism. In response to what came to be seen as the excess spending of the social welfare state from the 1930s to the 1960s, Western governments – led by Reagan in the US and Thatcher in the UK – moved to reinvent themselves in the 1980s by privatising national holdings, withdrawing regulation and governing 'at a distance' (see Chapter 2). According to Ouellette and Hay, this 'broad rethinking and remodeling of the Welfare State' has led to

> a greater reliance on the privatization and personalization of welfare than before as the State entrusts 'pastoralism' to private entities (including media) and emphasizes that citizens be not only active, but also 'enterprising' in the pursuit of their own empowerment and well-being. (Ouellette and Hay 2008: 12)

In the neoliberal climate of free individuals, free markets and entrepreneurship, citizens are required not only to do it for themselves but also to do it for others, since the care of those who are less fortunate is no longer considered a responsibility of the state. Along with other private entities, reality TV steps into the breach left by the dismantling of the social welfare state to distribute biopolitical resources and expertise among struggling citizens.

These struggling citizens are perhaps best exemplified on *Extreme Makeover: Home Edition* (*EM: HE*) (ABC, 2003–). First screened in late 2003, *EM: HE* was launched as a renovation spin-off of *Extreme Makeover*, with a team of carpenters and designers given the 'impossible' task of performing a radical makeover on a family home in only seven days (e.g. building an internal elevator for a family with a wheelchair-bound son). It soon became clear, however, that the success of the programme had less to do with temporal suspense than with 'telling the story of a deserving family' (Winslow 2010: 271). Renovations thus turned into spectacular demolition-and-rebuilding projects, yet houses could always be finished on time, no matter how many hundreds of workers it took (and it has taken ever greater armies of blue-shirted workers). The challenge of the makeover fell away and only opportunity remained as the show took on the mantle of charity provider and purveyor, promising to 'build a better community – one family, one house at a time' (from ABC's *A Better Community* website; see Ouellette and Hay 2008: 40–4). The show now openly operates as corporate philanthropy, answering the neoliberal injunction that private entities take over the task of social welfare and – in the going rhetoric – 'give something back' to the community.

As with *Extreme Makeover*, recipients of ABC's largesse have to be needy, but on *EM: HE* it is less about recipients needing than *deserving* the makeover. As Ouellette and Hay argue, the 'deserving poor' are marked by four characteristics: first, they must, through no fault of their own, be in financial need; second, they must be homeowners, no matter how down and out (2008: 45); third, they must have experienced some kind of traumatic familial hardship (death, disease, destruction); and, finally, they must exhibit an 'ethic of volunteerism' (2008: 48). Taken together, this means that the poor who deserve televisual philanthropy must be victims of circumstance who need charity but *do not depend* on it; they should be model citizens who are perfectly capable of self-governance – if not for the ill wind of disease, death and destruction – and have themselves 'given back' or provided charity to others. The families are thus both 'exemplary models for the viewer, capable of setting up patterns for imitation' (Winslow 2010: 280), and tearfully grateful recipients of charity from the generous media conglomerate ABC/Disney. The neoliberal privatisation of welfare is thereby modelled at both ends of the spectrum, with those who can afford it as well as those who cannot figured as Good Samaritans along neoconservative lines (McMurria 2008). Of course, ABC/Disney is not out of pocket for any of the goods and services required to build a house, no matter how huge, since these are solicited from local businesses and corporate sponsors in exchange for product integration and association with the 'A Better Community' brand (Ouellette and Hay 2008: 43).

Commercialism is thus positioned as both necessary and perfectly adequate to community maintenance, and familial trauma is given a commodity-based resolution. The message of just reward, for 'deserving families'[8] as well as sponsors, is clear: nobody gives without getting something back – except, perhaps, for the tens of thousands of applicants who are passed over by the private provider. But they, presumably, are the undeserving poor, who are either insufficiently moral or too dependent on welfare to gain neoconservative approval (McAlister 2010; Winslow 2010). As Joan McAlister argues, *EM: HE* represents a 'domestication of citizenship' that 'paradoxically combines the governmental and economic imperatives of neoliberalism with the moral and social norms of neoconservatism' (2010: 86, 85). Conservative family values ground community values, celebrities show up to add ideological support (including then-First Lady Laura Bush (finale, season 2)), and ABC/Disney combines corporate philanthropy with neoliberal governmentality in a feel-good formula to increase profits.

## Conclusion

This chapter has focused on the notion of *challenge* as a central organising principle of reality TV programmes in the flush of the second generation. In just a few short years, from 2001 to 2004, the challenge developed from a competition in an enclosed game world to an opportunity for self-realisation through love and the makeover to a means of transforming the family, the community and the nation through better governance. In genealogical terms, the houses built for deserving families on *EM: HE* have a link not only to the transformed properties and persons of makeover shows but also to what Ouellette and Hay refer to as 'reality TV's games of "group governance"' (2008: 8). By challenging participants to negotiate not just obstacle courses but also the difficulties of living within a group, *Survivor* laid the groundwork for the reality programming trends to come: relationship-based competition shows in 2001, real-love shows in 2002, extreme makeover shows in 2003 and self- and family regulation shows in 2004. Across this brief timeline, reality television sought to raise its commodity and cultural value by becoming more interventionist for supposedly greater social benefit. From arranging obstacles to arranging marriages, from managing travel to managing surgical procedures, from building confidence to building homes, second-generation reality TV discovered its capacity to intervene in people's lives, those of both viewers and participants, as an agent of reward and punishment, and a guidebook of good governance.

The chapter ends with biopolitics because one could argue that reality television, by intervening in people's lives on both sides of the screen to teach them strategies of governance, is a biopolitical apparatus. This is a provocative insight, but the tendency in biopolitical critiques is to argue that governmentality plays a totalising role in the personal transformation of participants in these shows. There are, however, shows that might also be considered 'life intervention' programmes which highlight a clash of difference between participants rather than a totalising intervention in the lives of ordinary citizens by state and corporate interests. We see this, for instance, in *Wife Swap* (Channel 4, 2003-9; ABC, 2004-9) and *Trading Spouses* (FOX, 2004-7), shows which are nominally about teaching families better modes of self-governance by forcing them to confront ways in which the 'other half' lives. In these programmes, which take two families and send the wife/mother of each to live with the other family for one or two weeks, the drama arises from radical differences in house rules, domestic routines and family values. In the UK format, *Wife Swap* casts the interactions and minutiae of everyday domestic life as markers of class difference and associated gender roles. In the US, where the myth of the classless society has long held sway (Winslow 2010), *Wife Swap* and *Trading Spouses* address class-and-gender roles indirectly, as manifested through the more visible identity markers of difference in race, religion and regionality. In each of these series, household management and parenting expectations are the means by which the swapped wives negotiate differences in class values, social status, belief systems and even sexuality.

Sarah Matheson (2007) has critiqued the US shows for endorsing a narrow band of appropriate forms of domestic citizenship, with the more normative family of each pair implicitly teaching the other half how to live. I would argue, however, that the domestic swap shows work in the opposite direction, loosening ideological strictures through the minutiae of difference rather than insisting on a universal application of middle-class, neoliberal norms. For instance, in a double episode of *Trading Spouses* (season 2, episodes 6/7), an African-American mother of four from Harlem is swapped with a white, upper-middle-class mother from a blended family in suburban Massachusetts: the result is a surprisingly searing critique of deep-lying racism in the US as sustained by class stratification. Thus, rather than building a domestic space of the same specifications for all participants, these shows are particularly attuned to the range and underpinnings of lifestyles, whether this is marked by the orderliness of a closet or repeated appeals to Jesus. The effect is anti-normatising, producing an abundance of possibilities for family organisation. The biopolitical model of neoliberalism, although it is useful in explaining the overlap between the commercial and pedagogical ends of much reality programming, masks the fact that the 'life interventions' of reality TV do not always result in political normativity. Other programmes suggest non-normative interpretations and counter-hegemonic negotiations of social identity and values. Not all reality TV shows build a one-size-fits-all house, and not all ordinary people are ordinary in the same way, as we shall see in the next chapter.

## Notes

1. Reality TV shows in the US, like other light entertainment programmes as well as violent films, were prone to postponement and even cancellation by industry executives in the wake of the 9/11 attacks, which left media organisations wondering how to respond appropriately to the devastation as well as the seismic shift in public

mood (see Spigel 2004). In addition to putting the second season of *The Mole* on hiatus, the ABC network cancelled its intended production of *The Runner*, to be produced by Matt Damon and Ben Affleck (Andrejevic 2004: 98–9).

2. At around the same time, NBC also came up with a concept combining a race with foreign travel. The NBC show *Lost*, which aired in 2001, divided contestants into three two-member teams and dropped teams off blindfolded in a remote area of an unknown country. Their goal was to race to the finish line at the Statue of Liberty supplied with nothing but a backpack of essentials. The show, which was scheduled directly against *The Amazing Race* and launched a week before the 9/11 attacks, rated very poorly and was not renewed.

3. The final episode of *Married by America* offered a house and cash prize to couples who actually got married on air. Although two of the four couples walked to the altar, neither wedding was completed as one partner ended up rejecting the other in both cases. A similar but earlier version of this format, where the selection process is followed by cohabitation, screened in the UK as *Perfect Match*, although this show was less staged because the selection was made by a panel of the bachelor/ette's friends and family, while the cohabitation period was documented by a diary cam controlled by the bachelor/ette.

4. Trista Rehn, the bachelorette of season 1, married Ryan Sutter in 2003, and Jason Mesnick, the bachelor of season 13, married Molly Malaney in March 2010. The latter, perhaps, does not count, since Mesnick had actually proposed to Melissa Rycroft and rejected Malaney in the final rose ceremony, but then split with Rycroft and proposed to Malaney on air in an 'After the Final Rose' special.

5. See Austin 1975. Austin classifies speech acts into constative acts, which describe a situation, and performative acts, which 'do' something rather than describing it. One of Austin's key examples of performative speech is the promise: 'I promise to' has no descriptive value because nothing has (yet) happened; its linguistic value lies in the performative power of the utterance.

6. A similar programme which attempts to dissociate romance from physical beauty was *Mr Personality* (FOX, April 2003), in which the male suitors had to wear masks when spending time with the bachelorette. Although that programme failed to last more than one season, the concept has been given a new spin by *Dating in the Dark* (RTL5/ABC, 2009–), a Dutch reality show which premiered in 2009 and has been successful as an international format sale.

7. 'RTL2 setzt Big Diet auf Nulldiät' (RTL2 puts 'Big Diet' on a zero diet), *Handelsblatt* 12 July 2001, <http://www.handelsblatt.com/archiv/rtl-2-setzt-big-diet-auf-nulldiaet;439493> (accessed 30 December 2010).

8. 'Deserving families' is a phrase that appears on the ABC website for *EM: HE*: <http://abc.go.com/site/a-better-community/show-outreach> (accessed 1 February 2001).

# 5 Third-Generation Reality TV (2002–): Economies of Celebrity

In recent years, television has been actively involved in what Graeme Turner has called 'a spectacular revival of the media's interest in manufacturing celebrity' (2004: 8). At the centre of this revival is the newest TV genre, reality television, which has enthusiastically adopted the processes of producing, promoting and benefiting from celebrity. In the popular imagination, however, television stars rarely achieve the heights of the Hollywood A-list, and a 'reality TV star' in particular is often taken to be a contradiction in terms. While popular discourse readily associates reality television with fame, it does so in a negative way, dismissing reality TV participants as fame-mongers, 'wannabes' and untalented nobodies looking for their fifteen minutes in the lime-light. In the rare cases when reality TV alumni manage to stretch their provisional fame into greater media visibility, they tend to be derided as 'D-list' celebrities who will do anything for attention (Palmer 2005). Because reality television is seen as a dumbed-down media form with a low entry threshold for participants, its diminished cultural value rubs off on participants' claims to fame, while its reputation for creating D-list celebrities confirms reality TV's low cultural value. But this popular dismissal of reality TV stardom fails to take into consideration the ways in which reality television illuminates and interlocks with the increasingly complex mechanisms of contemporary celebrity culture. Indeed, reality television is a driving force in recent transformations of this culture. As I shall argue, reality TV must be considered a key genre not only for understanding television celebrity but also for clarifying the processes through which contemporary celebrity is produced, maintained and consumed.

In genealogical terms, it may be premature to announce that a third generation of reality television is upon us, especially in the absence of a mould-breaking programme like *Big Brother* to mark the shift. Nonetheless, a gradual but noticeable change has been occurring in the reality TV genre, from an emphasis on documenting ordinary life to manufacturing celebrity out of the everyday. What in first-generation shows was a curious by-product of observational reality TV – the ordinary person becoming a celebrity, however temporarily – has increasingly been folded back into the casting and formats of second-generation shows, giving them a new role in the media economy. In the emergent third generation of reality television, talent formats pluck people off the street and thrust them into the spotlight; no-talent-required formats turn unlikely participants into overnight sensations; challenge formats are repurposed to extend celebrity shelf-life; and the family docusoap is made over into 'celebreality' as a steady stream of minor celebrities invite cameras into their homes. The result is that reality television now self-consciously functions as part of the celebrity-making apparatus, interacting with other media forms and entertainment industries to produce and promote fame.

As most critics agree, although the concept of fame has a long history (see Braudy 1997), contemporary celebrity is a media construction, with celebrities drawn largely from entertainment and sports industries. The term 'construction' indicates that celebrity is a product of media representation, which refers to the visibility accorded to people who become media images as well as to the discursive 'repertoires and patterns' used to make up these images (Turner 2004: 8). Reality television nurtures both of these aspects of representation. It offers participants a high degree of exposure to viewers nationally and internationally while drawing on cultural and generic discourses to produce certain images of participants. As Richard Dyer pointed out in his ground-breaking work on stardom (1998 [1979]), these discourses are notably contradictory: celebrities are both ordinary and special; they are both deserving and undeserving; they have worked hard and they have had a 'lucky break'; they are objects simultaneously of fascination, emulation and contempt. For its part, reality television offers a particularly potent mix of these contradictions because its own mechanisms place it on the cusp between the ordinary and the extraordinary. As a celebrity-making apparatus, reality television can turn ordinary people into celebrities just as easily as it can represent celebrities as ordinary people; the goal is to maintain the visibility of both in a mutually beneficial system.

Genealogically, the incursive, interventionist function of earlier reality TV modes has not disappeared in the third generation. However, in these programmes the focus is less on intervening in participants' personal lives than on using the material of personal lives to intervene in the economies of celebrity culture. 'Economy' is to be understood here in a broad sense, since celebrity serves a number of purposes in reality TV: it is the insubstantial but highly desirable commodity called 'fame'; it is a form of on-screen labour used to increase social status and promote material gain; it is a form of capital that can be invested in the production of further celebrity; and it is the embodiment of what Chris Rojek calls 'abstract desire', whose circulation is crucial to the 'market of sentiments' that sustains the 'market of commodities' (2001: 14).

Reality television has thus become a site where the celebrity-making logics of representation, desire and commodification meld. Consider as an example the fourteenth season of *The Bachelor* (ABC, 2010), whose man-at-the-centre, Jake Pavelka, had already accrued name recognition, not to mention audience investment in his innocent charm, during his stint as a suitor on the previous year's *The Bachelorette* (season 5). During the finale of *The Bachelor* with Pavelka, the cast of the upcoming *Dancing with the Stars* (season 10, ABC, 2010) was announced, which included – no surprise – Jake Pavelka, whose status had now risen to 'star' based on his exposure on *The Bachelor*. In a different discursive register, the same season of *The Bachelor* introduced contestant Rozlyn Papa, who was ejected from the programme in the second episode for having an 'inappropriate' relationship with a member of the production crew. The scandal drew some publicity, but hit its high mark after the end of the series when it was revealed by TMZ.com that Papa had made a sex tape – indeed, that she had more than one sex tape on the market. The result was a sudden leap for Papa from 'wannabe' to celebrity. As Cenk Uygur of The Young Turks internet news site wryly commented, the events seemed to constitute a lesson on how to achieve celebrity:

> You gotta give her credit, because she's going on the checklist of how to get famous in Hollywood. You first go on a reality show; second, cause some sort of massive trouble, like call attention to yourself by either being an unbelievable bitch – y'know, eight out of ten times – or sleeping with someone inappropriately, etc., that always works. And once you've done that – step one, on a reality show, step two, call attention to yourself – step three, sex tape. Boom, boom, boom. All of a sudden, we didn't know Rozlyn Papa a week ago and now – we're looking forward to her sex tape.[1]

In his ironic summary of the three-step celebrification process, Uygur emphasises the primacy of reality television: the first step, after all, is to go on a reality show. He concludes by pointing out the desirable economics of the Papa scandal: 'you . . . bring attention to the show and have everyone talking about it, in which case the show's ratings win, Rozlyn Papa gets famous, and we all get a hot sex tape – in which case, *everybody's* a winner'. Uygur's assessment of the win-win situation suggests the magical properties of contemporary celebrity: out of little else than 'attention' the show gains ratings, the participant achieves temporary fame and media audiences get their desire (which is likely to be more for the salaciousness of the event than to download a sex tape).

Seen more broadly, the case of Papa highlights three factors that are constitutive of contemporary celebrity. First, celebrity is based on media interest in the details of someone's *private* life rather than his/her professional role (Turner 2004: 3, 8). This might explain why the scandal of Papa's ejection from *The Bachelor* brought her some publicity but, in the absence of any private details about the affair, it took a putative sex tape to make her a celebrity.[2] Second, however central reality television is to the production of celebrity, it does not work alone. Modern celebrity formation is the collaborative product of multiple media forms and intersecting platforms, such as TMZ.com following the screening of *The Bachelor* finale with a report of Papa's sex tapes, which in turn is picked up by the TYT YouTube channel, which then sends internet users scrambling to find more on Papa, including the sex tape itself. Richard Dyer has pointed out in his study of Hollywood film stars that the 'star phenomenon' consists not only of screen performances but also of everything that is written and said about the star (2004 [1986]: 2–3). In the digital era of multiple platforms for performance, news and discussion, the extensiveness of the star phenomenon has radically increased. Third, although most celebrities, having achieved that status, strive to maintain their presence in the public eye, the dependence of celebrity on continued exposure in an overcrowded media terrain invests it with fragility and brevity. As Chris Rojek notes, the etymological root of celebrity in the Latin *celere*, meaning 'swift', indicates 'a social structure in which the character of fame is fleeting' (2001: 9). While some reality TV participants do achieve longevity (e.g. Jane McDonald, see Chapter 2), Rozlyn Papa is emblematic of the many who have been briefly lifted into public view, only to be forgotten after their fifteen minutes of fame.

Taking into consideration the conflicting discourses between earned and unearned fame, this chapter will examine the mechanisms used by reality TV to produce and maintain celebrity, as well as the economies in which celebrities circulate as commodities of markets and desires. The chapter is divided into three sections according to subgenre. The first focuses on the 'talent' formats, in which celebrity is construed as both deserved and the self-conscious product of hard work. This section will trace the development of the main reality TV music formats, *Popstars* and the *Idol* series. The second section turns to the 'no-talent' formats, or those reality shows which cast participants on the grounds of their apparent ordinariness. Drawing on international first seasons of *Big Brother*, the section will examine the processes of manufacturing celebrity from 'nothing' in terms of social status and class politics. Finally, the third section covers programmes which use existing celebrities, such as *I'm a Celebrity, Get Me Out of Here!* (UK, ITV), *The Osbournes* (US, MTV) and *Strictly Come Dancing* (UK, BBC), to investigate the celebrity's appeal to ordinariness in the 'market of sentiments' (Rojek 2001) as well as in the market of self-commodification.

## Fashioning Celebrity: Talent and Industry

Numerous approaches could be taken to the discussion of what I will here call reality talent formats, by which I mean reality shows that pitch contestants with a particular talent against one another in a competition to see who is the best. The talent in question may be singing (the *Idol* franchise (2001–)), dancing (*So You Think You Can Dance?* (FOX, 2005–)), modelling (the *Top Model* franchise (2003–)), cooking (*Top Chef* (Bravo, 2006–)), hairstyling (*Shear Genius* (Bravo, 2007–)) or fashion design (*Project Runway* (Bravo/Lifetime, 2004–)), to name just the most prevalent. One can analyse these shows as competitive formats, as opportunities for cross-sponsorship and brand loyalty (Jenkins 2006), as sites of convergence between entertainment and leisure industries (Kavka 2011), or as examples of format transfer in the global political arena[3] (Kraidy 2009). It seems appropriate to position such shows as the precedents of third-generation programmes, however, because the talent formats are first and foremost about *producing* celebrity, in all senses of the term: celebrity is produced putatively out of 'nothing' (that is, from ordinary people); its production requires the assistance of 'cultural intermediaries' (Rojek 2001: 10) such as judges, coaches, producers, choreographers, stylists, make-up artists, etc.; and celebrity is configured as an end-product that has commodity value after the life of the programme. We might add to this that the exposure of celebrity production mechanisms itself has celebrity effects, as exemplified by the cultural intermediaries who help to produce celebrity themselves often becoming celebrities (such as Simon Cowell, judge of *Pop Idol*, *American Idol* and *X-Factor*, or Tim Gunn, mentor and advisor on *Project Runway*). These shows are thus excellent formats for considering the economies of the celebrity industry and reality television's role within it.

At the same time, the talent formats are sites of discursive contradiction, particularly between the rhetoric of authenticity and that of manufacture. On the one hand, the shows purport to be literally searching for 'the next big thing' (the subtitle of the first *American Idol* was 'The Search for a Superstar'), as though star quality is an 'innate' substance that simply needs to be discovered. On the other hand, the narrative arcs of these programmes repeatedly expose the mechanics of celebrity production, emphasising the labour it takes to fashion a star out of ordinariness. As a reviewer wrote about the first season of *Pop Idol* in the UK, 'we've been treated to the sight of the [pop music] genre lifting up its glitzy miniskirt to show off its grubby knickers' (Raven cited in Holmes 2004b: 147). This contradiction between the language of authenticity and that of manufacture also structures the discourses of talent: on the one hand, judges on these shows praise raw talent, applauding participants for having the 'X-factor' or an 'eye for design'; on the other hand, participants are routinely criticised for not putting enough hard work into their self-presentation and not adapting to the standards of the industry. As Su Holmes has argued, the fact that these shows are reality TV means that 'claims to realism and authenticity become irrevocably intertwined' with discourses of manufacture (2004b: 155). Indeed, the many references to authenticity on these shows end up validating the production of celebrity while also mythologising its basis in 'natural' talent.

The programme *Popstars* (TVNZ, 1999) is of particular interest in this context not only because it was the first of the major reality talent formats but also because it was created explicitly to reflect on the manufacture of pop music stardom. The talent format has a long history on television, with early exemplars like *The Amateur Hour* in the US (DuMont Television/ABC, 1948–70) and *Opportunity Knocks* in the UK (Thames Television, 1956–78) having made the transition from radio. At least three characteristics, however, differentiate the reality talent format from its precursors. First, the reality talent competition is serialised, unfolding across an entire season rather than a single show (Jenkins 2006: 78). Second, the personalised aesthetics of reality television (e.g. close-ups, confessional interviews, extended emotion shots) enable audiences to form strong bonds of identification and intimacy with the contestants, particularly over the course of a series. Finally, the scopic technology of reality television adds 'backstage' information to 'frontstage' performances, thereby revealing the labour that goes in to celebrity production. It is this latter intent that drove the conception of *Popstars* in 1999 by New Zealand director and editor Bill Toepfer. Fascinated by the global success of the unashamedly manufactured Spice Girls, Toepfer decided to make what he calls a '"manipulated reality" documentary series' that would start with auditions for an all-girl group and then follow the band as they negotiated the music industry: 'Coming from a documentary background', Toepfer explains, 'I fancied it as some sort of Brechtian examination of the hype and machinations of the music business' (personal communication). With television producer Jonathan Dowling behind the scenes and music producer Peter Ulrich in front of the camera, the production team selected, styled and promoted the pop band True Bliss, guiding them through the recording and release of a single, which immediately went to no. 1 on the New Zealand pop charts.

Throughout the nine-part series, the programme self-consciously addressed the production as well as reception of pop stardom. The first episode, for instance, opens with intercutting between slick Spice Girls videos and excitable pre-teen girls mimicking their music and dance moves at home.[4] The voice-over goes on to make much of the fact that the head of Tierney Records, Mark Tierney, has signed the group before its members have even been selected, which gives him a voice in the selection process. Crucially, *Popstars* is the first talent format – not to mention the first reality television programme – to incorporate the casting calls into the series itself. As would become standard practice on the *Idol* format, open auditions were held in various cities, with hopefuls queuing up for the chance to sing a verse from a song of their choice without accompaniment. This paved the way for the reality talent format to entertain viewers with 'bad' auditions as well as good ones, but more importantly the casting process in *Popstars* introduced footage of the panellists' deliberations, which allowed them to articulate the criteria involved in the manufacture of pop celebrity. For instance, when considering a girl with a good singing voice and an abrasive style of self-presentation, record company executive Tierney asks music producer Ulrich, 'yes, but who would she appeal to?' Both agree that this is the ultimate question, indicating the importance of targeting consumers even at the casting stage. Later, in the final round of fifteen, Ulrich rejects a contestant because 'the pop thing just isn't there', even though she is '99% right' (TX, 27 April 1999).

From these initial stages, *Popstars* moves through a behind-the-scenes exfoliation of the various components involved in creating a pop group. After casting comes the work of rehearsal and song selection, followed by recording a single and making a music video. All the while the television camera oscillates between capturing the producers' explanations and the cast members' emotions. Moreover, the edit-to-air time is brief, so that the screening of the programme intersects with the real-time experience of viewers hearing the single on the radio, watching the video on music channels and having the opportunity to buy the band's music. This formula proved so successful for both the television and music industries that it was sold to Screentime Australia in 1999 and then licensed internationally,[5] producing chart-topping bands like Bardot (Australia, Seven Network, 2000), No Angels (Germany, RTL2, 2000), Hear'Say (UK, ITV, 2001), Eden's Crush (US, WB, 2001) and Bandana (Argentina, 2001), to name only the first few countries where the show was a hit. The broad appeal of the programme was twofold: on the one hand, it came with a near-guarantee of success for two media industries, television as well as music, while, on the other, as a reality programme it could make a claim to 'being real' precisely because it exposed the process of manufacturing a pop group (Holmes 2004b: 155). Of course, television celebrity brings with it a downside: in the rapid turnaround of visibility bestowed by the television apparatus, celebrity can go as easily as it comes (Gamson 1994: 44) and many *Popstars* bands found it impossible to sustain their stardom once the show had ended.[6]

*Popstars* had numerous imitators, such as the US series *Making the Band* (ABC, 2000–1; MTV, 2002–), but none have been so successful as *Pop Idol* (ITV, 2001–3) and the *Idol* franchise. Conceived in 2000 by British music manager Simon Fuller (whose previous experience included managing the Spice Girls), the *Pop Idol* format was produced by FremantleMedia and 19TV, a production company set up by Fuller specifically to develop 'cross-genre' music shows (Holmes 2004b: 150). The narrative arc of *Pop Idol* resembles that of *Popstars* but the manufacture of stardom is now focused on the individual, with the final ten contestants engaging in sing-offs to eliminate one contender each week in a separate show. The most important difference between the two formats, however, lies in *Pop Idol*'s 'invocation of audience interactivity' by drawing viewers themselves into the selection process (Holmes 2004b: 149). Although audience voting had been part of televised talent shows since the 1950s (namely, the 'clapometer' on *Opportunity Knocks*), *Pop Idol* drew on the cross-media voting model introduced by *Big Brother*, inviting audiences to vote for their favourite performer by telephone, SMS text, digital TV remote or internet and then eliminating the contender with the least votes. The promotional tagline of *Pop Idol* – 'this time, you choose!' – foregrounded the participatory role of viewers, implicitly democratising the selection process and allowing everyone 'to participate in politics as celebrity' (Andrejevic 2004: 113) – or, better yet, in the politics *of* celebrity. In *American Idol*, this nod to democratisation has often been articulated in the language of national ownership; winners of *American Idol* are heralded to the audience with the announcement, 'America, here is *your* idol!' (my emphasis).

Audience participation, however, has also had significant economic implications. The *Idol* franchise shares telephony revenues with service providers in each country. In the US, for instance, the FOX channel splits the proceeds of audience voting with AT&T and has even been lauded by AT&T for 'educat[ing] the public [about mobile phones] and get[ting] people texting' (cited in Jenkins 2006: 59). More importantly, the market aim of the *Idol* programmes is to sell 'their idol' back to the people who voted for him/her rather than simply promoting a particular series winner. That is to say, audience participation in the selection process makes viewers *invest* in their choice of an idol, emotionally as well as in the 99¢ phone call, so that they are then more likely to follow up their investment with the purchase of an iTunes song, a single, an album or a ticket to a live performance. It is this ability to leverage audience participation into emotional investment and financial outlay that has allowed some *Idol* winners – such as Will Young of the first *Pop Idol* series or Kelly Clarkson of the first *American Idol* series – to overcome the often temporary nature of television celebrity and enter the bonafide pop music scene. The principle of leveraging audience investment extends to sponsorship deals, product integration and merchandising of the *Idol* brand. As Henry Jenkins has argued, *American Idol* deftly propagates 'affective economics', turning *Idol* fandom into consumer loyalty for its corporate partners like Coca-Cola (whose brand name and recognisable colours are ubiquitous in the graphics of the show), Ford (which makes ads with *American Idol* finalists) and Mars/M&M's (2006: 59–87). The aim of such integrated marketing is to deliver viewers, wallet in hand, to the multiple sales arms of the *Idol* franchise, which in turn operates as capitalist microcosm.

In a discursively important difference from *Popstars*, the *Idol* format places less emphasis on behind-the-scenes preparation and more emphasis on the live performance itself. This moves the show closer to the traditional talent format while amplifying the effects of televisual liveness and grounding the discourse of authenticity specific to reality television. In economic terms, the live performance means that audiences can turn their positive response to a song or a performer into a musical purchase, while the performer is still 'hot'. Televisual affect is thus channelled into music consumption, with both industries converging neatly around the moment of performance. Of course, in reality television 'performance' is itself an ambiguous term. On the one hand, it means the presentation of one's 'natural' abilities and skills (as when participants are praised for how well they performed in a challenge); on the other hand, it invokes the inauthenticity of acting and putting on a show for the camera. In *Idol*, however, these two contradictory meanings are reconciled, since the point is precisely to 'put on a show' to the best of one's 'natural' ability. Moreover, in the discourse of authenticity common to pop music (Marshall 1997: 150), the live performance privileges natural ability over the highly constructed and edited performance of a recording. In a *Daily Mail* article entitled 'Talent that Makes Even a Cynic's Heart Sing', for instance, *Pop Idol* judge and British record producer Pete Waterman 'repeatedly invoked the concept of live performance as a guarantee of authenticity', arguing that the live performance allowed *Idol* contestants to display their superior level of talent (Holmes 2004b: 156). Implicit in this claim is the presumption that only a live performance will reveal whether a contestant has the 'X factor', that indefinable element lying somewhere between charisma and musical talent that differentiates the proto-celebrity from the wannabes. In the rhetoric favoured by judges on *American Idol*, this indefinable element marks the distinction between 'real' music and contestants who are just 'doing karaoke'. The reference to karaoke suggests not only bland mimicry of someone else's performance – and hence an inauthentic rendition – but also a pastime engaged in by the mass of wannabes, the undifferentiated people of daily life. To stand out as a potential star, one has to be original (despite singing cover tunes), authentic (despite having been coached, styled and choreographed) and extraordinary (despite manifesting the ordinariness required of reality TV participants). To successfully negotiate these contradictions is to make the most of the live performance as a moment of authenticity for which one has *laboured*.

The *Idol* format, however, goes one step further. Like *Popstars* it self-consciously adds the role of industry professionals to the celebrity 'myth of success', which contends that stars are ordinary but talented people who have made the most of lucky breaks through hard work (Dyer 1998 [1979]: 42). By weighting the judging panel with a record company executive (famously, Simon Cowell from Sony BMG Music) in addition to music producers (e.g. Randy Jackson) and erstwhile pop celebrities (e.g. Paula Abdul), the *Idol* series positions the judges not only as experts but also as those who can open doors in the industry (a promise manifested by the top prize being a limited recording contract with Sony BMG Music). On *American Idol*, celebrity guest judges and mentors appear every week to coach contestants, with footage from these sessions interspersed between the live performances. In the tenth season of *American Idol* (2011), after a format overhaul following the departure of Simon Cowell, music executive Jimmy Iovine serves as the 'in-house mentor' for contestants, a position which places even greater emphasis on the fact that participants can achieve pop celebrity only by being *fashioned* by professionals. As Iovine told a press conference in January 2011, 'The kids can't just be told, "O.K., sing better." Someone has to work with them every week on performance, on style, and also *make the songs they do have some kind of originality* as well' (Stelter 2011; my emphasis). The suggestion here that originality is actually 'made' by producers – whether this means that originality is constructed or that it is forced out of contestants – provides a good example of the discursive contradictions at play in the reality talent form. At the same time, the ease with which this statement rolls off Iovine's tongue indicates that the success myth of discovered talent melds neatly with the 'manufacture-of-fame' narrative (Gamson 1994). Indeed, *Idol*'s systematic production of celebrity thrives on the interaction of these competing discourses (Holmes 2004b: 155).

While *Idol* is the most conspicuous example of the subgenre, all of the reality talent programmes – whether to do with singing, dancing, cooking or design – are about adding industry to raw talent with the aim of producing and promoting celebrity. The term 'industry' here has a number of meanings: it refers to hard work, or the labour of earning one's celebrity, but it also refers to the extensive organisation of reality TV formats whose business it is to make and circulate celebrity as a commodity, as well as to the intersection of leisure and style services with the celebrity-making machinery of television. There are, of course, industries other than music that produce celebrities. The film industry, especially with regard to the Hollywood studio system, has received significant scholarly attention (Dyer 1998 [1979]; de Cordova 1990; Gledhill 1991), but the striking shift in recent years has been the convergence of reality television with a range of sister industries to promote their celebrities and produce new ones.

The industries of choice for reality TV are those which already belong to the media entertainment network, at least as its offshoots, and which lend themselves to 'glam' visualisation: modelling, fashion design, hairstyling, etc. This process of 'glamming up' suits the dramatic story arc required by reality TV but also neatly overlays the manufacture-of-celebrity narrative. The person on *America's Next Top Model* who best glamourises herself in response to the advice of Tyra Banks and a clutch of industry professionals will (usually) survive to the next round, as will the designer on *Project Runway* whose work best replicates – with originality – the sartorial aesthetics of Heidi Klum, Michael Kors and Nina Garcia, an editor of the fashion magazine that sponsors the grand prize. The one apparent exception in this narrative of celebrity production may be the cooking shows, like *Top Chef* or *Master Chef*, since food production has not been part of the media entertainment complex nor does it require participants to 'glam up' to achieve celebrity. But, of course, there is a long television history of how-to cooking programmes led by celebrity chefs, from Julia Child onward. Moreover, the talent-format cooking shows have developed in tandem with the recent explosion in the TV industry of on-air food preparation, restauranteurism and celebrity chefs, some of whom have themselves become industries with their own dizzying array of food labels, merchandise, books, DVDs and TV shows (e.g. Jamie Oliver). The talent-based cooking shows follow the same format as *Idol* or *America's Next Top Model*, similarly using expert panels to promote existing celebrities while seeking to produce the next celebrity chef. The only difference is that the participants' glam narrative is experienced through the visualisation of the food rather than their own or others' bodies. Of course, with so many shows in the business of producing celebrity, many of these newly minted reality TV stars simply become B-listers (or less) on casual contract in the media economy, as we shall see later in the chapter.

## Celebrity Wanted: No Talent Required

Reality talent shows represent only one aspect of the celebrity-making machinery of reality TV. Rather than being associated with the promotion of talent, after all, reality television has the opposite reputation, as a magnet for talentless wannabes who will do anything for a chance to be on TV. Richard M. Huff makes this a central point in his introduction to *Reality Television*: 'this new form of television has transformed everyday people with a hankering for attention into media stars. Many have little talent, leading to the suggestion that a willingness to make a fool of oneself is now enough to become a TV star' (2006: x). Huff's emphasis on 'new' and 'now' ascribes a revolutionary character to reality television based on its ability to transform ordinary people into celebrities, even if – or precisely because – this has little to do with their talent. All that seems to be required for celebrity is 'a hankering for attention', a will to be *seen* rather than having anything to be seen *for*. But this formulation is perhaps less revolutionary than Huff suggests, given how closely it recalls Daniel Boorstin's oft-repeated definition of the celebrity as 'a person who is well-known for his [*sic*] well-knownness', and hence is a 'human pseudo-event' without substance or qualities (1992: 57). Boorstin made this claim in 1961 as part of his indictment of the culture of artifice in 1950s America, where 'talk about "images"' was replacing 'talk about "ideals"' (1992: 181). Fifty years later, this indictment still has critical force. It provides the backdrop for the countless scathing critiques about the wash of supposedly talentless people on reality TV, critiques which manifest a grave sense of injustice that the reality apparatus produces celebrity out of 'nothing' – no talent, no just deserts, no exceptionality. Against this, some commentators celebrate the 'democratization of fame' by media (Braudy 1997), arguing that it gives everyone – at least in the abstract – the opportunity to achieve celebrity, while others point out that the rhetoric of equal opportunity simply masks the pervasive inequality of 'market meritocracy' (Tyler and Bennett 2010: 379). Whether or not it celebrates fools, reality television operates as a discursive terrain on which contemporary arguments about social recognition, status and cultural legitimation are vociferously played out.

While the celebrification of 'everyday people' may be most visible – and most derided – on reality TV, no television genre operates in a vacuum. Rather, discourses about ordinariness and celebrity traverse reality television, linking it to larger communication practices and positioning it within hierarchies of cultural and political value. Graeme Turner has convincingly argued that reality television is part of 'the demotic turn' of recent media culture, in which factual television, Web 2.0 and talk radio present ever greater opportunities for ordinary people to appear in the media (Turner 2004, 2010). Turner's study of the 'demotic turn' expands on what Jon Dovey investigated a decade earlier under the heading of 'first-person media' (2000). As both Dovey and Turner note, however, demotic (which means 'common people') is not necessarily the same thing as democratic, which refers to a political system based on equal representation of the people. The simple appearance of 'common people' in the media does not necessarily reflect equal representation, for visibility alone says nothing about either the political economic structures in which that visibility is achieved or the selection criteria for and content of what is made visible. While the Marxist cultural critic Walter Benjamin, writing in the 1930s, saw the political potential of demotic visibility in 'modern man's legitimate claim to being reproduced' on film (2006: 28), he also found that the common people's right to 'portray *themselves*' was denied by 'the capitalistic exploitation' of the European and Hollywood film industries (ibid.; original emphasis).

Jumping ahead seventy years, Benjamin would surely find a far greater degree of capitalistic exploitation in the current celebrity industry, where ordinary people arguably do not portray themselves so much as turn themselves into media content (Turner 2010: 2). Considered in terms of political economy, the relation between television and ordinariness can be characterised as one of mutual exploitation, where people with 'a hankering for attention' use reality TV for a chance at stardom, while reality TV thrives on 'ordinary people desiring "celebrification"' (Turner 2010: 13). In this view, celebrity depoliticises ordinariness, and reality television in particular is caught in the crosshairs. Depending equally on discourses of the ordinary and technologies of saturated surveillance, reality TV succeeds in fulfilling neither the political potential of the 'common people' nor the shimmery abstraction of 'true' celebrity. It thus holds a low ranking in the hierarchies of cultural value, which rubs off on its producers and participants. At the same time, reality TV's serialised, intensely intimate visualisation of individuals exposes the often ambiguous processes of celebrity production and reception. It reveals, as we shall see, the way in which particular combinations of identity attributes – gender, class, race/ethnicity, social role, even talent – come to be valued as the making, or undoing, of celebrity.

As a basis for the discussion of making celebrity out of 'nothing' on reality TV, we should note that there is a major difference between the reality talent and 'no talent' formats. While the goal of the talent formats is to produce celebrity as a commodity, the no-talent formats produce celebrity only as a *contingent* outcome, of interest to participants but not to producers. Indeed, casting directors often claim they look for people who do *not* want an industry career, since this makes them more 'ordinary' and hence more accessible for audiences (Turner 2004: 60). Although the celebrity effect is now an expected outcome of being on reality TV, it initially came as a surprise to producers and participants. Certainly, in the early 1970s the sudden celebrity status of the Loud family from *An American Family* (see Chapter 1) was a curious and uncomfortable side effect of making the documentary; as Lance Loud, the eldest son, later wittily put it, 'In 1970, television ate my family'.[7] In the crime and lifestyle formats of the early to mid-1990s, it was not uncommon for presenters like John Walsh of *America's Most Wanted* or Laurence Llewellyn-Bowen of *Changing Rooms* to gain celebrity, but their status as media professionals on popular shows made their celebrity a part of the programming strategy. It was not until the British docusoaps of the late 1990s that ordinary people, like the hapless Maureen Rees of *Driving School* on UK television, suddenly became household names (see Chapter 2). What was contingent about this occurrence was not only that the programme producers did not intend or control this production of celebrity, but also that no one could say in advance *which* reality TV participants would capture the public imagination. Removing talent as well as programming strategy from the equation meant that neither of the two celebrity narratives isolated by Gamson (1994) – the meritocratic or the manufactured – could predict or explain this new kind of celebrity.

The double contingency of unexpected celebrity bestowed on an unlikely person came to a head with the introduction of *Big Brother*. Given the massive ratings for early *Big Brother* series in various countries (see Chapter 3), it is perhaps no surprise that winners of the programme gained public visibility and received media attention. What did come as a surprise, however, was the *degree* and *objects* of this attention. Zlatko Trpkovski of the first German *Big Brother* (2000), Sara-Marie Fedele of *Big Brother 1* in Australia (2001) and Jade Goody of *Big Brother 3* in the UK (2002) all became widely recognised celebrities in their respective countries, even though none of them won their series and despite the fact that all three were treated as love-hate figures who, for many commentators, heralded the end of civilisation as we know it. Zlatko was evicted by public vote from the German Big Brother house in the fourth round, but on his exit he was greeted by several thousand people screaming so loudly that it left him and the studio crew dazed. Zlatko's popularity was even more incomprehensible in that he was known to viewers as the uneducated, tattooed auto mechanic from Macedonia who was outspoken and had never heard of Shakespeare. Jade in the UK had an unrivalled reputation for being ignorant and loud-mouthed, so much so that she was the target of a cruel hate campaign by the tabloid press before a sudden change of tone and heart turned her into 'the divine Ms Jade Goody' (*The Mirror*, cited in 'The Jade Goody Phenomenon' (2007)). Somewhat less dramatically, Sara-Marie, who had been nominated for eviction six times before finally being voted out, was greeted on her exit with screams of adoration by a nation keen on replicating her joyful 'bum dance' in pink pyjamas and bunny ears. None of these sudden celebrities could be described as having talent. On the contrary, the very thing they became famous for – ignorance, malapropisms, turning one's bottom to the camera and slapping it – could be better described as 'anti-talent'. It was as though the public imagination had been captured by precisely those attributes which resisted meritocratic definitions of celebrity.

That celebrity can arise from qualities other than merit is not a new idea among theorists of celebrity. Writing in the late 1970s, James

Monaco (1978) divided celebrity status into the 'hero', or the person who has done something to merit recognition; the 'star', or the media icon whom the public wants to see performing as him/herself rather than acting in a role; and the 'quasar', or the person who has become famous but has 'virtually no control over his or her image' (Marshall 1997: 16). This last category draws attention to celebrity as an effect of publicity rather than a status that has been merited, such as Monaco's examples of Patty Hearst, the media heiress kidnapped by terrorists in the 1970s, or Che Guevara, who might in the right time and place have been a 'hero' but whose iconic image on posters and T-shirts has made him into a 'quasar' (cited in Marshall 1997: 16–17). Chris Rojek also adopts a tripartite categorisation of celebrity, but he takes as his starting point the fact that 'celebrity status always implies a split between a private self and a public self' (2001: 11). Within this split, Rojek distinguishes between 'ascribed' celebrity, or fame inherited through blood relations (e.g. the royal family); 'achieved' celebrity, which is akin to Monaco's hero but emphasises 'the perceived accomplishments of the individual in open competition'; and 'attributed' celebrity, which results from 'the concentrated representation of an individual as noteworthy or exceptional by cultural intermediaries' (2001: 18). There is a similarity between Monaco's 'quasar' and Rojek's 'attributed celebrity' in that both address celebrity as an effect, but Rojek extends celebrity attribution to include the 'concentrated representation' generated by the media. This media product is what Rojek calls a 'celetoid', defined as an inevitable accessory of 'cultures organised around mass communications and staged authenticity' (2001: 20–1). The celetoid is distinguished by the brevity of his/her celebrity – here today, forgotten tomorrow – and is thus not only a literal product of cultural intermediaries like publicists but also a result of the interchangeability of commodities that defines late capitalism.

We will return to the evanescence of celebrity, but for the moment it is worth noting the ways in which the celetoid model does and does *not* fit the reality TV star. On the one hand, the ordinary person made famous by reality TV has gained 'a media-generated, compressed, concentrated form of attributed celebrity' (Rojek 2001: 18) which is the product of cultural intermediaries, from stylists to producers to agents. The reality TV participant's fame, moreover, is likely to be short lived. Rojek is also prescient in highlighting 'staged authenticity' as a condition for the manufacture of the reality TV star. What does not quite fit, however, is the idea that this individual is represented 'as noteworthy or exceptional'. As we have seen, the no-talent formats insist on ordinariness rather than exceptionality; the celebrity that arises from these formats is only noteworthy in terms of his/her anti-talent, or ordinariness in a negative sense. If anything, the exceptional-ity of the reality TV star kicks in only *after* the programme has ended and the struggle to maintain – and capitalise on – celebrity has begun.

Of the hundreds of participants appearing in *Big Brother* series in Germany, Australia and the UK – not to mention the tens of thou-sands who have appeared in reality television shows worldwide in the last decade – Zlatko, Sara-Marie and Jade stand out as exceptional examples of celebrity for two reasons. First, they arrived on the scene before celebrity was a taken-for-granted effect of reality TV, so their emergence as celebrities runs parallel with the emergence of the phenomenon of reality TV celebrity itself. Second, these three were amongst the first to leverage their *Big Brother* fame into media and merchandising contracts *after* the programme ended. Zlatko released two CD singles that went platinum and a best-selling album (pointedly called *I'm staying the way I am*) as well as appearing on TV shows and starring in a short-lived docusoap (*Zlatko's World*). Sara-Marie released a humour book, a CD single and a successful line of sleepwear (an offshoot of the pyjamas she wore in the *Big Brother* house), as well as appearing on Australia's *Celebrity Big Brother* (2002) and *Dancing with the Stars* (2005). The best known of the three, Jade Goody, arguably went on to set the standard for what it would mean to be a 'reality TV star'. She fronted reality shows about her own life (for LivingTV), appeared as a presenter or participant on numerous other programmes (including a stint on the UK *Celebrity Big Brother* in 2007 that caused national uproar (see Holmes 2009)), made a series of fitness DVDs, launched a perfume and – by the time of her death from cervical cancer in 2009 – wrote four autobiographies. By early 2007, less than five years after her initial appearance on *Big Brother*, an article pub-lished in *The Independent* bemoaned Goody's ubiquitous celebrity and astounding earnings:

> She is worth up to £4m; it is impossible to switch on a television without her featuring on some satellite channel somewhere; she is never out of the red-tops. She even has her own best-selling perfume. So how did this remarkable transformation come about? ('The Jade Goody Phenomenon' 2007)

This is a question worth asking, not least because it applies equally to Goody's own transformation through media celebrity as well as to the transformations in celebrity culture wrought by reality TV. If Goody's transformation from 2002 to 2007 involved the addition of celebrity to what appeared to be the dregs of ordinariness then celebrity culture in that same time frame underwent the inverse transformation, adding dreadful ordinariness to traditionally elevated notions of celebrity.

Every culture has its own terms for imagining the 'dregs' of ordinariness, a phrase I am using to capture the widespread disdain for participants who appear in no-talent formats, especially those who seem unjustly to have been promoted to public visibility. Celebrity is always about social status, but whereas earlier phases of celebrity culture measured status in terms of heights above the average (hence the term 'star' to denote those who inhabit the heavens, above the rest of us), the recent turn to ordinariness has plumbed the depths below, adding a C-list, D-list and even Z-list to the rankings. In the UK, such hierarchies are inextricably linked to discourses and meanings of social class. Arguing against claims that social class is no longer relevant to contemporary consumer society, Imogen Tyler and Bruce Bennett, writing in a British context, argue that 'class remains central to the constitution and meaning of celebrity' (2010: 376). They even define celebrity in terms of class, as 'a class pantomime through which the establishment of social hierarchies and processes of social abjection . . . are acted out figuratively' (ibid.). In this class-based staging of celebrity, Tyler and Bennett are particularly fascinated by a recent construction they refer to as 'the celebrity chav', where 'chav' is slang for young members of the white working class who are 'shiftless, tasteless, unintelligent, immoral or criminal' (2010: 379). Crucially, their examples of the celebrity chav – Jade Goody and Kerry Katona, to which we could easily add Katie Price – emphasise the role of reality TV in propelling these unlikely figures into public visibility and unexpected wealth. (Katona, who had been a minor celebrity in the band Atomic Kitten and then a television presenter, became highly visible when she won *I'm a Celebrity, Get Me Out of Here* in 2004. In that same season of *I'm a Celebrity*, former topless model Katie Price, a.k.a. Jordan, was propelled to fame when she began a relationship with pop singer Peter Andre, whom she later married.)

It is not just that these 'chav' figures come from a working-class background. Rather, they fascinate the public because they represent the *underclass* of the stalwart working classes, in ways that are now tied to media hypervisibility. For the celebrity chav, the social decorum of class-based discretion is traded in for the spoils of media attention, with the events of the celebrity chavs' upbringing and private lives obsessively repeated in the press and auto/biographies like a national bedtime story. As *The Guardian* interviewer Simon Hattenstone noted archly about his interview with Katie Price, those who are acquainted with *OK!* Magazine . . . know all about the cosmetic surgery, the rubbish boyfriends, the feuds with Victoria Beckham, the abuse she once suffered as a child at the hands of a stranger, the occasional threesome, the abortion, the jungle, the televised courtship, the televised marriage, the miscarriage, the postnatal depression, her disabled son, Harvey, and Pete's 'cockalicious' trouser snake. (2008)

Tyler and Bennett point out, moreover, that the hypervisibility of the chav draws on an intersection between categories of class and gender (2010: 380–2). Usually female, the celebrity chav is coded in the recognisable terms of monstrous femininity; she has an unruly body of too-large proportions, either because she struggles with weight, has surgically enhanced body parts, flaunts her sexuality, or – in the case of Jade Goody – all of the above. The technology of intense visualisation on which reality TV thrives, and through which celebrity is produced, is thus read as obscene exhibitionism in the figure of the chav. Flaunting her body, her ignorance and her prejudices, she maintains a celebrity career only by dint of being the 'bad object', according to Tyler and Bennett, that mobilises viewer community through 'class hatred' (2010: 379). Certainly, during her appearance on *Celebrity Big Brother* in 2007 Jade Goody notoriously caused national outrage – not to mention national soul-searching – when she fired racial epithets at fellow housemate and Bollywood star Shilpa Shetty (see Holmes 2009). Indicating just how much reality TV can matter in the 'real' world, the fall-out was serious: Goody lost media and merchandising contracts, Channel 4 cancelled the next season of *Celebrity Big Brother*, and then Prime Minister Gordon Brown made a public apology on behalf of Britain in India. As Su Holmes notes about the outcry, it 'became quickly apparent that the articulation of classism and sexism were more "acceptable" than racism to many British commentators' (2009: par. 5), which is to say that the public condemnation of Goody's racism was frequently expressed in the unselfconscious terms of misogyny and class hatred.

At the same time, celebrity culture is nothing if not mutable. This applies to both the social status of anti-talent celebrities as well as their availability for recoding as figures of empowerment. Anita Biressi and Heather Nunn, writing in the British context in 2004, have convincingly argued that celebrity through reality TV makes available 'the sartorial and material signifiers of class transformation', which 'mark both working-class origins and the move away from them' (2005: 145–6). Celebrity is thus a route to social mobility played out through what

Biressi and Nunn call 'classed cross-dressing' (2004: 145). Goody's media career is exemplary of this cross-dressing, but the shifting public reception and representation of Goody also indicates the mutability of celebrity status itself. After nearly ruining her career on *Celebrity Big Brother*, Goody began the painstaking process of recuperating herself, which included public apologies to Shilpa Shetty, a 2008 appearance on Living TV's *Living with* . . . series and a planned stint on India's *Bigg Boss*, an Indian *Big Brother* hosted by Shetty. The success of the recuperation campaign is difficult to measure, since Goody left *Bigg Boss* on the second day, having learned (on camera) of her diagnosis with cervical cancer, which was then also incorporated into the *Living with Jade* episode. Once she regained media interest as a result of her illness, Goody never left the public eye. In fact, she found herself at the centre of a maelstrom of competing celebrity discourses, with public opinion torn between harsh criticism of her self-commodification and sentimental sanctification of her role as mother to two young boys and public advocate for cervical screenings (Kavka and West 2010). Arguably, the respect owed to the dying won out, and Goody was lauded for the dignity and courage she showed as she went into terminal decline. What is of particular interest in this celebrity trajectory is not simply the ups and downs that were compressed into less than a decade but also the fact that Goody managed to live out the *mutable* fortunes of celebrity at the same time as she mobilised discourses of *authenticity*. Goody was equally excused and excoriated for 'being herself', which is precisely the paradoxical condition of ordinary-celebrity that Goody helped bring into being. It was this ability to 'be herself', despite class expectations and social strictures, that made her available for recoding as a figure of self-empowerment, as someone in whom the *demos*, the common people, could invest their own fantasies of anti-elitism.[8]

   I pointed out earlier that every culture has its own way of imagining the 'dregs' of ordinariness and configuring the fantasies of populist empowerment that such ordinariness might represent. This does not always occur strictly in terms of class. In the US, for instance, where the myth of the American Dream in a classless society prevails, the negative side of ordinariness is more likely to be expressed through particular intersections of race, regionality and religion.[9] In Germany, the situation is different again. The anti-talent of the original ordinary celebrity of German *Big Brother*, Zlatko Trpkovski, was marked in terms of his ethnicity and (lack of) education. On the one hand, the celebrification of Trpkovski allowed viewers to imagine a 'new' unified Germany that would have room for an accented Macedonian immigrant, as a recuperation of Germany's racist past. On the other hand, Trpkovski's outspokenness was read as an expression of authenticity, as confirmed by research with focus groups carried out by the Rheingold Institute: 'In contrast to the other *Big Brother* housemates, Zlatko turns out to be a non-conformist with the courage to call a spade a spade, without concern for possible consequences, and to say what he thinks, what he likes and what he finds tedious' (Grüne n.d.; my translation). This outspoken authenticity, when combined with his ignorance of Shakespeare, became a mark of his freedom from the oppressive strictures of a society that measures success in terms of education and achievement. In effect, Zlatko became 'a stand-in for the many viewers who in their daily lives could not or would not dare to admit that Shakespeare's language is incomprehensible twaddle' (ibid.). He thus offered viewers the opportunity to recode his 'authenticity' as resistance to the norms of behaviour and social success: 'While others achieve success by working at it, his talent consists in just successfully being himself' (ibid.).

This brings us back to our two key terms in this section: talent and ordinariness. It is worth noting that in the focus groups on German *Big Brother* carried out by Rheingold, the researchers found that viewers saw Zlatko as a stand-in, literally a deputy (*Stellvertreter*), for themselves. He thus functioned, in an important sense, as their representative in an implicit confrontation with a social hierarchy determined by levels of education and occupation. Although Zlatko's celebrity was short-lived, his name is still recognised in Germany as an icon of resistance and anti-elitist achievement. It is true that social structures do not change as a result of the visibility of the ordinary celebrity – at least not explicitly – but at the same time we should not discount the political potential of the imagined selves that are animated by the anti-talented celebrity stand-in.

## Celebreality and the Art of Celebrity Maintenance

No discussion of celebrity and reality television would be complete without considering the range of celebrity formats, which arguably constitute the core of third-generation reality TV. Unlike the talent or no-talent formats, the celebrity shows dispense with the appeal of ordinary people in favour of participants who already have name or face recognition, usually because of their place in entertainment, sports or even politics. There is a particular limitation on celebrity in these formats, however, for the celebrities never come from the A-list (or even B-list).[10] They tend to be 'minor' celebrities, or what

Gareth Palmer calls the D-list, which he defines as 'a space between the unknown mass of ordinary people and the celebrity' (2005: 41). Considered in temporal terms, the participants on these shows are people whose fame is in flux; they are either on their way down and out, like the ageing/fading star, or on their way up from obscurity, like the pop starlet or reality TV star. The celebrity-making apparatus of reality television is here put to a particular use; it does not fabricate celebrity out of 'nothing' so much as foster the increase of a pre-existing dose of fame. I am using the language of quantity deliberately to highlight the fact that these shows participate in an economy of maximising value: the exposure gained from reality TV increases the celebrity value of the participants in direct proportion to the popularity of the programme, while the programme increases its ratings and market value in direct proportion to the popularity of the celebrity participants. This sets up a relation of mutual benefit – also called a win-win situation – in which both the celebrities and the show attempt to heighten their own commodity value through an association with the value of the other. For instance, during the finale of the US *The Celebrity Apprentice 3*, Australian celebrity chef Curtis Stone – who had probably taken part in the programme to increase his profile with American audiences – was congratulated by Donald Trump for securing a clutch of publicity deals, including a spot on the judging panel of NBC's newly announced *America's Next Great Restaurant*. Stone jokingly offered Trump 10 per cent of his earnings, in recognition of *The Celebrity Apprentice*'s role in raising his commodity value – to which Trump shot back with a demand for 25 per cent.

Traversing this win-win economy is another, indispensable logic, which aims to increase the participants' celebrity status by paradoxically representing their ordinary, real-person qualities. This revelation of ordinariness nods to the backstage effect of reality TV, but in the celebrity formats the 'behind the scenes' view does not necessarily expose the mechanics of celebrity production; rather, it is instrumental in fostering and maintaining celebrity by offering intimate access to the stars. In his book *Celebrity and Power*, P. David Marshall argues that the institution of television positions celebrity very differently to the film industry, because on television 'celebrity is configured around conceptions of familiarity' (1997: 119). In contrast to the film celebrity, whose magical aura of unattainability is sustained by emphasising distance from the audience, the television celebrity 'embodies the characteristics of familiarity and mass acceptability' (ibid.). In making this claim, Marshall echoes John Ellis, who distinguishes between the film celebrity as a 'star', constructed through competing discourses of distance and closeness, and the television celebrity as a 'personality' who 'exists very much more in the same space as the television audience, as a known and familiar person' (Ellis 1992: 106). Although Ellis was writing before the era of reality television, Su Holmes points out the suitability of these discursive constructions for the genre: 'if familiarity and ordinariness are fundamental to the construction of televisual fame, then reality TV, in fact, exemplifies this rhetoric to the extreme' (2004b: 152). It is for this reason that reality TV can serve to normalise celebrity, bringing stars into close and familiar quarters. This normalisation of celebrity is necessary to what John Ellis, borrowing from Roland Barthes, calls the 'photo effect' of celebrity, an oscillation between ordinariness and extraordinariness, between presence and absence that makes celebrities both accessible and unattainable to fans (1992: 97).

In and of itself, this is nothing new, since the function of normalising the celebrity is performed by women's magazines, the tabloid press, talk shows (where celebrities can 'be themselves') and most recently celebrities' own Twitter accounts (where they can share their thoughts, just 'like us'). None of the other media avenues for making a star ordinary, however, not even Twitter, offers the sustained, intimate access of a reality TV series, which invites viewers to enter celebrities' lives over the course of weeks or even months. This long-form normalisation creates intimacy but also causes a loss of the aura supported by distance: in being made ordinary, the celebrity on reality television is hyper-familiarised, shown sprawling on a couch and being lazy, stupid, bitchy, etc. We might take this one step further: if familiarity breeds contempt, and reality TV sits at the devalued end of the cultural spectrum, then the cost of access to the celebrity apparatus of reality TV must be the perpetual possibility of audience affection slipping into audience contempt. The reality TV celebrity, not to mention his/her cultural intermediaries, must constantly navigate this unstable affective terrain.

This difficult terrain is home to the denizens of the D-list, a category which can springboard its occupants into the B-list or, more likely, serve as 'a cautionary tale of representations of the ordinary' (Palmer 2005: 45). For Palmer, the denizens of the D-list are the 'replaceable, expendable, interchangeable units of celebrity' (2005: 44). They are the people most susceptible to realising Andy Warhol's promise that 'in the future, everyone will be world-famous for 15 minutes' as little more than a threat of impending obscurity. Chris Rojek also touches on the turnover temporality of celebrity, but he links it to the machinery of desire at the capitalist base of celebrity culture. For Rojek, a necessary part of every capitalist system is the exchangeability of commodities, which drives consumers to continue to want and buy more things; when celebrity is one such commodity, then it too must be exchangeable. The competitive principle in capitalism thus not only leads producers to maximise their market share (Rojek 2001: 188), but also 'renews celebrity culture and elicits the transference of desire to new celebrity figures' (Rojek 2001: 197). Caught in this loop of consumption, fans, or the end-users of celebrity, thus experience an 'abstract desire' in relation to celebrities. This desire is abstract because, first, it operates at a distance, without face-to-face contact; second, it is alienable, meaning that the logic of capitalism requires it to be transferable from one commodity to the next; and third, it is subconscious, open to manipulation but not strict regulation by either the systems of celebrity production or the fans/ end-users themselves. Through this notion of abstract desire, Rojek connects the evanescent temporality of celebrity to the spatiality of distance and the logic of capital and the economy of desire. This undercuts claims that television celebrity is always about familiarity, since constructions of distance are at play in abstract desire, but it also undermines D-list gloom-mongering that reality TV celebrities can only elicit contempt and condemnation. Rather, reality TV is able to mobilise the affections involved in abstract desire as well as the instabilities. And, like capitalism, it is able to keep going on the principle of transferability. Celebrity reality TV thus offers to write the next chapter in the manufacture-of-fame narrative described by Gamson (1994). Once fame is manufactured, the pressing question is, how does one keep up celebrity in an overcrowded marketplace? The answer: go on a reality TV show – and then another and another.

We should note that there are two quite different types of formats that fall under the heading of celebrity reality TV. In keeping with the split between observational reality shows, in which cameras follow participants in their 'natural habitat', and situationist shows, in which participants are brought into constructed environments, the celebrity formats have developed along similar lines. On one side are those shows we might call the celebrity docusoap, in which cameras capture celebrities in their own environments (e.g. *Scott Baio is 45 . . . and Single* (VH1, 2007)), and on the other are programmes that function as celebrity versions of constructed-environment formats (e.g. *Celebrity Big Brother*). Coincidentally, both of these types of celebrity reality TV initially appeared in 2002, with MTV in the US screening the celebrity docusoap *The Osbournes* and ITV in the UK trialling *I'm a Celebrity . . . Get Me Out of Here!*

Innovation-conscious MTV pitched *The Osbournes* as 'the first reality sitcom' (Morreale 2003), making explicit the permeability between factual and fictional programming that had been suggested as far back as the *Brady Bunch*-like opening credits of *An American Family* (see Chapter 1). Self-consciously exploiting the hybridisation of documentary and fiction, *The Osbournes* began as a popular 2000 segment of *Cribs*, the MTV show on which celebrities show off their luxurious homes, before morphing into a docusoap series framed by the aesthetics and narrative strategies of 1950s/1960s US sitcoms. Despite the updating of family values to include the 'ignominious bodies' (Kompare 2004) and foul language of ageing rock musician Ozzy Osbourne and his brood, Derek Kompare notes the genealogical links between *The Osbournes* and *An American Family* (and, we might add, *Sylvania Waters* (see Chapter 1)), which in the early 1970s attempted to investigate the 'real' family by setting it within and against the generic codes of television fiction. The difference between then and now, of course, lies in the celebrity element: for MTV, the draw-card was Ozzy Osbourne's iconic (if somewhat faded) reputation as a hell-raising heavy metal rocker prone to biting the heads off living things on stage. By resituating Ozzy as 'the Dad' of sitcom history, the show milked the irony of the gap between old-fashioned, fictional family values and current, actual family practices, as well as humorously highlighting the labour that goes into maintaining celebrity reputation (as Ozzy complains to his wife when he sees the set for an upcoming stage show, 'I'm the Prince of fucking Darkness, Sharon, I can't have bubbles!' (season 1, episode 5)). At the same time, Kompare is right to point out that the 'hook' of the programme lies in the fact that 'the family somehow still functions as a normative, loving unit' (2004: 108), not unlike the juxtaposition of crass behaviour and sentimental relationships exploited so successfully by *The Simpsons* (Gray 2006: 55–65). *The Osbournes* thereby insists on the continuity of family values from then to now, from television to 'real' life, and from the ordinary to the celebrity.

By the middle of its first season, the programme was MTV's all-time highest-rated series[11] (Kompare 2004: 97) and its popularity soon led to imitations that confirmed the arrival of the celebrity docusoap. Although there have since been few 'reality sitcoms' and none that achieved the success of *The Osbournes*,[12] the celebrity docusoap has spawned a monstrously rich tradition. From the derided *The Anna Nicole Show* (E!, 2002–3) with former Playboy Playmate and notorious May–December bride Anna Nicole Smith, to the surprise hit *Newlyweds: Nick and Jessica* (MTV, 2003–5) and more recent E!

favourites such as *Keeping Up with the Kardashians* and its multiple Kim/Khloe/Kourtney spin-offs, all of these programmes take minor celebrities from the world of music, modelling or sports and increase their visibility and commodity value by purportedly revealing who they are 'at home'. Moreover, all of these shows present a carefully modulated public face as the 'real' personality, balancing the generic conventions of television with the 'raw' appeal of documentary aesthetics. Pop starlet Jessica Simpson, for instance, cultivated her 'dumb blonde' image (or had it cultivated for her) so successfully on *The Newlyweds: Nick and Jessica* that by the end of the first season she had become a household name. She then parlayed her increased celebrity value into a re-release of her album *In this Skin* in 2004 and the role of dumb-blonde Daisy Duke in the 2005 blockbuster *The Dukes of Hazzard* – itself a film remake of a popular early 1980s US TV series, which contributed to the cultural construction of the dumb blonde that Simpson mobilised in her reality show.

The second major type of celebrity format is the celebrity repurposing of a constructed environment format. Although the premise first appeared as a celebrity version of the UK *Big Brother* in March 2001, this initial short series was intended by broadcaster Channel 4 as a one-off tie-in with the BBC's Comic Relief charity appeal in that year. As a format concept, the actual progenitor of the celebrity challenge series appeared in the UK in August 2002 with the first season of *I'm a Celebrity . . . Get Me Out of Here!* Far less mould breaking than *The Osbournes*, *I'm a Celebrity* is less about innovation than about repetition with a celebrity twist. Admittedly, it is not strictly a spin-off of a prior 'ordinary' series, like *Celebrity Big Brother*, but the idea of placing ten people in a jungle to survive in the wild while undergoing challenges and facing elimination no doubt proved familiar. In fact, Castaway Productions, owners of the worldwide copyright to *Survivor*, sued the Granada Media Group (producers of *I'm a Celebrity*) for copyright infringement in 2002, quickly followed by CBS filing an injunction against ABC to prevent it from producing or broadcasting the US version of *I'm a Celebrity* (both attempts failed) (Billings 2002: 'CBS loses fight'). The repeated element in *I'm a Celebrity* and other shows of this type is the recognisable format of placing people in a particular constructed situation; the twist, however, is that these shows place celebrities in the spots that ordinary people would otherwise occupy. The celebrity is thus literally made ordinary, not by revealing how he/she might behave 'at home', as on the celebrity docusoap, but rather the obverse: the claim to authenticity in the celebrity competitive format lies in putting celebrities in an unfamiliar situation, under stress, in order to show who they 'really' are. *I'm a Celebrity . . . Get Me Out of Here!*, in its title alone, draws attention to the appeal of status-mixing: as celebrities, the participants should presumably not have to spend two weeks living in a jungle camp on the Australian Gold Coast undergoing tests of fitness and gastronomic endurance, but these are minor, or D-list, celebrities and their prize is the chance to raise their public profile and resuscitate an often flagging career.

The notion of a challenge in which celebrities become ordinary through their struggle with an unfamiliar setting is also the driving force of *Strictly Come Dancing/Dancing with the Stars*. Launched in 2004, six years after the end of the long-running ballroom dancing competition show *Come Dancing* (BBC, 1949–98), *Strictly Come Dancing* (BBC, 2004–) pairs celebrities from television, music and sports with professional ballroom dancers to learn and perform a new dance every week before a panel of judges. Although the participants have celebrity status, the fact that they have to do something in which they have no experience – ballroom dancing – makes them ordinary, on a level with the rest of 'us'. This format has proven so popular with audiences, who have a vote in the weekly elimination rounds, that it has resulted in numerous spin-off specials and been licensed to over thirty countries, as well as generating a great deal of discussion in the press and on websites. Although the participants on *Strictly Come Dancing* also arguably hail from the D-List, these celebrity anti-talent dancers tend to generate more respect and affection among audiences than the participants on *I'm a Celebrity*. While the celebrities on the latter are associated with tawdriness and tabloid fodder (as exempli-fied by season 3, which gave rise to the very public relationship of Katie Price and Peter Andre), the TV presenters, soap actresses and singers of *Strictly Come Dancing* are seen to be investing labour week after week, resulting in impressive dance moves and newly trim physiques (e.g. Kelly Osbourne of *Dancing with the Stars* and Pamela Stephenson of *Strictly Come Dancing*). This is not exactly an exposure of the mechanisms of celebrity maintenance but it does resound with the age-old success myth of celebrity: hard work produces success, and success translates into celebrity value. This venerated formula also explains why politicians are sometimes to be found participat-ing in this format, such as then ACT party leader Rodney Hide on New Zealand's *Dancing with the Stars* (TVNZ, 2005–9) or ex-Shadow Home Secretary Ann Widdecombe on season 8 of *Strictly Come Dancing* (2010).

To return to economics, two final points should be taken into con-sideration. First, the celebrity challenge format is a repurposing of the ordinary format not only because it replaces ordinary participants with celebrities but also because it replaces the individual econom- ics of prize-winning with the social economics of charitable giving. The celebrities are presumed to have enough money of their own (although they do receive an undisclosed 'lost earnings' stipend on *I'm a Celebrity*) and hence, in the neoliberal economy where private dona- tions compensate for a weakened welfare state, they become a magnet for attracting money out of the private system and channelling it to charities. This began with the first series of *Celebrity Big Brother*, whose aim was to provide publicity for the BBC's Comic Relief telethon, but it has continued in some form with most celebrity challenge formats; on *I'm a Celebrity* and *Strictly Come Dancing*, for instance, the money earned from phone-in voting goes to a particular charity each season. In a programme like *The Celebrity Apprentice*, each celebrity represents a particular charity and any money earned by that celebrity as project manager goes to his/her charity. As with other celebrity challenge formats, *The Celebrity Apprentice*, which appears only in a US version with Donald Trump, relies heavily on the sentimentalised discourse of giving while masking the commodification of the celebrities them- selves. In the studio finale of each season, celebrities are given the chance to thank Trump for the opportunity to raise money for their deserving cause. The fact that, for instance, Cyndi Lauper of the third season was also invited to perform a single from her newly released album during the finale is not discussed.

The second point about the economics of these programmes is that celebrity has become more than a career choice; it is now big, multi- media business. Writing in 2004, Graeme Turner points out that 'celebrity is increasingly possible as a career option' (2004: 63), but he is referring specifically to reality TV celebrity as a career option for 'ordinary' people. What changes in the third-generation reality pro- grammes is that reality TV becomes a viable career option for celebri- ties themselves. Rather than being a springboard into media celebrity, reality TV is now instrumental in sustaining the field of media celeb- rity itself. Sharon Osbourne provides a good case in point. Although she had worked in the media industry as a music manager since taking over Ozzy's management in her late teens, she was unknown to a wider audience at the start of the series *The Osbournes*. After the success of two seasons of *The Osbournes*, she became a judge on *The X-Factor* and later *America's Got Talent*, before hosting *Rock of Love: Charm School* and appearing as a grande dame on *The Celebrity Apprentice*. Her daughter Kelly Osbourne followed up *The Osbournes* with minor pop stardom before making a career- and body-changing appearance on

*Dancing with the Stars* season 9; losing her trademark plumpness, she gained red-carpet credence and a contract to join Joan Rivers presenting *The Fashion Police* (E!, 2010–). The poster child of this new reality TV celebrity career, however, has to be glam rocker Bret Michaels. Appearing in four seasons of his own celebrity version of *The Bachelor*, *Rock of Love* and *Rock of Love Bus* (VH1, 2007–9), Michaels then won *The Celebrity Apprentice* season 3 while filming his own celebrity docu-soap, *Bret Michaels: Life as I Know It*. The first episode of the docusoap conveniently premiered in the week after the *Apprentice* finale, even though the full season did not go to air until late 2010. In a further sign of media industry integration, the theme song for *Life As I Know It* was a single from Michaels' latest album, *Custom Built*, while the music video shot for the single made liberal use of footage from the docusoap. Reality television and multi-media celebrity, in other words, now come as a package deal.

## Conclusion

This chapter has examined reality TV as an integral apparatus of celebrity production and maintenance. Itself positioned at the intersection of discourses of ordinariness and extraordinariness, authenticity and inauthenticity, reality TV thrives on the competing discourses that construe celebrity as the product of both merit and manufacture, talent and (the) industry. I have suggested that celebrity production operates through three different types of reality TV formats: the talent format, the no-talent format and the pre-existing celebrity format. Each of these programme types has a different relation to the economy of celebrity. In the talent format, as exemplified by the *Idol* series, the mechanisms of reality TV are self-consciously mobilised to fashion a celebrity out of nothing but 'raw' talent. Celebrities in these programmes are produced and marketed as cross-industry commodities, for the mutual benefit of the TV show, the sister industry and the ordinary person who has been raised from obscurity. In the no-talent format, such as *Big Brother*, celebrity is produced as a contingent effect of the scopic technology of reality TV: the extensive visibility afforded by the cameras turns an unlikely person, with no particular talent, into an unexpected celebrity. This celebrity-making apparatus not only runs counter to meritocratic discourses of celebrity but seems to revel in anti-talent. The extraordinarily ordinary person, raised to the dubious heights of 'reality TV star', becomes the site of unstable audience affect, hated by some for being talentless attention-seekers and loved by others for dismantling the hierarchical codes of fame.

Affective instability also characterises the abstract desire that swirls around the D-listers on pre-existing celebrity formats. The clutch of has-beens, wannabes and minor celebrities are the epitome of replaceable commodities in the celebrity system, but their commodity value can be heightened by appearing in a reality TV show or, better, by threading numerous shows together in a new kind of celebrity career. Instead of fabricating celebrity out of ordinariness, celebrity docusoaps and competition shows offer up the 'ordinary' face of the celebrity as a means of maintaining fame in a fickle economy.

This chapter has also addressed the democratic potential of populist celebrity constructions on reality TV. It continues to be debated whether giving ordinary people access to the media apparatus promotes self-representation or simply self-commodification in a culture of consumption. On the one hand, critics of reality TV argue that celebrity has depoliticised ordinariness, so that politics means little more than equal access to the celebrity sphere, where 'everyone [can] actively participate in self-commodification' (Andrejevic 2004: 112–13). On the other hand, proponents argue that no-talent celebrities throw into relief a hegemonic culture of education, achievement and meritocracy which is exclusionary because its rules are set by those who meet the criteria. When someone like Jade Goody or Zlatko Trpkovski achieves celebrity through other means, s/he offers hope of empowerment and social change. These two positions represent the double bind of reality TV's politics, which has critics alternately denigrating its role in celebrity-driven capitalism and lauding the potential political resistance of celebrity populism.

Whichever position one takes, there is little doubt that celebrity works as the new currency of individuation. Reality television participates in the capitalist economy that feeds on this currency. At the same time, because it produces celebrities as familiar, differentiated individuals – just like 'us' but different – reality television holds out the promise that participants as well as viewers will also be able to articulate themselves as differently ordinary. Whether this means making room in German society for an uneducated Macedonian auto mechanic who is made ordinary through familiarity or creating a space in American culture for the foul-mouthed family of an ageing British rocker whose ordinariness is celebrated as different, celebrity culture has an elasticity that is breaking down the traditional reasons for being 'seen'. Reality television has been instrumental in promoting the increase of celebrity culture: there are more shows, more channels, more disposable celebrities than ever before. It is also worth noting that reality TV has increased the range and kinds of celebrities on our screens: there are now more people engaged in more ways of being differently ordinary.

I do not mean to lose sight of the fact that such representations of celebrity are careful constructions. After all, this chapter has focused on the work that goes into constructing celebrities on reality TV. However, I am suggesting that reality TV has been instrumental in expanding the range of constructions of ordinariness, which in turn is bound to have political effects, whether positive or negative. In an apparent recognition of shift, even 'real' politics has begun to harness the celebrity potential of reality TV, such as in the thinly veiled political campaign called 'Sarah Palin's Alaska' (TLC, 2010–11), in which Palin, the Republican vice-presidential candidate in the 2008 election, takes her family on various adventures across her home state. No doubt Palin's self-representation as 'Mama Grizzly', which is pitched to appeal to her conservative constituency's interest in hard-line politics, is far from what media theorists would call democracy in action. One thing is clear, however: the conjunction of celebrity culture and reality TV is not apolitical, and warrants further study.

## Notes

1. TYT, The Young Turks YouTube Channel, March 2010, <http://www.youtube.com/watch?v=Mt3NnskdVgU&NR=1&feature=fvwp> (accessed 3 January 2011).
2. Papa herself seemed to consider that, while on *The Bachelor*, she was performing in a professional role. When confronted on-camera by presenter Chris Harrison about the affair, she responded, 'I don't think that my personal life is really anybody's business' (season 14, episode 2).
3. See also *Afghan Star* (dir.: Marking 2009), an illuminating documentary about the third season of the adaptation of the *Idol* concept in Afghanistan, the popular programme *Afghan Star* (Tolo TV, 2005–).
4. This opening references Toepfer's inspiration for the *Popstars* concept, which came from watching a 'gaggle of girls commandeer the microphone' of the hired band at his daughter's eighth birthday party and sing 'an endless number of Spice Girls songs', to which they seemed to know every word (personal communication).
5. Jonathan Dowling and Bill Toepfer sold the international rights to Screentime for what is suspected to be very little money, since in 1999 no one yet knew what formats could be worth. Notably, it

was Screentime who then figured out how to package and market the *Popstars* format for substantial international earnings, thus joining Endemol as pioneers of global format sales (see Ch. 3). In 2001, Screentime threatened to sue Fremantle Media and 19TV, the makers of *Pop Idol*, over *Idol*'s format similarity to *Popstars* (Wilkes 2001); the issue was presumably settled out of court. Ironically, three years later 19TV's Simon Fuller, creator of *Pop Idol*, filed a copyright infringement suit against Simon Cowell and Fremantle Media in protest against the similarities between the *Idol* format and Cowell's new show *The X-Factor* (ITV, 2004–); the lawsuit also settled out of court ('Pop Idol Format Lawsuit Settles' 2005).

6. The German group No Angels is perhaps the exception to this rule, as is the British group Girls Aloud (created through the ITV1 spin-off show *Popstars: The Rivals* in 2002). Both have achieved relative longevity in the pop music industry.

7. See <http://www.aidshealth.org/news/in-the-media/archive/lance-loud-obituary.html> (accessed 10 June 2011).

8. Much the same could be said about the appeal of Katie Price as a feminine role model for 'large numbers of young girls and grown women' (Aitkenhead 2010), who seem to appreciate her not as a walking advert for cosmetic surgery but rather as 'just a really nice, normal girl' (Cadwalladr 2006) whose story reverberates with their own lives.

9. Of myriad possible examples, one might turn here to Marty Piombo, a Californian technology executive on *Survivor: Nicaragua* (2010) whose contempt for fellow participants Jane and Chase was articulated in terms of their South Carolina background, their accents and their putative lack of intelligence.

10. News agencies and gossip magazines lit up in late July 2010 with excitement at the rumour that A-listers Tom Cruise and Katie Holmes would make a reality TV show to prove to the world that they are 'normal' (<http://tvnz.co.nz/entertainment-news/tom-katie-turn-reality-tv-prove-normality-3661630>; accessed 30 July 2010). Although no such Cruise/Holmes vehicle has yet appeared, Victoria and David Beckham did make a one-off reality special called *Coming to America* in 2007, which was not particularly well received.

11. *The Osbournes* (season 1) was superseded as the highest-rated show in MTV's history seven years later by *Jersey Shore* (see Ch. 6).

12. The notable exception might be VH1's *Hogan Knows Best*, a docu-soap about ageing wrestler Hulk Hogan and his family, which

premiered in 2005 and had four seasons before being cancelled in 2007 because of the break-up of the parents and a serious car accident leading to criminal charges for the son. The title of the show is a play on the classic 1950s sitcom *Father Knows Best* (CBS, 1954–60).

# 6 Legacies: The New MTV Generation

Twenty years on, reality TV has grown from crimewatch shows and docusoaps into a bewildering array of programmes. At the same time, its generic identification has shrunk to a one-word tag: 'reality'. Having redefined industry practices and audience expectations, reality TV now seems poised to redefine reality itself – and, in a sense, it has. It is no longer so easy to demarcate 'real life' from life on camera, or to think of the TV screen as a hard line of separation between media professionals on one side and ordinary people on the other. Mediation has entered reality, and reality legitimates itself through mediation. As Graeme Turner notes, our age is marked by 'the growing importance of the camera as a means of constituting and validating everyday reality' (2004: 62). To see ourselves on screen, or at least to imagine seeing ourselves there, is a way of being real.

These observations may help us to understand the influence of reality TV on media culture but not necessarily its constitution as a genre. Whereas television scholars may have concerned themselves five years ago with questions about whether such a hybrid form of programming could even be called a genre, now the question seems to be whether there is a limit to this genre which blends so easily with other media forms and reaches beyond the screen into the lived spaces of social reality. With so many innovations, derivations, interventions and cross-media collaborations, it is difficult to know how to define reality TV at this point in its development. I am tempted to borrow the pragmatic approach of Supreme Court Judge Stewart Potter who, in an often-quoted judgement on an obscenity trial, refused to define hard-core pornography but claimed to 'know it when I see it'.[1] Setting aside for the moment the implicit comparison between reality TV and pornography, I too would prefer to deflect the question of definition and simply say that I know reality TV when I see it. But the more interesting part of the comparison might be that Judge Potter did not refuse to define hard-core pornography because he found it distasteful – as many find reality TV – but rather because there was *too much* of it to 'encompass intelligently' in a definition. One could say the same of reality TV. Like it or leave it, condone it or condemn it, we must recognise that its rapid growth and protean extensions have played a central role in the changing profile of television as medium, industry and text form. It is the ongoing job of media scholarship to study and contextualise this role within larger social, cultural and political frameworks.

This book has attempted to trace the genealogical developments of reality TV as a clustering of discursive, formal and technological hallmarks that make it 'knowable' as a genre. Discursively, reality TV makes claims about ordinariness, authenticity and the social value of accessing private lives. These claims continue to be mobilised not because they can be taken for granted but precisely because they are located at points of contradiction. For all of its claims about giving viewers access to a 'backstage' reality, there is always a producer off-camera whom we do not see; for all of its emphasis on 'being real', participants nonetheless perform themselves in spectacular ways; for all of the language of ordinariness, participants are consistently positioned as extraordinary. Formally, too, reality TV relishes contradictions. It shamelessly mixes the generic attributes of fact and fiction. It uses (largely) unscripted interactions among participants placed in carefully constructed environments and controlled situations. It magnifies private acts for consumption by a (trans)national public. It challenges participants to perform yet rewards them for being themselves. It treats celebrities as ordinary people and ordinary people as celebrities. Technologically, the scopic mechanisms of reality TV have gone from being perceived as a threat to civil liberties and a tool for voyeurism to being embraced as an apparatus for self-expression, to being enthusiastically pursued as a means of self-legitimation. Not content to observe, the production mechanisms of reality TV have shifted the appeal of television 'from truth to use' (Goodwin 1993), seeking to change the conditions of individual lives and blurring the divide between representation and intervention. These key themes of authenticity, hybridisation, surveillance, privacy, performance and commodity consumption have structured the academic study of reality TV. Addressed by scholars working with methods of industry analysis, audience studies, textual criticism and cultural studies, reality TV has proven to be rich territory for analysing contemporary media concepts as well as practices. If the camera is truly becoming 'a means of constituting and validating everyday reality', as Turner has argued, then reality TV is the most visible – and arguably the most controversial – manifestation of this shift in media function.

In keeping with my method throughout this book, however, I do not wish to end with a large-scale conclusion but rather with attention to the particular. To do this, it makes sense to return to where it all (or at least one strand of it) began, on MTV. As a locus of reality TV, MTV represents an interesting case for future study. Ten years after its launch as a music-video channel in 1981, it established the conditions for branded regular programming by giving the green light to *The Real World*. Since then, there have always been reality TV shows on MTV, including, of course, *The Real World* itself. From the start, MTV shows have been anti-naturalistic and openly interventionist, importing aesthetic and narrative techniques from fiction in a self-conscious attempt to appeal to the youth demographic. Its sister channel, VH1, has taken this further by gleefully embracing the debased elements of reality TV – its inauthenticity, commodifiability and pornographic appeal – in highly stylised celebreality shows that trade on the thin line between the Hollywood A- and Z-lists. Recently, however, MTV has begun to introduce a different kind of reality show, a throwback to the social-interest documentary that seeks to send a responsible message to young people by showing what life is like for their less fortunate peers. This is the trajectory begun by *16 and Pregnant* in 2009 and continued with *Teen Mom* (2009) and *Teen Mom 2* (2011); it has also given rise to a more interventionist version, *If You Really Knew Me* (2010), which presents workshops in high schools across the country about the effects of social prejudice. These shows do not, however, represent a programming overhaul or a market repositioning of the channel, for MTV has not given up on its homegrown brand: the youth-antics reality TV show that sets a culture's teeth on edge. After all, in 2009 MTV launched the first seasons of both *16 and Pregnant* and *Jersey Shore*.

There will perhaps soon be an academic industry around *Jersey Shore* to match the cultural industry that it has become in just a few seasons. For my more limited purposes, though, I will note only that *Jersey Shore* is a very useful programme for reviewing the themes of this book. In terms of scopic technologies, *Jersey Show* marks a return to the surveillance techniques introduced by *The Real World*, with the additional mounted cameras and low-gauge aesthetics that are now so recognisable from *Big Brother*. The grainy video aesthetic is both a marker of the show's authenticity and a sign of cool style: the 1970s 'look' of hazy outlines and muted colours suggests nothing so much as a hipstamatic updating of analogue platforms (now available as an app on your iPhone). As the participants move freely in and out of the house, especially to go to bars and clubs, the programme maintains a multi-character intercutting between events while pursuing a particular narrative arc per episode. Formally, the show thus mixes the style of observational documentary with the narrative content and structure of the soap opera, creating a constructed 'family' of sibling rivalry and sexual tensions for the purposes of drama. In aesthetic and formal terms, then, we see in *Jersey Shore* the genealogical legacy of *An American Family*.

As with programmes since *Big Brother*, the issues of authenticity and performance also come into play, but *Jersey Shore* self-consciously marks how little this now has to do with concerns about what is 'actually' real. The programme does not lead viewers to question the authenticity of the participants or their actions. Rather, authenticity is confirmed by the show's aesthetic combined with the emotional intensity of the participants' interactions. Performance is thus not about acting 'up' (for the cameras) but about extreme versions of acting 'out'. Fuelled by hormones, emotion and quite a bit of alcohol, the participants frequently end up in screaming matches, physical brawls and sexual entanglements, with outsiders as well as each other. As a measure of just how authentic these performances are seen to be, the show has met with extensive criticism about having cast extreme exhibitionists in order to appeal to the voyeurism of viewers. I have argued in Chapter 3 that, theoretically speaking, voyeurism and exhibitionism are not flip sides of the same coin. However, given the out-sized physical endowments of both the boys and girls on *Jersey Shore*, not to mention the way that such spectacularisation of muscle and cleavage invites audiences to ogle, this may well be the time to reconsider the view common to second-generation reality TV that participants perform to the cameras. On *Jersey Shore*, the cameras have become so naturalised, for both viewers and participants, that the participants perform *directly* to the gaze of the audience, in a loop of fascination and validation that reflects the larger economies of social desire.

The notable difference that sets *Jersey Shore* apart from earlier reality TV shows is the way in which the programme and its participants are self-consciously, and quite comfortably, integrated into such larger economies. Although they may initially have been cast as ordinary people for an Italian-American version of *The Real World*, the cast members have since turned themselves and their lives into a cultural industry. MTV's promotional use of the term 'guido' (derogatory slang for Italian Americans), which initially caused great controversy,[2] has now been recoded as an idiom of celebratory self-identity: guidos/guidettes are proudly claimed by Nicole 'Snooki' Polizzi to be 'people who take care of themselves'. There is an interesting study yet to be done about shifting notions of care and reality TV's role in this, but one thing that is already clear is that discourses about identity and self-care are becoming disconnected from 'us vs. them' stereotyping and now provide the basis for self-commodification. The acronym 'GTL' – short for gym, tanning, laundry – that has been popularised by the *Jersey Shore* cast is a reminder of television's active role in shifting discourses and social practices. 'GTL' has literally become a term of cultural currency, meaning not only that it circulates broadly in culture but also that it functions as an exchangeable token, something that can be traded in for celebrity. Thus, seven of the eight original participants of *Jersey Shore* have been promoted from and by reality TV into celebrity culture, and have now begun the work of merchandising self-maintenance.[3]

We do not have to look further for evidence that the third generation of reality TV is upon us. Exhibitionism pays, self-commodification is everyone's bread and butter, and we must perform ourselves to be seen, let alone to be validated. This is a far cry from the motivations of twenty and even forty years ago for putting ordinary people on camera, but it is proof, if any were needed, that reality TV is a genre in flux.

## Notes

1. *Jacobellis v. Ohio*, 378 U.S. 184 (1964).
2. The strongest protest has come from Unico National, a service organisation of Italian Americans. Along with other ethnic-identified organisations, Unico National has repeatedly called on MTV to cancel *Jersey Shore* as a result of its derogatory stereotyping of Italian Americans, a call which led in the first season to some advertisers pulling their sponsorship of the show. None of these protests, however, has dented the runaway popularity of the show, with the opening season 3 episodes posting ratings that made them the most watched broadcasts in MTV's history. The entire cast, meanwhile, was included in Barbara Walters's '10 Most Fascinating People List' of 2010.
3. For instance, Mike 'The Situation' Sorrentino has made workout DVDs, Jenni 'Jwoww' Farley has a line of body supplements and bronzers, Vinny Guadagnino has a clothing line and Nicole 'Snooki' Polizzi has (ghost) written a novel (Williams 2011). This is, of course, in addition to their numerous cross-over appearances in other media genres (e.g. Nicole Polizzi's appearance on *The Tonight Show*).

# Bibliography

Aitkenhead, Decca (2010), 'Katie Price: "People think I'm not normal"', *The Guardian* 16 August, <http://www.guardian.co.uk/media/2010/aug/16/katie-price-jordan> (retrieved 17 August 2010).

Alexander, Ben (2004), 'Reality TV is a dangerous art form', in Karen F. Balkin (ed.), *Reality TV*, Farmington Hills, MI: Greenhaven Press, pp. 44–7.

Andrejevic, Mark (2004), *Reality TV: The Work of Being Watched*, Lanham, MD: Rowman & Littlefield.

Andrejevic, Mark, and Dean Colby (2006), 'Racism and reality TV: the case of MTV's *Road Rules*', in David S. Escoffery (ed.), *How Real Is Reality TV?*, Jefferson, NC, and London: McFarland, pp. 195–211.

Armstrong, Stephen (2008), 'Back to reality', *The Guardian*, 1 September, <http://www.guardian.co.uk/media/2008/sep/01/channel4.realitytv?> (retrieved 15 February 2009).

Austin, J., and A. D. McVey (1989), *NCCD Prison Population Forecast, 1989: The Impact of the War on Drugs*, Rockville, MD: National Institute of Justice/ National Criminal Justice Reference Service.

Austin, J. L. (1975), *How to Do Things with Words: The William James Lectures Delivered at Harvard University in 1955*, Oxford: Oxford University Press.

Bancel, Nicolas, Pascal Blanchard and Gilles Boëtsch (eds) (2008), *Human Zoos: Science and Spectacle in the Age of Colonial Empires*, trans. Teresa Bridgeman, Liverpool: Liverpool University Press.

Barnouw, Erik (1993), *Documentary: A History of the Non-Fiction Film*, Oxford: Oxford University Press.

Barthes, Roland (1993 [1957]), *Mythologies*, trans. Annette Lavers, London: Vintage Books; orig. Éditions du Seuil.

Benjamin, Walter (2006), 'The work of art in the age of mechanical reproduction', in Meenakshi Gigi Durham and Douglas Kellner (eds), *Media and Cultural Studies: Keyworks*, rev. edn, Malden, MA, and Oxford: Blackwell Publishing, pp. 18–40.

Berlant, Lauren, and Michael Warner (1998), 'Sex in public', *Critical Inquiry* 24.2, pp. 547–66.

Bignell, Jonathan (2005), *Big Brother: Reality TV in the Twenty-First Century*, Basingstoke: Palgrave Macmillan.

Billings, Claire (2002), 'Geldof sues Granada for ripping off *Survivor* format', brandrepublic.com, 27 September, <http://www.brandrepub lic.com/news/159133/Geldof-sues-Granada-ripping-off-Survivor-format/> (retrieved 20 January 2011).

Biltereyst, Daniël (2004), '*Big Brother* and its moral guardians: reappraising the role of intellectuals in the *Big Brother* panic', in Ernest Mathijs and Janet Jones (eds), *Big Brother International*, London and New York: Wallflower Press, pp. 9–15.

Biressi, Anita, and Heather Nunn (2005), *Reality TV: Realism and Revelation*, London and New York: Wallflower Press.

Bondebjerg, Ib (1996), 'Public discourse/private fascination: hybridization in "True-Life-Story" genres', *Media, Culture and Society* 18.1, pp. 27–45.

Bonner, Frances (2003), *Ordinary Television: Analyzing Popular TV*, London and Thousand Oaks, CA: Sage Publications.

Bonner, Frances (2009), 'Fixing relationships in 2-4-1 transformations', in Tania Lewis (ed.), *TV Transformations: Revealing the Makeover Show*, London and New York: Routledge, pp. 107–17.

Boorstin, Daniel J. (1992 [1961]), *The Image: A Guide to Pseudo-Events in America*, New York: Vintage Books.

Bratich, Jack Z. (2007), 'Programming reality: control societies, new subjects and the powers of transformation', in Dana Heller (ed.), *Makeover Television: Realities Remodelled*, London and New York: I. B. Tauris, pp. 6–22.

Braudy, Leo (1997), *The Frenzy of Renown: Fame and Its History*, New York: Vintage Books.

Brenton, Sam, and Reuben Cohen (2003), *Shooting People: Adventures in Reality TV*, London: Verso.

Brunsdon, Charlotte (2004), 'Lifestyling Britain: the 8–9 slot on British television', in Lynn Spigel and Jan Olsson (eds), *Television after TV: Essays on a Medium in Transition*, Durham, NC, and London: Duke University Press, pp. 75–92.

Bruzzi, Stella (2000), *New Documentary: A Critical Introduction*, London and New York: Routledge.

Bruzzi, Stella (2001), 'Docusoaps', in Glen Creeber, Toby Miller and John Tulloch (eds), *The Television Genre Book*, London: British Film Institute, pp. 132–4.

Buchanan, Ian (2001), 'Enjoying "Reality TV"', *Australian Humanities Review* 22, <http://www.lib.latrobe.edu.au/AHR/archive/Issue-June-2001/buchanan3.html> (retrieved 10 October 2002).

Cadwalladr, Carole (2006), 'All because the ladies love Jordan', *The Observer* 12 February, <http://www.guardian.co.uk/theobserver/2006/feb/12/features.review47> (retrieved 17 August 2010).

Caillois, Roger (2001), *Man, Play and Games*, trans. Meyer Barash, Urbana and Chicago: University of Illinois Press.

Carter, Bill (2001), 'Survival of the pushiest', *New York Times Magazine*, 28

January, <http://www.nytimes.com/magazine/20010128mag-burnett.html> (retrieved 27 January 2001).

Cassidy, Marsha F. (2006), 'The Cinderella makeover: *Glamour Girl*, television misery shows, and 1950s femininity', in Dana Heller (ed.), *The Great American Makeover: Television, History, Nation*, New York and Basingstoke: Palgrave Macmillan, pp. 125–40.

Clissold, Bradley D. (2004), '*Candid Camera* and the origins of reality TV', in Su Holmes and Deborah Jermyn (eds), *Understanding Reality Television*, London and New York: Routledge, pp. 33–53.

Coles, Gail (2000), 'Docusoap', in Bruce Carson and Margaret Llewellyn-Jones (eds), *Frames and Fictions on Television: The Politics of Identity within Drama*, Bristol: Intellect Books, pp. 27–39.

Cooke, Rachel (2008), 'Family fortunes', *New Statesman*, 22 September, p. 70.

Corner, John (1996), *The Art of Record: A Critical Introduction to Documentary*, Manchester: Manchester University Press.

Corner, John (2002), 'Performing the real: documentary diversions', *Television and New Media* 3.3, pp. 255–69.

Corner, John (2004), '*An American Family* and *The Family*', in Glen Creeber (ed.), *Fifty Key Television Programmes*, London: Arnold, pp. 6–10.

Corner, John (2000), 'Documentary in a post-documentary culture? A note on forms and their functions', *European Science Foundation 'Changing Media – Changing Europe'* Programme, <http://www.lboro.ac.uk/research/changing. media/John%20Corner%20paper.htm> (retrieved 2 April 2010).

Cummings, Dolan (ed.) (2002), *Reality TV: How Real Is Real?*, Oxford: Hodder and Stoughton.

Dauncey, Hugh (1994), 'Reality shows on French television: Télé-vérité, Télé-service, Télé-civisme or Télé-flicaille?', *French Cultural Studies* 5.1.13, pp. 85–98.

De Cordova, Richard (1990), *Picture Personalities: The Emergence of the Star System in America*, Urbana and Chicago: University of Illinois Press.

Dehnart, Andy (2000), 'CBS allowed to continue production of global adventure', RealityBlurred.com, <http://www.realityblurred.com/reality tv/archives/the_amazing_race/2000_Nov_27_cbs_allowed_to_continue> (retrieved 28 December 2010).

Dehnart, Andy (2008), 'Casting director: *Amazing Race* "is a relationship show, period"', RealityBlurred.com, <http://www.realityblurred.com/realitytv/ archives/the_amazing_race_13/2008_Dec_04_casting_former_survivors> (retrieved 12 August 2011).

Delisle, Jennifer Bowering (2003), 'Surviving American cultural imperialism: *Survivor* and traditions of nineteenth-century colonial fiction', *Journal of American Culture* 26.1, pp. 42–55.

Donaher, Noeline (1993), *The Sylvania Waters Diary: Noeline's Own Story*, Melbourne: Bookman Press.

Donovan, Pamela (1998), 'Armed with the power of television: reality crime programming and the reconstruction of law and order in the United States', in Mark Fishman and Gray Cavender (eds), *Entertaining Crime: Television Reality Programs*, New York: Walter de Gruyter, pp. 117–38.

Dovey, Jon (2000), *Freakshow: First Person Television and Factual Media*, London: Pluto Press.

Dovey, Jon (2004), 'It's only a game show: *Big Brother* and the Theatre of Spontaneity', in Ernest Mathijs and Janet Jones (eds), *Big Brother International*, London and New York: Wallflower Press, pp. 232–49.

Doyle, Aaron (2003), *Arresting Images: Crime and Policing in Front of the Television Camera*, Toronto: University of Toronto Press.

Dyer, Richard (1998 [1979]), *Stars*, London: British Film Institute.

Dyer, Richard (2004 [1986]), *Heavenly Bodies*, 2nd edn, London and New York: Routledge; orig. Macmillan.

Eby, Margaret (2010), 'The "real world" creator has some explaining to do', Salon.com, 30 June 2010, <http://www.salon.com/entertainment/tv/reality_tv/index.html?story=/ent/tv/2010/06/30/jon_murray_king_of_reality_tv> (retrieved 1 July 2010).

Ellis, Jack C., and Betsy A. McLane (2005), *A New History of Documentary Film*, New York and London: Continuum Books.

Ellis, John (1992), *Visible Fictions: Cinema, Television, Video*, rev. edn, London and New York: Routledge.

Ellis, John (2001), 'Mirror mirror', *Sight and Sound* 11.8, p. 8.

Ellis, John (2005), 'Documentary and truth on television: the crisis of 1999', in Alan Rosenthal and John Corner (eds), *New Challenges for Documentary*, 2nd edn, Manchester: Manchester University Press, pp. 342–60.

Eschholz, Sarah, et al. (2002), 'Race and attitudes to the police: assessing the effects of watching "reality" police programs', *Journal of Criminal Justice* 30, pp. 327–41.

Escoffery, David S. (ed.) (2006), *How Real Is Reality TV?*, Jefferson, NC, and London: McFarland.

Feuer, Jane (1983), 'The concept of live television: ontology as ideology', in E. Ann Kaplan (ed.), *Regarding Television*, Frederick, MD: University Publications of America/American Film Institute, pp. 12–22.

Feuer, Jane (1992), 'Genre study and television', in Robert C. Allen (ed.), *Channels of Discourse, Reassembled*, Chapel Hill, NC: University of North Carolina Press, pp. 138–60.

Fishman, Mark (1998), 'Ratings and reality: the persistence of the reality crime genre', in Mark Fishman and Gray Cavender (eds), *Entertaining Crime: Television Reality Programs*, New York: Walter de Gruyter, pp. 59–75.

Fishman, Mark, and Gray Cavender (eds) (1998), *Entertaining Crime: Television Reality Programs*, New York: Walter de Gruyter.

Fiske, John (1987), *Television Culture*, New York: Routledge.

Flusser, Vilém (1999), *The Shape of Things: A Philosophy of Design*, trans. Anthony Mathews, London: Reaktion Books.

Foucault, Michel (1979), *Discipline and Punish*, trans. Alan Sheridan, New York: Vintage Books.

Foucault, Michel (1984), 'Nietzsche, genealogy, history', in Paul Rabinow (ed.), *The Foucault Reader*, New York: Pantheon Books.

Foucault, Michel (2011), 'Society must be defended, 17 March 1976', in Imre Szeman and Timothy Kaposy (eds), *Cultural Theory: An Anthology*, Malden, MA, Oxford and Chichester: Wiley-Blackwell, pp. 124–33.

Friedman, James (ed.) (2002), *Reality Squared: Televisual Discourse on the Real*, New Brunswick, NJ: Rutgers University Press.

Friend, Tad (2006), 'Letter from California: the pursuit of happiness – L. A. loves its televised car chases', *New Yorker*, 23–30 January, pp. 64–71.

Funt, Allen (1971), 'What do you say to a naked lady?', in Alan Rosenthal (ed.), *New Documentary in Action: A Casebook in Film Making*, Berkeley: University of California Press, pp. 251–63.

Funt, Allen, and Philip Reed (1994), *Candidly Allen Funt, a Million Smiles Later*, New York: Barricade Books.

Fyfe, Nicholas R., and Jon Bannister (1998), 'The eyes upon the street – closed-circuit television surveillance and the city', in Nicholas R. Fyfe and Jon Bannister (eds), *Images of the Street: Planning, Identity and Control in Public Space*, London and New York: Routledge, pp. 254–67.

Gamson, Joshua (1994), *Claims to Fame: Celebrity in Contemporary America*, Berkeley and Los Angeles: University of California Press.

Gledhill, Christine (ed.) (1991), *Stardom: Industry of Desire*, London and New York: Routledge.

Glynn, Kevin (2000), *Tabloid Culture: Trash Taste, Popular Power, and the Transformation of American Television*, Durham, NC: Duke University Press.

Goffman, Erving (1959), *The Presentation of Self in Everyday Life*, New York and Toronto: Anchor Books.

Goodwin, Andrew (1993), 'Riding with ambulances: television and its uses', *Sight and Sound* 3.1, pp. 26–8.

Gray, Jonathan (2006), *Watching with* The Simpsons*: Television, Parody and Intertextuality*, New York: Routledge.

Grüne, Heinz (n.d.), 'Big-Brother-Phänomen Zlatko: Sumpfblüte aus dem Container oder Forrest Gump der @-Generation?', Rheingold Institut für qualitative Markt- und Medienanalysen, <http://www.rheingold -online.de/veroeffentlichungen/artikel/Big-Brother-Phaenomen_Zlatko_ Sumpfbluete_aus_dem_Container_oder_Forrest_Gump_der_-_Generation _.html> (retrieved 10 January 2011).

Haralovich, Mary Beth, and Michael W. Trosset (2004), '"Expect the unexpected": narrative pleasure and uncertainty due to chance in *Survivor*', in Susan Murray and Laurie Ouellette (eds), *Reality TV: Remaking Television Culture*, New York and London: New York University Press, pp. 75–96.

Hattenstone, Simon (2008), 'Who wants to be a billionaire?', *The Guardian*, 22 March 2008, <http://www.guardian.co.uk/lifeandstyle/2008/mar/22/ healthandwellbeing> (retrieved 22 April 2011).

Heller, Dana (ed.) (2006), *The Great American Makeover: Television, History, Nation*, New York and Basingstoke: Palgrave Macmillan.

Heller, Dana (ed.) (2007), *Makeover Television: Realities Remodelled*, London and New York: I. B. Tauris.

Hendrie, Alison (1993), *Rescue 911: Amazing Rescues*, Random House Children's Publications.

Hill, Annette (2002), '*Big Brother*: the real audience', *Television and New Media* 3.3, pp. 323–40.

Hill, Annette (2004), 'Watching *Big Brother* UK', in Ernest Mathijs and Janet Jones (eds), *Big Brother International*, London and New York: Wallflower Press, pp. 25–39.

Hill, Annette (2005), *Reality TV: Audiences and Popular Factual Television*, London and New York: Routledge.

Hill, Annette, and Gareth Palmer (2002), '*Big Brother*', *Television and New Media* 3.3, pp. 251–4.

Holmes, Su (2004a), '"All you've got to worry about is having a cup of tea and doing a bit of sunbathing": approaching celebrity in *Big Brother*', in Su Homes and Deborah Jermyn (eds), *Understanding Reality Television*, London and New York: Routledge, pp. 111–35.

Holmes, Su (2004b), '"Reality goes pop!" Reality TV, popular music, and narratives of stardom in *Pop Idol*', *Television and New Media* 5.2, pp. 147–72.

Holmes, Su (2008a), *The Quiz Show*, Edinburgh: Edinburgh University Press.

Holmes, Su (2008b), '"Riveting and real – a family in the raw": (re)visiting *The Family* (1974) after reality TV', *International Journal of Cultural Studies* 11.2, pp. 193–210.

Holmes, Su (2009), '"Jade's back and this time she's famous": narratives of celebrity in the *Celebrity Big Brother* "race" row', *Entertainment and Sports Law Journal* 7.1, <http://www2.warwick.ac.uk/fac/soc/law/elj/eslj/issues/volume7/number1/holmes> (retrieved 2 December 2009).

Holmes, Su, and Deborah Jermyn (eds) (2004), *Understanding Reality Television*, London and New York: Routledge.

Huff, Richard M. (2001), 'CBS puts foot down: Fox, *Boot Camp* face *Survivor* ripoff suit', *New York Daily News*, 11 April, <http://www.nydailynews.com/archives/entertainment/2001/04/11/2001-04-11_cbs_puts_foot_down_fox___boo.html> (retrieved 28 December 2010).

Huff, Richard M. (2006), *Reality Television*, Westport, CT, and London: Praeger.

Huizinga, Johan (2000 [1938]), *Homo Ludens: A Study of the Play-Element in Culture*, London: Routledge.

'The Jade Goody phenomenon' (2007), *The Independent*, 9 January, <http://www.independent.co.uk/news/people/profiles/the-jade-goody-phenomenon-431370.html> (retrieved 20 January 2010).

Jenkins, Henry (2006), *Convergence Culture: Where Old and New Media Collide*, New York and London: New York University Press.

Jermyn, Deborah (2004), '"This *is* about real people!": video technologies, actuality and affect in the crime appeal', in Su Holmes and Deborah Jermyn (eds), *Understanding Reality Television*, London and New York: Routledge, pp. 71–90.

Jermyn, Deborah (2007), *Crime Watching: Investigating Real Crime TV*, London and New York: I. B. Tauris.

Jones, Janet (2003), 'Show your real face: a fan study of the UK *Big Brother* transmissions (2000, 2001, 2002)', *New Media and Society* 5.3, pp. 400–21.

Jones, Janet (2004), 'Emerging platform identities: *Big Brother* UK and interactive multi-platform usage', in Ernest Mathijs and Janet Jones (eds), *Big Brother International*, London and New York: Wallflower Press, pp. 210–31.

Kavka, Misha (2006), 'Changing properties: the makeover show crosses the Atlantic', in Dana Heller (ed.), *The Great American Makeover: Television, History, Nation*, Basingstoke: Palgrave Macmillan, pp. 211–29.

Kavka, Misha (2008), *Reality Television, Affect and Intimacy*, Basingstoke: Palgrave Macmillan.

Kavka, Misha (2009), 'Reaching tentacles into reality', in Robert Leonard (ed.), *Artur Zmijewski*, Brisbane: Institute of Modern Art and Te Tuhi Centre for the Arts, pp. 2–7.

Kavka, Misha, and Amy West (2010), 'Jade the obscure: celebrity death and the mediatised maiden', *Celebrity Studies* 1.2, pp. 216–30.

Kilborn, Richard (1994), 'How real can you get? Recent developments in "reality" television', *European Journal of Communication* 9.4, pp. 421–39.

Kilborn, Richard (2003), *Staging the Real: Factual TV Programming in the Age of Big Brother*, Manchester and New York: Manchester University Press.

Kilborn, Richard (2006), '"Mixing and matching": the hybridising impulse in today's factual television programming', in Garin Dowd, Lesley Stevenson and Jeremy Strong (eds), *Genre Matters: Essays in Theory and Criticism*, Bristol: Intellect, pp. 109–22.

King, Barry (2006), 'Training camps of the modular: reality TV as a form of life', in David S. Escoffery (ed.), *How Reality Is Reality TV? Essays on Representation and Truth*, Jefferson, NC: McFarland, pp. 42–57.

Kompare, Derek (2004), 'Extraordinarily ordinary: the Osbournes as *"An American Family"*', in Susan Murray and Laurie Ouellette (eds), *Reality TV: Remaking Television Culture*, New York and London: New York University Press, pp. 97–116.

Kraidy, Marwan M. (2009), *Reality Television and Arab Politics: Contention in Public Life*, Cambridge: Cambridge University Press.

Kraszewski, Jon (2004), 'Country hicks and urban cliques: mediating race, reality, and liberalism on MTV's *The Real World*', in Susan Murray and Laurie Ouellette (eds), *Reality TV: Remaking Television Culture*, New York and London: New York University Press, pp. 179–96.

Langer, John (1998), *Tabloid Television: Popular Journalism and the 'Other News'*, London and New York: Routledge.

Lewis, Tania (2008), *Smart Living: Lifestyle Media and Popular Expertise*, New York: Peter Lang.

Lewis, Tania (ed.) (2009), *TV Transformations: Revealing the Makeover Show*, London and New York: Routledge.

Lotz, Amanda (2007), *The Television Will Be Revolutionized*, New York and London: New York University Press.

Luo, Wei (2010), 'Chinese reality TV: a case study of GDTV's *The Great Challenge for Survival*', PhD thesis, University of Waikato (New Zealand).

Maas, James B., and Kathleen M. Toivanen (1978), 'Candid camera and the behavioral sciences', *Teaching of Psychology* 5.4, pp. 226–8.

McAlister, Joan Faber (2010), 'Domesticating citizenship: the *Kairotopics* of America's post-9/11 home makeover', *Critical Studies in Media Communication* 27.1, pp. 84–104.

McAllister, Matthew P. (2006), 'Selling *Survivor*: the use of TV news to promote commercial entertainment', in Angharad N. Valdivia (ed.), *A Companion to Media Studies*, Malden, MA, and Oxford: Blackwell Publishing, pp. 209–26.

McCarthy, Anna (2004), '"Stanley Milgram, Allen Funt, and me": postwar social science and the "first wave" of reality TV', in Susan Murray and Laurie Ouellette (eds), *Reality TV: Remaking Television Culture*, New York and London: New York University Press, pp. 19–39.

McGrath, John Edward (2004), *Loving Big Brother: Performance, Privacy and Surveillance*, London and New York: Routledge.

McMurria, John (2008), 'Desperate citizens and Good Samaritans: neoliberalism and makeover reality TV', *Television and New Media* 9.4, pp. 305–32.

Magder, Ted (2004), 'The end of TV 101: reality programs, formats, and the new business of television', in Susan Murray and Laurie Ouellette (eds), *Reality TV: Remaking Television Culture*, New York and London: New York University Press, pp. 137–56.

Maron, Linda (1993), *Rescue 911: Extraordinary Stories* (Longmeadow Press).

Marshall, P. David (1997), *Celebrity and Power: Fame in Contemporary Culture*, Minneapolis: University of Minnesota Press.

Marwick, Alice (2010), 'There's a beautiful girl under all of this: performing hegemonic femininity in reality television', *Critical Studies in Media Communication* 27.3, pp. 251–66.

Matheson, Sarah A. (2007), 'The cultural politics of *Wife Swap*: taste, lifestyle media, and the American family', *Film & History* 37.2, pp. 33–47.

Mathijs, Ernest (2002), 'Big Brother and critical discourse: the reception of *Big Brother* Belgium', *Television and New Media* 3.3, pp. 311–22.

Mathijs, Ernest, and Janet Jones (eds) (2004), *Big Brother International: Formats, Critics & Publics*, London: Wallflower Press.

Meijer, Irene, and Maarten Reesink (eds) (2000), *Reality Soap! Big Brother en de opkomst van het multimediaconcept*, Amsterdam: Uitgeverij Boom.

Mikos, Lothar (2004), '*Big Brother* as television text: frames of interpretation and reception in Germany', in Ernest Mathijs and Janet Jones (eds), *Big Brother International*, London and New York: Wallflower Press, pp. 93–104.

Milgram, Stanley, and John Sabini (1979), 'Candid Camera', *Culture and Society* 16.6, pp. 72–5.

Miller, Toby (2006), 'Metrosexuality: see the bright light of commodification shine! Watch Yanqui masculinity made over!', in Dana Heller (ed.), *The Great American Makeover: Television, History, Nation*, New York and Basingstoke: Palgrave Macmillan, pp. 105–22.

Mittell, Jason (2004), *Genre and Television*, New York and London: Routledge.

Monaco, James (ed.) (1978), *Celebrity: The Media as Image Makers*, New York: Delta.

Monaco, Paul (2001), *The Sixties: 1960–1969*, Berkeley and Los Angeles: University of California Press.

Moran, Albert (1998), *Copycat Television: Globalisation, Program Formats and Cultural Identity*, Luton: University of Luton Press.

Moran, Albert, with Justin Malbon (2006), *Understanding the Global TV Format*, Bristol: Intellect Books.

Morreale, Joanne (2003), 'Revisiting *The Osbournes*: the hybrid reality sitcom', *Journal of Film and Video* 55.1, pp. 3–15.

Moseley, Rachel (2000), 'Makeover takeover on British television', *Screen* 41.4, pp. 299–314.

Murray, Susan, and Laurie Ouellette (eds) (2004), *Reality TV: Remaking Television Culture*, New York and London: New York University Press.

Museum of Television and Radio (1994), Seminar: *The Real World* (1994), New York: Museum for Television and Radio, 28 December.

Museum of Television and Radio (2001), Seminar: 'From *An American Family* to *Survivor*', New York: Museum of Television and Radio, 7 May.

Nadis, Fred (2007), 'Citizen Funt: surveillance as Cold War entertainment', *Film and History: An Interdisciplinary Journal of Film and Television Studies* 37.2, pp. 13–22; rpt in Julie Anne Taddeo and Ken Dvorak (eds) (2010), *The Tube Has Spoken: Reality TV and History*, Lexington: The University Press of Kentucky, pp. 11–26.

Neale, Steve (1990), 'Questions of genre', *Screen* 31.1, pp. 45–66.

Neale, Steve (2000), *Genre and Hollywood*, London and New York: Routledge.

Neupert, Richard John (2007), *A History of the French New Wave Cinema*, 2nd edn, Madison: University of Wisconsin Press.

Nichols, Bill (1994), *Blurred Boundaries: Questions of Meaning in Contemporary Culture*, Bloomington: Indiana University Press.

Nichols, Bill (2001), *Introduction to Documentary*, Bloomington: Indiana University Press.

Norris, Clive, and Gary Armstrong (1999), *The Maximum Surveillance Society: The Rise of CCTV*, Oxford and New York: Berg.

Ogdon, Bethany (2006), 'The psycho-economy of reality television in the "Tabloid Decade"', in David S. Escoffery (ed.), *How Real Is Reality TV? Essays on Representation and Truth*, Jefferson, NC: McFarland, pp. 26–41.

O'Loughlin, Dean (2004), *Living in the Box: An Adventure in Reality TV*, Halesown: The Gamesford Files.

Ouellette, Laurie, and James Hay (2008), *Better Living through Reality TV*, Malden, MA, and Oxford: Blackwell Publishing.

Palmer, Gareth (1998), 'Police shows on British television: new police blues', *Jump Cut* 42, pp. 12–18.

Palmer, Gareth (2005), 'The undead: life on the D-List', *Westminster Papers in Communication and Culture* 2.2, pp. 37–53.

Purser, Philip (1974/5), 'Approximately themselves', *Sight and Sound* 44.1, pp. 48–9.

Rabinow, Paul, and Nikolas Rose (2006), 'Biopower today', *BioSocieties* 1.2, pp. 195–217.

Raphael, Chad (2004), 'The political economic origins of Reali-TV', in Susan Murray and Laurie Ouellette (eds), *Reality TV: Remaking Television Culture*, New York and London: New York University Press, pp. 119–36.

Redden, Guy (2007), 'Makeover morality and consumer culture', in Dana Heller (ed.), *Makeover Television: Realities Remodelled*, London and New York: I. B. Tauris, pp. 150–64.

Rojek, Chris (2001), *Celebrity*, London: Reaktion Books.

Roscoe, Jane (2004), 'Watching *Big Brother* at work: a production study of *Big Brother* Australia', in Ernest Mathijs and Janet Jones (eds), *Big Brother International: Formats, Critics & Publics*, London and New York: Wallflower Press, pp. 181–93.

Ruoff, Jeffrey (2002), *An American Family: A Televised Life*, Minneapolis: University of Minnesota Press.

Rupert, Laurie, and Sayanti Ganguly Puckett (2010), 'Disillusionment, divorce, and the destruction of the American Dream: *An American Family* and the rise of reality TV', in Julie Anne Taddeo and Ken Dvorak (eds), *The Tube Has Spoken: Reality TV and History*, Lexington: The University Press of Kentucky, pp. 83–97.

Scannell, Paddy (2002), '*Big Brother* as television event', *Television & New Media* 3.3, pp. 271–82.

Schlesinger, Philip, Howard Tumber and Graham Murdock (1991), 'The media politics of crime and criminal justice', *British Journal of Sociology* 42.3, pp. 397–420.

Sella, Marshall (2000), 'The electronic fishbowl', *New York Times*, 21 May, <http://query.nytimes.com/gst/fullpage.html?res=9A07E7DE1E3BF932A 15756C0A9669C8B63&&scp=2&sq=sella%20big%20brother%202000& st=cse> (retrieved 30 January 2011).

Sender, Katherine (2006), 'Queens for a day: *Queer Eye and the Straight Guy* and the neoliberal project', *Critical Studies in Media Communication* 23.2, pp. 131–51.

Smith, Kyle (2000), 'TV's reality check', *People* 53.9, <http://www.people. com/people/archive/article/0,,20130638,00.html> (retrieved 28 December 2010).

Spigel, Lynn (2004), 'Entertainment wars: television culture after 9/11', *American Quarterly* 56.2, pp. 235–70.

Stelter, Brian (2011), 'Smug's out, talent's in at *Idol*', *New York Times*, 18 January, <http://www.nytimes.com/2011/01/19/arts/television/19idol. html?hpw> (retrieved 19 January 2011).

Stempel-Mumford, Laura (1995), *Love and Ideology in the Afternoon: Soap Opera, Women and Television Genre*, Bloomington: Indiana University Press.

Straayer, Chris, and Tom Waugh (eds) (2005), 'Queer TV style', *GLQ* 11.1, pp. 95–117.

Stratton, Jon, and Ien Ang (1994), '*Sylvania Waters* and the spectacular exploding family', *Screen* 35.1, pp. 1–21.

Taddeo, Julie Anne, and Ken Dvorak (eds) (2010), *The Tube Has Spoken: Reality TV and History*, Lexington: The University Press of Kentucky.

Thackaberry, Jennifer (2003), 'Mutual metaphors of *Survivor* and office politics: images of work in popular *Survivor* criticism', in Matthew J. Smith and Andrew F. Wood (eds), *Survivor Lessons: Essays on Communication and Reality Television*, Jefferson, NC, and London: McFarland, pp. 153–81.

Turner, Graeme (2004), *Understanding Celebrity*, London and Thousand Oaks, CA: Sage Publications.

Turner, Graeme (2010), *Ordinary People and the Media: The Demotic Turn*, London and Thousand Oaks, CA: Sage Publications.

Tyler, Imogen, and Bruce Bennett (2010), '"Celebrity chav": fame, femininity and social class', *European Journal of Cultural Studies* 13.3, pp. 375–93.

Van Zoonen, Liesbet (2004), 'Desire and resistance: Big Brother in the Dutch public sphere', in Ernest Mathijs and Janet Jones (eds), *Big Brother International: Formats, Critics & Publics*, London and New York: Wallflower Press, pp. 16–24.

Von Braun, Christina (2000), '*Big Brother* oder Der frei zirkulierende Eros', *Tages-Anzeiger* (Switzerland), 5 December, p. 57.

Weber, Brenda (2009), *Makeover TV: Selfhood, Citizenship, and Celebrity*, Durham, NC, and London: Duke University Press.

West, Amy (2005), 'Caught on tape: a legacy of low-tech reality', in Geoff King (ed.), *The Spectacle of the Real: From Hollywood to Reality TV and Beyond*, Bristol: Intellect Books, pp. 83–92.

Wilkes, Neil (2001), 'Popstars: legal row over Pop Idol series', *digital spy*, 4 April, <http://www.digitalspy.ie/tv/s102/popstars/news/a2459/popstars-legal-row-over-pop-idol-series.html> (retrieved 15 August 2010).

Williams, Mary Elizabeth (2011), 'Who wants to buy *Jersey Shore*?', Salon.com, 5 January, <http://www.salon.com/entertainment/tv/jersey_shore/index. html?story=/mwt/feature/2011/01/05/jersey_shore_industry> (retrieved 6 January 2011).

Wilson, Pamela (2004), 'Jamming *Big Brother USA*: webcasting, audience intervention and narrative activism', in Ernest Mathijs and Janet Jones (eds), *Big Brother International*, London and New York: Wallflower Press, pp. 194–209.

Winslow, Luke (2010), 'Comforting the comfortable: *Extreme Makeover Home*

*Edition*'s ideological conquest', *Critical Studies in Media Communication* 27.3, pp. 267–90.

Winston, Brian (2000), *Lies, Damn Lies and Documentaries*, London: British Film Institute.

Wolf, Naomi (1991), *The Beauty Myth: How Images of Beauty Are Used against Women*, New York: HarperCollins.

Woods, Gaby (2004), 'Meet Marnie ... ', *The Observer*, 18 July, <http://www.guardian.co.uk/theobserver/2004/jul/18/features.review7?INTCMP=SRCH> (retrieved 7 December 2005).

Wright, Christopher J. (2006), *Tribal Warfare:* Survivor *and the Political Unconscious of Reality Television*, Lanham, MD: Lexington Books.

Xie, Y. G., and H. Chen (2007), *Zhenrenxui jiemu: lilun, xingtai he chuangxin* (Reality TV Programmes: Theory, Form and Innovation), Shanghai: Fudan University Press.

Yesil, Bilge (2001), 'Reel pleasures: exploring the historical roots of media voyeurism and exhibitionism', *Counterblast: The e-Journal of Culture and Communication* 1.1 (n.p.).

Young, Colin (1974), '*The Family*', *Sight and Sound* 43.4, pp. 206–11.

Zimbardo, Philip G. (1985), 'Laugh where we must, be candid where we can', *Psychology Today* 119, pp. 43–4.

# Index